Diaspora and Law

Europäisch-jüdische Studien – Beiträge

European-Jewish Studies – Contributions

On Behalf of the Moses Mendelssohn Center for European-Jewish Studies, Potsdam

In Cooperation with the Selma Stern Center for Jewish Studies Berlin-Brandenburg

Edited by Miriam Rürup and Werner Treß

Volume 66

Diaspora and Law

Culture, Religion, and Jurisprudence beyond Sovereignty

Edited by
Liliana Ruth Feierstein and Daniel Weidner

DE GRUYTER
OLDENBOURG

ISBN 978-3-11-106184-9
e-ISBN (PDF) 978-3-11-106263-1
e-ISBN (EPUB) 978-3-11-106304-1
ISSN 2192-9602

Library of Congress Control Number: 2023938194

Bibliographic information published by the Deutsche Nationalbibliothek
The Deutsche Nationalbibliothek lists this publication in the Deutsche Nationalbibliografie; detailed bibliographic data are available on the internet at http://dnb.dnb.de.

Printing and binding: CPI books GmbH, Leck

www.degruyter.com

Table of Contents

Liliana Ruth Feierstein, Daniel Weidner
Introduction: Law beyond Sovereignty — 1

I. Diaspora

Susannah Heschel
An Exile of the Soul: A Theological Examination of Jewish Understandings of Diaspora — 13

Ino Augsberg
Diaspomenos: Hermeneutics of Exile — 37

II. Traditions of Plurality

Suzanne Last Stone
Law without Nation? The Ongoing Jewish Discussion — 51

Charlotte Elisheva Fonrobert
***Dina de-malkhuta dina* and Talmudic Divorce Law: A Challenge for Rabbinic Law in Diaspora — 83**

Serdar Kurnaz
The Transformation of Sharia from a Law-Centered Understanding to Ethics: An Overview — 99

III. Law and Religion

Martin Heger
Der Wandel von einem personalen zu einem territorialen Rechtsverständnis in Mittelalter und früher Neuzeit — 119

Elisa Klapheck
Towards a Jewish Theology of Secular Law — 135

IV. Legal Pluralism in Concrete Action

Stephan M. Probst
Halacha and Medical Law at the End of Life — 151

Liliana Ruth Feierstein
"He was lain to rest in the Darkening of the Tides ...": Death and Burial in the Field of Tension between Competing Laws in Latin America — 171

V. Law and Literature in the Diaspora

Klaus Stierstorfer
Law and Literature in Diaspora: Gandhi's Autobiography — 191

Caspar Battegay
Star Trek: Diaspora and Law in the German-Jewish Imagination — 205

About the Authors — 219

Index — 223

Liliana Ruth Feierstein, Daniel Weidner

Introduction: Law beyond Sovereignty

The triumphal story of "the law" is one of the most enduring myths of Western modernity. From its Roman roots, the law had continued to evolve during the dark Middle Ages, it became more universally accepted in the early modern period when it also "emancipated" itself from local customs and religion to become an autonomous sphere of formal rationality that allows modern societies to solve their conflicts in less violent ways. Today, the rule of law creates powerful political bodies, the nation states, and continues to work for a global society, since human rights politics are becoming more and more important also on an international scale – a politics in which the reference to the story mentioned becomes political, legitimizing hegemonic claims as part of the universal project of "the law."

There is a certain irony, in this story, however; namely that today, when it seems to come to its fulfillment, "the law" tends to dissolve itself. Today, law is no longer homogenous nor unquestioned. Different overlapping legal regimes constantly interfere with one another, both on an international level, in complex transnational contexts such as the European Union or human rights law, but also in the context of cultural diversity or conflicts between religious norms and civil institutions. On the other hand, the neutrality of law is also under growing pressure, be it from different global transnational players, or from within nation states where populist calls are made to adapt law to the "will of the people." The heated European debate on the "refugee crisis" has made it manifest that law is more necessary than ever and yet fundamentally contested, perhaps even caught in contradictions and self-limitations. At the same time, the current perspective on legal problems allows us to address issues of diversity and the role of Europe in the globalized world more clearly.

Legal pluralism is, of course, not without precedents. The legal order has rarely been as homogenous as the modern nation state imagined it to be. Even within classical nation states there have always been different, at times multiple, forms of legal practice that interact and usually compete with one another. Residues of older corporate institutions remain such as the university, the church, or the military. Different legal cultures overlap in the border zones of imperial expansion, leading to practices of negotiation and improvisation. Moreover, different religious and cultural minorities such as the Jews, the Sinti and Roma, the Armenians, or the Huguenots had different degrees of juridical autonomy with respect to their own legal rulings or even negotiations with the state. We believe that recent debates on legal pluralism, multinormativism, and diversity have much to learn from these historical examples. For they also provide a more concrete understand-

https://doi.org/10.1515/9783111062631-001

ing, more detail, and color to discussions that, when limited to the most pressing actual debates, quickly run into dead ends: into abstract distinctions as between "us" and "them" or equally abstract appeals that one "could not" or "has to." Concrete cases and a vivid memory might help here.

The plurality of different orders which no longer coincide with homogenous territories can be discussed in the context of diaspora. Diaspora, usually denoting the dispersion of a certain population and the loss of a political center, has become a powerful concept that refers to deterritorialization and the non-coincidence of different layers of social and cultural practice. Diaspora thus offers a conceptual framework that might help to unsettle presuppositions about modernity, modern states and communities, and their relation toward the modern subject. The very relation of diaspora and law comes with its own tensions, which we consider fruitful: law, that might seem a simple, single, homogenous, albeit somewhat abstract entity becomes multifaceted, even kaleidoscopic when seen from a diasporic perspective; diaspora, with which we might associate a colorful, multicultural, creative form of life, becomes more serious and problematic when normative and legal issues are raised.

Refiguring law

> Before the law sits a gatekeeper. To this gatekeeper comes a man from the country who asks to gain entry into the law. But the gatekeeper says that he cannot grant him entry at the moment.
>
> Franz Kafka, "Before the Law"

Modern attempts to understand the law usually begin with a sort of astonishment, or estrangement, that something so familiar and so rational remains somewhat uncanny – a feeling that finds expression in Franz Kafka's "Before the Law," a parable that has proven essential for so many thinkers of the twentieth century. Maybe we, the moderns or postmoderns, are no longer at home with the law. We approach it as a stranger, as a man from the country, and we do not really get to it. We do not pass from our displaced and diasporic identities towards the center towards which we are drawn. The little story that contains and unfolds the tensions of law in modernity can thus help us to articulate the questions that our subject implies.

For Kafka, law is indeed displaced, for first, there is a doorkeeper who would not let the man enter. Law, we are told, is a complex issue, something that modern societies are justly proud of, but which also bears strange ambivalences. It seems to be something abstract, but it also has a location, a series of rooms or rather doors; it is a body of law, and it is even guarded. Law is not only a principle, but also an institution the German calls *Zwangsanstalt* – a 'coercive institute,' a form of power, that is usually most manifest in the fact that modern law has become bound to the state. With its doorkeepers, the law does not only draw boundaries in the world, as the boundary between the "legal" and the "illegal"; it also draws boundaries around itself, excluding the "extralegal," e.g., questions of taste, of mere morality, or of religion. These issues, at least in the liberal model, fall outside of law, or rather in the parable, have to be kept out of law by the very doorkeeper who would not let the man from the country enter. Having a location, law also seems to contain – or not. Though the law is general (it should be accessible to anyone at any time, as the man in Kafka's parable wonders), some are "within" the law and some are not. Maybe, one might suspect, the force of the law rests on that very distinction; at least this distinction, or the promise that you might enter, but not now, keeps the man waiting.

Second, the man keeps waiting, among other things because there is a radiance shining from the inner realms of the law. There is a moment of fullness, substance, or even sacrality at stake, and indeed, the relation of law and religion might be much more central than the modern myth of law as a rational form suggests. Remember that, within the larger frame of *The Process,* Kafka's parable is narrated in a church. This setting suggests that something, or someone, is in the law, that there are not merely doorkeepers but something that they protect and also represent: the lawgiver, the spirit of law, the sovereign – or something even loftier such as justice, redemption? Moreover, law is translucent because of this radiance; it has its own transcendence, visible in its procedures even in modern societies – or maybe especially in modern society, where legal rituals might still hold a remainder of transcendence, ritual, and absoluteness. Historically, law often emerged from religious context. Religion and law share the issue of normativity, and in many legal regimes, religious norms are indistinguishable from legal ones. To be sure, modern law pretends to be secular; as the doorkeeper, it shows neither affect nor preference but simply does its duty. Yet does it? Is it really that neutral? At least in Germany, the relation of religion and law has never been so easily determined, since the relation of church and state is determined by what legal theory calls – in an aptly Kafkaesque image – the "hinkende Trennung" ('limping separation') in which the state grants some religious groups considerable privileges. Again, at least some have already entered the law, have been incorporated, although others are being warded off. And today, in our postsecular time, the reemerging conflicts between religious values and secular laws seem to indicate that the latter are maybe not that secular or that their secularity is driven by other energies than we assumed.

Thirdly, towards the end of the parable, the dying man asks the doorkeeper why, even though everyone strives for access to the law, no one else has ever come along to request entry. The doorkeeper responds: "No one else could gain admittance here, because this entrance was meant solely for you. I'm going to go and shut it now." As norms in general, law is not only a social institution, they also concern the subject in its innermost intimacy. They do not only regulate society, but also constitute legal subjects, and since political subjectivity is bound to its legal form, it is of utmost importance how and in what respect the legal subject is constituted, and what parts of dimensions are recognized by the law: one's gender, affiliation, community, longing, identity, etc.

Moreover, the very question remains: why did no one come along? Was this law really still in practice, or is it rather an abandoned thing, more a memory than an institution, rather a story than a site of power? For law is not only prescriptive, but also descriptive; it exists as a text, even, as we have argued, as a myth. It can be upheld even though not in practice, as in the rabbinic discussions about the temple-cult that debate with utmost precision the proper practice, even though – or perhaps even *because* – there is no temple in sight. As Walter Benjamin in an interpretation of Kafka once remarked, a law that is no longer practice becomes life, that is, human activity in all its complexity and messiness as a way to establish a world even under adverse conditions.

The volume presented here consists of the proceeding of a conference held at the *Selma-Stern Center for Jewish Studies in Berlin-Brandenburg* in the winter of 2019. It took recent developments and debates both in legal and diaspora studies as a springboard to discuss the pressing question of how to live together in the new millennium and how to figure the long history of law before, besides, and after the dominant paradigm of state law. We would like to thank the participants of that conference for their engagement in the discussion and the willingness to contribute to this volume. Thanks also to Monika Schärtl, Nadja Fiensch and Simone Damis for their help in preparing the event, to the Selma Stern Zentrum für Jüdische Studien for support and funding. To Sonja Andersen for her careful proofreading of the text, Julia Brauch and Alice Meroz for the editing work and De Gruyter for welcoming us in this collection.

I Diaspora

Stepping outside the law, taking one's position to observe it not in its inner chambers but on the very threshold implies a shift, or displacement that can be associated with the turn to diaspora in cultural studies. For diaspora not only steers our attention towards migration, cultural contact, and hybridity, but it also comes along with a broader displacement of ideas of culture, society, and anthropology. Seen from the perspective of diaspora, cultures are no longer conceived as containers, life-worlds or spheres that only occasionally get into touch with each other; instead, both cultures and culture in general is never in its "own" place but always somewhere else, always determined by cultural difference, a difference that is continually performed in thought and deed, in ideas as well as events and actions, artworks and discourses. Diaspora, however, can mean a host of things, not all of which are related to difference and hybridity. It also comes with strong identities, especially in the imaginative realm: the longing for a "homeland" might produce a sense of belonging that is, as an affect, much stronger than the feeling of being at home. Nor does it come without ambivalence towards its cultural "other." Connected to cultural memories and bearing religious overtones, diaspora both relates to the complex interplay between religious and secular in traditional societies and to modern law's difficulties in dealing with culture, the imaginary, and religion.

This complexity of meanings is discussed in Susannah Heschel's contribution on the political, religious, and existential implication of diaspora in Judaism and its history. The meaning and valorization of diaspora emerged in answer to Christian supercessionism and quickly developed into a complex discourse. Its tensions became all the stronger in modernity, especially facing Zionism, which itself has an ambivalent and changing attitude towards the diaspora that continues to create conflicts and – no less importantly – continues to relate to other conflicts, such as the (post-)colonial ones. In a similarly genealogical approach, Ino Augsberg shows that ideas of the diaspora, of dispersion, difference, and alterity can be found in the oldest layers of Western thought, namely when Greek rhetors and philosophers discuss the understanding of the other, the distant, and the stranger – figures that threatened the univocality of meaning and became especially problematic when related to the idea of the legal subject that always tends to exclude, suppress, or render invisible that which does not fit into the homogenous juridical space.

II Traditions of Plurality

Jewish cultures have long had experiences with forms of law beyond the state. The specific rabbinic form of legal reasoning and the specific halachic way of life emerged in the very moment when Jewish sovereignty was lost. During the history of exile, there have been multiple forms of legal self-determination, as in the *kahal*, the Jewish community that took at least part of legal procedures into its own hands, or in different forms of multireligious rulings. The Talmudic principle of *dina de malkhuta dina* ("the law of the kingdom is law") was employed not only to accept the laws of the respective countries where Jews settled but also to integrate secular rulings into Jewish legal reflection, and to articulate the precarious balance between political participation and cultural autonomy.

These practices are not limited to Judaism, however. In most European countries, arguably, we are merely experiencing an uncanny transfer: accusations typically directed against Jews during the nineteenth century – that they do not integrate but rather constitute a "state within the state," that they lack loyalty and rationality, that they promote problematic archaic morals and customs – now, more often than not, are directed at other groups such as the Sinti and Roma or Muslims. Debates about the headscarf, circumcision, or *kosher/halal* slaughter reveal familiar fault lines between the state and its legal apparatus on the one hand, and cultural "minorities" on the other. Here, cultural and religious norms of majorities and minorities seem to interfere with each other in ways that seem to be difficult to handle legally, politically, and discursively.

The contributions in this section analyze ways in which the religious traditions used to deal with those differences. We are pleased to reprint Suzanne Last Stone's by now classical essay, which already in 2013 asked to what extent the Jewish law can be viewed as a paradigm for a "law without nation," in which universality and particularity take a decisively different form than in the nation state. At the same time, the founding of the state of Israel also affects the development of modern Jewish law and results in decidedly different – national, cosmopolitan, transnational – understandings of Jewish law, which today concur and interact with each other. Charlotte Elisheva Fonrobert analyzes the complexities of one of the most extreme cases of legislative competence in Talmudic law: divorce. She shows that beyond the more practical needs to compromise, the rabbis tried to reserve for themselves whatever had to do with relations among humans, such as family laws and regulations concerning slavery. Facing the Muslim legal Tradition, Serdar Kurnaz shows how different layers of law interact and how potential conflicts are dealt with in different models, as in the proposal of a European Islam that shifts the attention from positive laws to ethical norms, whereas other voices continue to emphasize the difference between the believer and the non-believer. The parallel with developments in Jewish law may be revealing since Muslim law was less codified and not intended for a minority situation in the diaspora. And, on the other hand, Judaism has two millennia of history of adaptations to its cultural (and therefore legal) minority status.

III Law and Religion

Seen from a diasporic perspective, law is neither a coherent system nor a mere technique we need in order to live together. A diasporic law is always a law with qualification, a law involved in processes of translation, negotiation, or even abrogation, and it rests on institutions other than the legal apparatus of the nation state. Quite often, actual legal practice is conceived against the horizon of an idealized past (or even divine) law or a law to come, surrounded by narratives, legends, and myths. Thus, thinking law from the perspective of diaspora and, conversely, focusing on the legal moments of modern, diasporic existence might enrich our perspective on the phenomenon of law.

Especially the relation of law and religion does easily align with the great narratives of modernity. In fact, the relation between law and religion differs widely even in different "secular" European countries, e.g., with the French programmatic secularism, the remnants of royal religions in the British monarchy, or the "limping" separation mentioned earlier that consists of complex agreements the German state forges with some (but not all) religious communities. Even more complex are the implications of this relation: does the law come with implicit or even explicit promises, with fantasies of cultural hegemony as well as utopian imaginations of ethics and justice? And how did the present relation between law and religion emerge and develop? How does legal secularism relate to its religious past?

The contributions in this section present different and complex accounts of the relation between religious and secular law. Martin Heger shows that personal and territorial law did not necessarily coincide in premodern Europe, which allowed very different legal regimes, among them the relative autonomy of Jewish communities who would build their own legal bodies through a network of responsa. Even the emerging nation-state employed different legal regimes in its own territory and in its colonies, where again the conflict of different legal principles might offer possibilities of negotiation. Elisa Klapheck illuminates such contradiction in a theological reading of Jewish law, in which the rabbis not only repeatedly emphasize human responsibility for legal development but also use the Noachide laws, or the difference between the two tablets of the Sinaitic laws to articulate tensions between different legal layers: the secular and the theological. Conceiving law not as a fixed entity allows them to place it also into dialogue with the legislation of other cultures.

IV Legal pluralism in concrete action

Diversity, the living together of different people with different preferences and values, imaginations and dreams, has become a pressing issue for our societies. While a plurality of ways of life is generally accepted and appreciated, these ways of life do not always go together well, especially when it comes to legal regulation. Diasporic communities endeavor to uphold their way of life in surroundings that might prove hostile or simply hegemonic; others, who think of themselves not as diasporic but rather "at home" might similarly worry about their way of life as being threatened. Herein lies a symmetry that does not lead to mutual understanding, but obviously, and sadly, rather heightens mutual suspicion.

Quickly, people call for the law to mitigate the situation – but is the law really the best instrument to do so? At least in the nineteenth and early twentieth centuries, law became closely bound to the nation state and more often than not developed into an instrument of the majority to suppress cultural difference. Even the universality of the law is often associated with standards to which the individual and his or her community must conform. But, as stated previously, such an emphasis on the law and conformity does not offer a complete picture, for legal practice was, at times, more creative than theory or ideology. Can the law be put into practice in other ways besides the universal? Are there possibilities to recognize difference, plurality, and diversity, in positive ways? The issues of how to rule a multireligious and multicultural society or how to imagine and conceptualize religion and its different forms have become major challenges in postsecular society.

The contributions in this section trace these different paths in quite concrete, borderline situations. Stephan Probst addresses the problem of death in Judaism, where a large body of traditional Jewish legal thought sees itself confronted with the debates and dilemmas of complex medical decisions in the Diaspora. The radically individual character of death poses the central problem of cultural acceptance, since what might be negotiable in life is fully nonnegotiable when it comes to the end of life. Here again, the long Jewish experience over the centuries and the work of Jewish physicians can be a model and inspiration for a more flexible law. In a similar direction, Liliana Ruth Feierstein's contribution addresses conflicts about the Jewish burial in Latin America where the community tried to conceive of the Jewish cemetery as an *extra-territorial space*, where Jewish law rules. The text points out how hard and at the same time empowering the friction is between both traditions and their disputes around the dead, where one legal system often has the possibility of limiting and "correcting" the other.

V Law and literature in the Diaspora

Considering law through the eccentric perspective of diaspora, we will not be surprised to arrive at literary realism as one potential pathway of understanding, for the literary text does have a specific relation towards law. In the Jewish tradition, the interrelationship between the genres *halakha* and *agada*, of the legal debates and the legendary parts of rabbinic literature, that runs across very single treatise of the Talmud and every Mishnaic commentary illustrates this interweaving: normative decision-making and narrative elaboration both need each other and cannot exist without each other. Stressing this relationship, the cultural, but also literary and textual embeddedness of law into a much wider tradition of myth and even fairytale and humor offers another way to question the myth of the rise of "the law," which is mostly also a story of purification, formalization, and abstraction, in which the legal rationality gets rid of its cultural particularities and its narrative shells.

The contributions in this section demonstrate how literary texts can remember and represent the literacy of the law: its imaginative, contingent, and also playful dimensions. Klaus Stiersdorfer's reading of Ghandi's autobiography reveals how the experience of diaspora does not only permeate Ghandi's idea of law and of an Indian "national" identity that continues to bear diasporic traces. The diasporic experience also shapes the literary form that Gandhi gives his life: as that of a lawyer trained in British law, whose plea for the political liberation of the Indian people emerged in yet another space, namely in the Indian Diaspora of South Africa. Caspar Battegay illuminates in his contribution the fascinating displacement of exile in the German-Jewish literature in the Diaspora. Reading Alfred Wolfenstein, Alfred Döblin and Franz Werfel, he depicts an imaginary geography located in time – a refuge in (science) fiction that allows an escape from the world that, after the First World War, becomes more and more critical for Jewish existence. It is, we might add, precisely the utopian moment of this text, that might allow us to reconceive law once more: to imagine the moment when the Law(keeper) opens its doors to Kafka's countryman. Perhaps it is the recovery of the relationship between the word and justice, between the writing system and the legislative, between minorities and majorities, that restores the possibility of not having to die every time in front of the door that will never be open. Because only the diaspora – only the margin and the difference – can afford the center the possibility of its own survival.

I. Diaspora

Susannah Heschel

An Exile of the Soul: A Theological Examination of Jewish Understandings of Diaspora

At the conclusion of a Jewish wedding ceremony, just before the groom smashes a glass, he declaims a verse from a Psalm: "If I forget you, Jerusalem, let my tongue be cut off" (137:5). Breaking the glass – which is immediately followed by exuberant calls of "Mazel Tov" and lively music – is purportedly to remember the destruction of the Temple and the exile from the land of Israel. The tragedy of exile is symbolically present even at a joyous occasion to iterate that in a state of exile, nothing can be perfect and whole. Breaking the glass affirms that the physical connection to the land of Israel is broken, making a religion of exile the portable homeland of the Jews, a state of mind as much as a theological principle.

Exile constitutes Jewish political and religious identity, yet it is based on a paradox. After the Romans destroyed the Second Temple in Jerusalem, the Jews were not forcibly exiled from the land of Israel; no edict of expulsion was issued by the Romans after their destruction of the Jerusalem Temple in 70 CE, and by that time Jews already had been living in diaspora for centuries.[1] Rabbinic depictions of exile, some paradoxically written in the land of Israel, were formulated as meditations on the Babylonian exile of the sixth century BCE that had been overcome. The destruction of the northern kingdom of Israel in the eighth century BCE by the Assyrians, who deported the entire population (who then disappeared from history) is simply forgotten in Jewish history. Only the destruction of the southern kingdom of Judah, where the Temple was located in the capital, Jerusalem, is remembered. The Babylonian exile of Judah, in turn, was also paradoxical: a few decades later, Cyrus the Great offered the Israelites safe passage back to Jerusalem, but relatively few returned while the majority remained in Babylonia for over 2,500 years, composing the Babylonian Talmud, medieval Jewish philosophy, and turning Israelite religion into Judaism. All the while, rabbis in the land of Israel composed the Palestinian Talmud, various Midrashic texts, and, in the sixteenth century, a Code of Jewish Law along with Lurianic mysticism.

1 Eric Gruen, *Diaspora: Jews amidst Greeks and Romans* (Cambridge, MA: Harvard University Press, 2002), 3.

https://doi.org/10.1515/9783111062631-002

Was any of this an "exile"?

Exile became a theological doctrine defining Judaism not in response to a political decree banning Jews from living in Israel, but rather, as the historian Israel Yuval argues, emerged in the fifth century CE in response to the rise of Christianity and its supersessionist claims.[2] Religious polemics faded but exile remained as a Jewish mentality: being a Jew is to be exilic. Jews not only live in exile (galut), exile lives in them – indeed, exile has come to define the condition of the collective Jewish people and the self-understanding of the individual Jew. Exile is not only a theo-political doctrine, it is also a regime of affect, defining the subjective, emotional experience of individual Jews. The combination of doctrine and affect have reinforced one another and been fortified by rituals, such as breaking a glass at a wedding, fast days of mourning, such as Tisha B'Av, which commemorates the destruction of the Temple in Jerusalem, numerous references to exile in Jewish prayers, and various customs, such as leaving a tear in a wall covering or table cloth to indicate that nothing can be perfect while Jews remain in exile.

On the other hand, exile is the condition of life, according to the account in Genesis of the banishment of Adam and Eve from the Garden of Eden. Elsewhere, exile is suggested in a positive way, with the Exodus story in the Hebrew Bible as a liberation from Egyptian slavery. Hellenistic writers reinterpreted it as the banishment of the Israelites from Egypt by the Pharaoh during a plague. The Bible next relates the destruction of the northern kingdom, laid waste by the Assyrians and its inhabitants taken away, only to disappear. The more important exile came after the Babylonian destruction of Judah and the First Temple in 586 BCE when Israelites were forcibly taken to Babylonia. The emotions of that exile are portrayed in Psalm 137 which captures the trauma felt by the Israelites in Babylonia and sets forth a pattern of affect repeated by Jews liturgically and politically to the present day:

> By the waters of Babylon, there we sat down and wept, when we remembered Zion.
> 2 On the willows there we hung up our lyres.
> 3 For there our captors required of us songs, and our tormentors, mirth, saying, "Sing us one of the songs of Zion!"
>
> 4 How shall we sing the LORD's song in a foreign land?
> 5 If I forget you, O Jerusalem, let my right hand wither!

2 Israel Yuval, "Christianity in Talmud and Midrash: Parallelomania or Parallelophobia?," in *Transforming Relation: Essays on Jews and Christians throughout History in Honor of Michael A. Signer*, ed. Franklin T. Harkins and John van Engen (South Bend, IN: University of Notre Dame Press, 2010), 68.

> 6 Let my tongue cleave to the roof of my mouth, if I do not remember you, if I do not set Jerusalem above my highest joy!
>
> 7 Remember, O Lord, against the Edomites the day of Jerusalem, how they said, "Raze it, raze it! Down to its foundations!"
> 8 O daughter of Babylon, you devastator! Happy shall he be who requites you
> with what you have done to us!
> 9 Happy shall he be who takes your little ones and dashes them against the rock!

Perhaps a sense of guilt combined with the trauma of the conquest of Jerusalem, of being captured and forcibly taken into captivity produced the psalm, which formulates the mixed emotions of exile: rage, despair, humiliation, desire for revenge, sorrow, and yearning. The psalm also introduces the river as a metaphor for the tears of the exiles, its flow bearing their pain. Through the psalm and its enormous influence, these emotions came to define exile not only for Jews, but in a universal arena as well, borrowed by poets and freedom fighters throughout history, most notably by African slaves and their descendants in the United States.

Exile is a prerequisite for messianic redemption, a trauma accompanied by hope. Psalm 137 does not mention redemption and the custom of breaking a glass at a wedding ceremony does not suggest hope for the future. Messianism is central to Judaism yet exile and its trauma are far more important in defining Jewish historical and existential experience than hope for the future. Perhaps deflection from imagining the promised messiah was another response to Christianity and its intense focus on its messiah.

The puzzle of Jewish exile is that a majority of Israelites did not leave Babylonia and return to Israel when they were offered the opportunity to do so, preferring to remain in the exile and turning it into a fruitful diaspora. In that Babylonian diaspora, Israelites learned to worship without a Temple, the Bible was put together from various oral traditions, and ultimately rabbinic Judaism was created. Yet the choice to remain in Babylonia was not celebrated in the biblical account, as it implies that exile was not so bad and could be transformed into a peaceful and even lively diasporic existence. The prophet Jeremiah, who lived through the Babylonian conquest, advised turning exile into diaspora: "Build houses and live in them; plant gardens and eat what they produce .... Work for the good for the city to which I have exiled you, since on its welfare yours depends" (Jeremiah 9:4–7). If messianic redemption does not arrive, exile, Jeremiah urges, should be turned into diaspora, into an acceptance of present conditions and an effort to "work for the good for the city." If exile is a withdrawal into one's own traumatic condition, seasoned with a desire for revenge, as the psalmist portrays, diaspora, in Jeremiah's depiction, should bring acceptance, engagement and improvement of the entire society. Not exile, but diaspora is the condition necessary for prophetic justice, yet for theological reasons, exile has been favored over diaspora in the Jewish religious imagination.

Exile as Competition with Christianity

The post-biblical Jewish understanding of exile as a political event with theological and emotional significance is assumed to be linked to the Roman destruction of Jerusalem and the Second Temple in 70 CE. In liturgy and theology, exile is not only geographic, but comes to represent a state of consciousness that defines being a Jew and that is invested with religious meaning: "Because of our sins, we were exiled from our land," we pray over and over in the words of the prayerbook.[3] Perhaps it is not surprising; already in the Bible political developments are linked to religious behavior.[4] Politics is transformed into theology, and exile is linked to sin, an existential state analogous to the original sin of Christianity, not so much an expulsion from Israel by the Romans, but a human condition of alienation combined with the anticipation and hope that God would send the messiah one day.

Christianity turned the destruction of the Jerusalem Temple into a key element demonstrating Christian supersessionism; the Temple was destroyed and replaced by Christ, proving Christianity's triumph over Judaism. From the Christian perspective, the destruction of the Temple was willed by God to demonstrate that Judaism, the carnal Israel, had been superseded by Christianity, which calls itself Israel in the spirit. The rabbinic theology of galut, argues the historian Israel Yuval, arose in the fifth century in response to Christianity, which had given Jews a sense of "religious inferiority vis a vis the rival religion" and served as a "vital apologetic function in the everyday encounter."[5] Jews felt "rejected, expelled, and accursed" in the face of Christian sovereignty and claims that the messiah had already come – "a fatal blow to Jewish self-consciousness," Yuval writes. The two faiths were rival interpretations of the Hebrew Bible, writing the Talmud and New Testament proleptically, as fulfillment of biblical prophecies. The result was a kind of theological competition: which religion best fulfilled the predictions and promises of the Bible? For the Jews, the destruction was a sign of divine wrath in response to Israel's sins but also an affirmation that the covenant remained intact, albeit now in an exilic state until messianic times.

3 The phrase appears, with elaboration, in the Musaf (additional) service liturgies of Jewish festivals, new months, and Rosh Hashanah.

4 See, for instance, see 2 Kings 17:7–17.

5 Israel Yuval, "Christianity in Talmud and Midrash: Parallelomania or Parallelophobia?," 68.

The Gospels conflate the death of Jesus with the destruction of the Temple; at the moment of his death, writes the Gospel of Matthew 27:51, "the veil of the temple was torn in two from top to bottom." The rabbis were well aware of that claim and responded to it in a Talmudic passage, Gittin 56a. In the Talmudic account, it is Titus who enters the holy of holies with a prostitute, has sex with her on the Torah scroll, and punctures the *parochet* (veil) with his sword, causing it to bleed, a rape image that symbolically expresses how the rabbis viewed Christianity's supersessionist theology: as a rape of Judaism. Some early Christian texts claim that Jesus himself destroyed the Temple and identify him with the parochet (Matthew 27:50–51; Hebrews 10:19–20) and the catastrophe with God's punishment of the Jews for crucifying Christ and rejecting Christianity, a fulfillment of biblical warnings (Lev 26:41; Isaiah 1:7); Jews were punished with galut, exiled from the land of Israel and forced to wander the earth to demonstrate the superiority of Christianity. When the Gospels write that Jesus was "despised and rejected," fulfilling Isaiah 53, Jews claim that they embody the exilic condition, regardless of where they are living or what diasporic conditions might be.

That Jews live in galut, not diaspora, begins to appear in Jewish texts in response to Christian polemics, Yuval argues.[6] The Christian claim that Jews live in exile, and that the exile is a punishment for refusing to accept Jesus as the messiah, turned the events of 70 CE from a political conflict into a theological confrontation. Was this an exile or a continuation of the diasporic existence of Jews that had begun centuries earlier? If exile, what was its cause and purpose? Some Jewish texts, such as the Book of Esther and the writings of the first-century Jewish philosopher Philo and the Jewish historian Josephus, refer to diaspora positively, even as a blessing. According to Christians, the Jews were placed into exile as punishment by God for killing Christ; according to Jewish understanding, Jews are indeed in exile, but as self-sacrificial atonement for the sins of all human beings; one hears the echoes of Christ as atonement. In some sense, then, it is Christianity that created the trope of Jewish exile – as opposed to diaspora – so that the Jewish theology of exile, in response, was in itself an adoption of Christian tropes.

The ambivalence in Jewish understanding of their exilic condition, which shifted the exile in Babylonia into a flourishing diaspora, is reflected in Talmudic passages. Yuval notes that the Palestinian Talmud refers only to the destruction of the Temple, not to a forced exile – after all, these rabbis remained in Palestine since there was no edict of expulsion from the land. By contrast, the Babylonian Talmudic and Midrashic literatures link the destruction of the Temple to exile from the

6 Israel Yuval, "The Myth of the Jewish Exile from the Land of Israel," *Common Knowledge* 12:1 (2006): 16–33.

land. Sorrow over the destruction is certainly expressed; the Babylonian Talmud attributes to Rabbi Yochanan, who lived in third-century Palestine, the mournful statement: "Our House has been destroyed, our Temple burnt and we ourselves exiled from our land" (Gittin 56a).[7] Yet a different Talmudic passage is sympathetic to diaspora, explaining that there are four winds in the world: "Just as it is impossible to think of the world without those four winds, it is impossible to think of Israel not residing in all of them," (Ta'anit 3b) a sentiment echoed frequently in rabbinic literature.

By the Middle Ages, whether Jews lived in peaceful or persecutory conditions, exile was internalized as an existential state and as a fundamental doctrine of Jewish theology: the historical exile that never happened was transposed into a cosmic state of Judaism's *Heilsgeschichte*. Jews developed various explanations that attributed religious significance to exile and discussed the ways in which life in galut could have religiously meaningful consequences, such as sacrificial atonement on behalf of all humanity, expiation for sin, soteriological penance, and a mission to spread knowledge of God: "God exiled Israel so that they would gather souls" (Pesachim 87b).

But what kind of sin would bring galut in the first place? Adam and Eve were exiled from the Garden of Eden, says the Midrash Genesis Rabbah 20:1, because they spoke *lashon hara,* wicked words, against God, portraying God as a jealous deity who wanted to prevent them from sharing in His knowledge. In another Midrash, Moses says the Jews, enslaved in Egypt, deserve their exile because of their malicious talk mischaracterizing his efforts to protect them.[8] The Talmud says the First Temple was destroyed because of the sins of idolatry, immorality, and bloodshed, while the Second Temple was destroyed because of the sin of groundless hatred, sinat hinam, toward one another (Yoma 9b). As God created the world with words, Jews spoke exile into being through their misuse of words. Their words were not physical acts of sinful behavior, but cruel words of malice that bring emotional hurt to others. The emphasis on punishment for cruel words demonstrates that galut moved from physical dislocation to exile as an existential condition as punishment for bringing emotional suffering to others.

7 Yuval, "The Myth of the Jewish Exile," 20; Claiming that the Roman exiled Jews from the land of Israel also had helpful legal implications: by arguing that they had lived in exile since 70CE in the Roman Empire, medieval Jews could claim ancient rights allegedly bestowed by Titus or Vespasian (Yuval). Moreover, Jews in Christian lands could present their community as a "kehillah kedosha", a holy community, a local embodiment of ancient Jerusalem.

8 Exodus Rabbah 1 and Tanhuma Shemot 10; see also Rashi to Ex. 2:14; Daniel Feldman, 19.

Where is God for Jews when in Exile?

When the rabbis shift from political to existential galut, they do not abandon the politics of exile, but shift it to the theological realm. The theological transformation of a political state of exile, namely, the lack of political sovereignty, is most startling in the Jewish theological claim that God, too, is in exile. Jews may have no sovereignty, and even the ultimate sovereign of the world is also in exile. The theme is found in the Talmud and Midrash and receives centrality in medieval Kabbalistic literature: Jews are not alone in exile because God is in exile with them and also requires redemption. The idea is distinctive in Jewish theology and has no comparable claim in Christianity or Islam. This enabled the covenant to remain operative in an exilic state. The Talmud declares (TB Megillah 29a), "In every exile into which the children of Israel went, the Shekhinah (divine presence) was with them."[9] Even more directly, the Mishnah proclaimed, "Ani va ho hoshia na," "I and 'ho' may we be redeemed" (Mishnah Sukkah 4:5).[10] Who is "ho"? Talmud BT Shabbat 104a tells us that "ho" is a designation for God. The Midrashic sources elaborate: "Rabbi Ishmael said, You find that whenever Israel is enslaved, the Shekhinah is with them, as it says, 'In all their affliction, God is afflicted' (Isaiah 63:9): wherever Israel is exiled, Shekhinah is with them." (Sifre Be'Ha'alotecha 84). The destruction of the Temple brings suffering to God as well as Jews. The Babylonian sage Ulla sorrowfully declared, "Since the day the Temple was destroyed, all that remains for the Holy One, Blessed Be He, in His world are the four amot of halakha" (Talmud, Berachot 8a). No more Temple; all that is left is Jewish law and Jews must accommodate life without a Temple, without Jewish sovereignty, and create a Judaism viable even outside the land of Israel.

---

9 Sifre Be'Ha'alotecha 84: "Rabbi Ishmael said, You find that whenever Israel is enslaved, the shekhinah is with them, as it says, "In all their troubles, God is troubled" (Isaiah 63:9). ... wherever Israel is exiled, Shekhinah is with them."

10 Every day they went around the altar once, saying, "O Lord, save us, O Lord, make us prosper" (Psalm 118). Rabbi Judah says: "Ani vaho, save us." On that day they went round the altar seven times. When they departed, what did they say? "O altar, beauty is to you! O altar, beauty is to you!" Rabbi Eliezer said: [they would say,] "To the Lord and to you, O altar, to the Lord and to you, O altar."

בְּכָל יוֹם מַקִּיפִין אֶת הַמִּזְבֵּחַ פַּעַם אַחַת, וְאוֹמְרִים, אָנָּא ה' הוֹשִׁיעָה נָּא, אָנָּא ה' הַצְלִיחָה נָּא. רַבִּי יְהוּדָה אוֹמֵר, אֲנִי וָהוֹ הוֹשִׁיעָה נָּא. וְאוֹתוֹ הַיּוֹם מַקִּיפִין אֶת הַמִּזְבֵּחַ שֶׁבַע פְּעָמִים. בִּשְׁעַת פְּטִירָתָן, מָה הֵן אוֹמְרִים, יֹפִי לְךָ מִזְבֵּחַ, יֹפִי לְךָ מִזְבֵּחַ. רַבִּי אֱלִיעֶזֶר אוֹמֵר, לְיָהּ וּלְךָ, מִזְבֵּחַ. לְיָהּ וּלְךָ, מִזְבֵּחַ:

The exile of Israel in the Midrash and the exile of the soul from its original home fused in Kabbalah with the exile of the *Shekhinah.*[11] In classical Kabbalah exile is represented by asserting that the transcendent masculine aspect of God is exiled from the immanent feminine aspect, the *Shekhinah* from the *Kadosh Baruch Hu,* and awaits reunion and redemption. Thus, before praying, a meditation is said: "for the sake of the reunion of the *Kadosh Baruch Hu* and the *Shekhina,*" may my prayers redeem God from exile.

That God is in need of redemption is a theologoumena unique to Judaism. Islam would never speak of God being into exile or having his omnipotence limited in any way; in classical Sunni Islam, God is everywhere and is not subject to affect or need. Moreover, divine omnipotence is eternal. Christianity emphasizes the suffering of Christ, but not of God the Father. In fact, the early Church condemned theopaschism, that God the Father suffers, as heretical, though some Protestant theologians in the 1970s, such as Jürgen Moltmann, tried to revive the idea.[12]

From the Bible to the Zohar, there is hope: piety may influence God to send redemption; in classical Kabbalah, piety may even redeem God, unifying the sefirot, the divine emanations of Malchut and Tiferet, though Lurianic kabbalah in the sixteenth century, redefined exile as a calamity that occurred at the very moment of creation, woven into the fabric of the cosmos when God initiated the creation of the world. The hopelessness of redeeming a world born in exile led to ever greater calamity, the despair of pan-European Sabbatianism and ultimately to the idea that one can be a Jew without Judaism. This was a diaspora trying to overcome galut altogether, yet both Sabbatians and secular Jews, as Gershom Scholem argued, ended up in exile from Judaism.[13] Exile remains in a state of relation to that which is elusive, redemption, but nonetheless present. Once the state of being in exile loses its connection to redemption, the object of its longing, it simply becomes hopelessness and despair.

From Exile to Diaspora: The Ambivalences of Modernity

Modernity did not so much bring an end to Jewish exile as an end to the anxiety over exile. For Jews in Europe and the United States, life was increasingly a com-

11 Gershom Scholem, *Major Trends in Jewish Mysticism,* trans. George Lichtheim (Jerusalem: Schocken Publishing House, 1941), 107.

12 Jürgen Moltmann, *Experiences of God,* trans. Margaret Kohl (Philadelphia: Fortress Press, 1980).

13 Gershom Scholem, *On Jews and Judaism in Crisis* (New York: Schocken Books, 1976).

fortable diasporic integration into the wider society and the land of Israel receded in importance and the Jews as a nation were repudiated. Overcoming exile meant obtaining the rights of citizenship, not anticipating the messiah or building a Jewish state. For modern European Jews seeking emancipation and integration, the ghetto was a metaphor for galut. Jews were not only kept in galut, but they had also internalized a galut mentality, argued the Maskilim, the proponents of Enlightenment, and that galut mentality led rabbis to create elaborate laws that confined Jews in narrow mindedness. Emancipation, Enlightenment, and religious reform would allow Jews to break out of the ghetto and enter European society, they believed. In Eastern Europe, by contrast, home could be found in precisely the piety and Torah study rejected by the Maskilim. The traumas of exile were brought to the Torah; engrossed in pious study, Jews transcended the surrounding political and economic culture and found their home in texts.

The seventeenth-century rabbi of Venice, Simone (Simcha) Luzzatto (1583–1663), caught the mood well when he described a calm Jewish immersion in the cultural waters of Christian Europe: "For the Jews are scattered around the whole world like a river running through a long stretch of countryside, whose waters receive a coloration from the soils of the various lands through which they pass. This is how the Jews acquire different ways from the nations in which they settle... [They have] a firmness and inexpressible tenacity in the observance of their faith and a uniformity of dogma regarding their beliefs during the course of 1,550 years of dispersion in the world. This is a remarkable steadfastness." The river metaphor, presented in Luzzatto's Italian work, "Discourse," written for a Christian as well as a Jewish readership, is a far cry from Psalm 137's account of the trauma of exile. For Luzzatto, Jews are immersed and affected by their surroundings, changing aspects of Jewish culture just as a river changes color as it is immersed in the soils it traverses. In Luzzatto's metaphor, Jews are a calm river: scattered, flowing, and yet always retaining their essential nature; the assimilation that takes place in diaspora does not affect the core of Jewish identity, just as the consciousness of being in exile is not affected by living in peaceful diasporic conditions. In fact, in diaspora, Jewish exile created a religious tradition that is more, and not less, able to survive and thrive.

Modernity brought three major changes in Jewish understandings of exile. Hasidism transformed physical exile into an existential state. German-Jewish thinkers created a postcolonial moment by rejecting Christian supersessionism and calling for a liberation from the confines of Jewish law. Zionism transformed exile as theological into exile as a political condition that had to be overcome through Jewish statehood. Yet all three movements also understood exile as a Jewish mentality that had to be excised from Jewish consciousness. Exilic consciousness was deeply ingrained, and it is striking that all three movements sought its excision by reference to gender identity, perhaps understanding that exilic mentality, like gender, cannot be easily altered. As the right-wing American rabbi Meir Kahane once observed, "Removing the exile from Israel is ten times harder than removing Israel from the exile, and this is the reason that even in the Land of Israel a nation has arisen that trembles at flesh-and-blood gentiles, a nation lacking in trust in G-d."[14]

Hasidism

For Judaism to be superseded by Christianity is not easy, and it sparked a Jewish fascination with Christianity not despite, but precisely because it had been rejected. The growing political triumph of the daughter religion, Christianity, evoked a set of complex emotions in Jews, including anger, shame, and contempt, but also envy and imitation. As much as Christianity was rooted in a theological supersession of Judaism, Judaism, despite presenting itself as the "mother" religion, was fascinated by certain Christian claims and often defined itself by deploying Christian metaphors. The twelfth-century Hebrew Chronicles, for example, echo Christian motifs of martyrdom in describing mass Jewish suicides as the Crusaders poured through the Rhineland, demanding conversion or death. Classical Kabbalistic depictions of God in the Zohar, composed in the thirteenth century, display introjected Trinitarian images for the Sefirot, the divine emanations, and depict the Shekhinah, the divine presence, as if it were the Virgin Mary. Jewish immersion in Christian culture was not simply a process of "assimilation," but an intricate and often byzantine process of introjection, a process of Jewish self-representation through fantasized interpretation of Christian metaphors.

Over time, Jewish consciousness of living in galut grew stronger and more positive; exile came to be seen as an existential state of being, especially in the Hasidic theology that emerged in the late eighteenth century. In Hasidism, exile defined human subjectivity and life in exile and homelessness was turned into an experience of home and a source of identity. For example, the Bible relates that Abraham is told by God to leave his home in Ur to journey to his homeland, the promised land of Israel; that is, he goes into exile to find his home. The Hasidic thinker Levi Yitzchak of Berdichev, in his commentary, *Kedushas Levi*, interprets God's command to Abraham, "*Lech l'cha*" ("go forth"), as "go within yourself," that is,

14 Meir Kahane, *The Jewish Idea* (Institute for Publication of the Writings of Rabbi Meir Kahane, 1998) vol. 1, 504; cited by Shaul Magid, *Meir Kahane: An American Jewish Radical* (Princeton: Princeton University Press, forthcoming).

as a universal human journey to the interior of the self, finding oneself in the exile within. In a similar vein, the Hasidic rebbe Menachem Mendel of Kotzk insisted that Judaism has to be authentic and unique to each individual, so that knowing oneself intimately is crucial to being a Jew. Far from a punishment or suffering, galut becomes an inner state of human beings, to be plumbed through the self-understanding that can be achieved through prayer and religious passion. Exile is less a state to be overcome than a state of being to be mined for its religious meaning.

German-Jewish Thought

Modernity brought a new dimension to European-Jewish understandings of galut. In their quest for assimilation, secular education, and social acceptance, leading Jewish proponents of Enlightenment argued that galut was a mentality that had been internalized by Jews and produced narrow-minded, confining laws, a ghetto of the mind. A galut mentality, argued the theologian Abraham Geiger, had caused the petrification of what had been liberal, progressive Jewish law until it became stultifying.[15] One of the leading Maskilim of the eighteenth century, Herz Wessely, argued that galut had brought a deformity in Jews' own understanding of Judaism by emphasizing Talmud to the neglect of the Bible and its poetry.[16] For these thinkers, modernity meant an end to galut and the dawn of Jewish engagement with the world at large.

If the Jewish theology of exile began in the fifth century in response to Christian supersessionism, as Yuval has argued, it also lost its theological importance with the development in modern Jewish thought of a reverse supersession. Modern Jewish claims that Jesus was a Jew who promoted the progressive religious Judaism of his day functioned to define Christianity as a religion about Jesus invented by Paul. The actual faith of Jesus was to be found in the modern, liberal Judaism that flourished once medieval persecutions ended and Jews gained emancipation and citizenship. Judaism's theology of exile ended as it began its project of undermining Christian claims of supersession.

The problem is that Zionism arose in the same era, making claims to exile's deleterious effects on Jews. For Jews to live in diaspora and not in exile is not only a challenge to Zionism, but also a theological challenge to normative Judaism

15 Abraham Geiger, *Das Judentum und seine Geschichte* (Breslau: Schlettersche Buchhandlung, 1864).

16 Herz Wessely, *Divrei Torah v'Emet* (Berlin, 1782).

more generally because it obviates the need for messianic redemption, or geulah; certainly, Zionism does not place messianic redemption at the center of Jewish collective belief. Here Zionism was in accord with assimilationism: Jews needed to rid themselves of a longing for messianic redemption. During the course of the nineteenth century, German Jews removed messianic prayers from the prayer book because they were settled, happy with their lives, expecting to remain permanently, and would not pray for a messianic return to the land of Israel and the reconstitution of the Temple and Davidic kingship.[17] Reform Jews redefined messianism as an end to injustice and suffering, a fair and equal society brought about through human effort, not by the messiah sent by God. Zionism promised an end to messianic anticipation by reaching the messianic goal through human hands.

Zionism

Zionism appeared with a stated goal of ending Jewish exile. Not the messiah, but Theodor Herzl, the founder of political Zionism, would lead the Jews out of exile. Yet Zionism's relationship to classical Jewish theological doctrines was ambivalent. Even as Christianity takes a supersessionist relationship to the Hebrew Bible and Judaism, Zionism, too, functions in a supersessionist fashion to Jewish understandings of exile. Zionism demands a negation of exile for the sake of fellow Jews, but unless those Jews have a sense of being in exile, the Zionist project has no meaning. Just as Christianity cannot destroy the Hebrew Bible or it will lose its own theological foundation as the fulfillment of divine promises, Zionism requires a retention of an exilic sensibility that it promises to overcome in order to maintain its *raison d'être*. The problem is retaining that sense of exile not only while in diaspora, but also once statehood has been achieved and even while most Jews live outside Israel. What does Israel offer Jews who remain in diaspora? In recent politics, the state of Israel presents itself as a dominant Jewish husband of a submissive diasporic Jewish wife; or perhaps she is his agunah, chained to him even while living apart, affected by Israeli politics even though unable to change the political culture and leadership. The relationship between Israelis and diaspora Jews gives rise to a new Orientalism. In the diasporic Jewish imagination, the exile/redemption paradigm reflects Edward Said's Orientalist gaze that oscillates between the erotic and the repugnant, a widespread conviction among diaspora Jews that Israel offers a way to solidify Jewish identity and yet also undermine Jewish ethical sta-

17 Michael Meyer, *Response to Modernity: A History of the Reform Movement in Judaism* (Detroit: Wayne State University Press, 1995).

tus. Israeli Orientalism has its own set of erotic possibilities as it regards diasporic Jewish flourishing; there is a longing for the cosmopolitan realm of the Gentile, but also a wish for the remote East, for India and Asia, the siren of the forbidden female, as an escape from all that is both Jewish and Israeli.[18]

The gendered nature of exile also contributes to its tenacity. Exile is reinforced through symbolic enactment. If breaking the glass is a classic symbol of a husband breaking his new wife's hymen, the heteronormativity of the Jewish wedding service affirms at the wedding – in a ceremony first developed during Jewish exile – that the man has the power to shift halakhic control of a woman from father to husband, perhaps from Gentile to Jew; breaking the hymen functions, as Avital Eshed argues, as a female equivalent of circumcision, turning the woman into a Jew.[19] To be a daughter or a wife is to lack independence and autonomy, according to rabbinic law, and be subject to father or husband, a status of exile from oneself. Yet the theology of Jewish exile is so important that even symbolic recognition of exile is entrenched. Thus, although halakha, Jewish law, has managed to create a variety of legal fictions, such as eruv, and edicts, such as the prohibition against polygamy, and cope with changing circumstances, such as the Shoah and Zionism, one item has resisted change despite its toxic effects on Jewish women: the laws of divorce that create the agunah. The agunah, the chained woman whose husband has disappeared or who refuses to grant her a divorce, remains chained to a marriage without a husband, unable to remarry or gain her freedom, and can be subjected to bribery from her husband in exchange for granting her a divorce precisely because she is the quintessential exilic person and symbolizes the trapped, exilic Jew. She is shackled to a man in a non-relationship, unable to free herself, as the Jew is shackled to exile and must passively await redemption. The problem of the agunah has remained unresolved for centuries not only because of rabbinic intransigence, but also because the agunah is the ultimate symbol of exile. If Zionism arrived to redeem Jewish men from the emasculating nature of exile, the agunah remained intact, demonstrating that neither return to the land nor establishment of a state overcomes the exilic nature of being a Jew.

Galut can be understood on the personal level as enticing the Jewish man with an offer of freedom from constraints of all kinds as well as hearing the demand of the land to return home to the Jewish people. Galut is the id of Judaism, as ex-

---

18 Israeli politician Avrum Burg has written of the allure of cosmopolitan Europe, in contrast to the Jewish monoculture of Israel. Avrum Burg, "A Zionist Changes His Mind," *Tikkun* 22:6 (2007): 53–57.

19 Avital Davidovich Eshed, "'How then could I gaze at a virgin?' The Concept of Virginity in Medieval Ashkenazi-Jewish Culture in Christendom," ([Hebrew] PhD diss., Tel Aviv University, 2014).

pressed, for example, by the early Hebrew writers Saul Tchernichovsky and Micah Joseph Berdichevsky, rebelling against the constraints of the law, whereas Zionism demands a negation of exile out of solidarity with fellow Jews, building and defending the state like a man. Many of us live in both realms. Galut functions metaphorically as the primal mother before being instructed by the law of the Father, the legal and political regime that commands return to the land.

To overcome the diaspora ("l'hitgaber" in Hebrew) literally means to become a man. As a slogan for Zionism, what meaning does it offer to women? If galut is to be conquered by a Zionism that classically presents itself as the conquest of the effeminate diasporic Jewish men and the creation of a new masculine Jewish male, what is the role for women? The identification of galut as female suggests that women, coming to Israel, bring the problem of exile to the land itself. Indeed, the Tosafists, medieval commentators on the Talmud, warned that we cannot extricate ourselves from galut simply by moving to Israel. For them, exile is a divine decree whether one lives in the land of Israel or not.

If exile functions for Jews as both a theological premise and a subjective experience constituting Jewish consciousness, can it be overcome by a political movement? Zionism seeks to transfer theology into politics, human subjectivity into passion for land and state. Theologically, Zionism renders messianic hope mute, and statehood in the land of Israel is supposed to overcome the sense of exile.

There is a paradox at the center of the Zionist project: Zionism promises to end two thousand years of Jewish exile and it simultaneously claims Jewish indigeneity in the land of Israel. Zionist supersessionism wants not only to overcome galut but to lay claim to the land. Settler colonialism,[20] the establishment by Europeans of permanent homes in inhabited lands outside Europe but as extensions of Europe, has a double goal: "the suppression or effacement of the indigene" and the indigenization of the settler.[21] If Zionism claims to be redeeming Jews from their exile, how can Jews claim to be native in the land of Israel? How can nativism be created out of exile? Can an immigrant be a native? Zionist nativism is fueled by the antisemitism of diaspora that says the Jew belongs to that land, not this one, and nativism replies that Jews have always been in that land, in our souls if not bodily, and were torn away from it, exiled into a melancholy that the State of Israel will supposedly redeem. Erotic desire for the land and historical violence against the body became intertwined.

20 Caroline Elkins and Susan Pedersen, "Settler Colonialism: A Concept and Its Uses," in *Settler Colonialism in the Twentieth Century: Projects, Practices, Legacies*, ed. Caroline Elkins and Susan Pedersen, 1–20 (New York: Routledge, 2005).

21 Anna Johnston and Alan Lawson, "Settler Colonies," in *A Companion to Postcolonial Studies*, ed. Henry Schwarz and Sangeeta Ray (Malden, MA: Blackwell, 2000), 369.

The great tragedy is that, at the same time that the Israeli nation-state created a Jewish homeland, a new diaspora emerged of Jews expelled from Arab countries, and Christians and Muslims from Palestine. This raises the moral question: how do Jews come "home" to Israel while simultaneously creating homelessness for Palestinians? It also questions the relationship between diaspora and nativism: if Israeli Jews come from a two-thousand-year diaspora that created Judaism and Jewishness, it is problematic if we also speak of Jews upon our return to a land of Israel as native.

The American Challenge

The great challenge to Zionism as well as the greatest guarantor of the State of Israel is the United States. Once Jews started arriving in large numbers during the nineteenth century, life in the United States turned them promiscuous. Unfaithful to age-old theological commitments, including exile, Jews arrived and soon no longer felt themselves in an existential – or political – state of exile. They engaged instead in what we might call a "plumpes Leben," a freedom from traditional Judaism, if not an anarchist repudiation of Judaism's authority. After World War II, conditions began to change, as American Jews turned increasingly observant and Zionist. Contradictions exist: liberated from a sense of galut, American Jews nonetheless insist they are Zionists; emphasizing the importance of the State of Israel as the main pillar of Jewish identity, they nonetheless cultivate Christian evangelical support for Israel.

As Ben Gurion once said, for the State of Israel, the biggest challenge is a robust, happy Jewish community outside Israel: who will want to make aliyah? The United States presented a frightening specter to Zionism: it was too comfortable. For Zionism to be the redemption of Jews from galut, Jews had to feel they were, in fact, living in galut. Yet at the famous Biltmore Hotel gathering of Zionist leaders in New York City in 1942, Israeli Prime Minister David Ben Gurion came to an agreement with Jacob Blaustein, an American industrialist and president of the American Jewish Committee: they agreed that Jews in America were not in galut, but in golah (diaspora). As a multicultural country, the United States was welcoming, and Jews were flourishing; this was golah. American Jews did not feel they were in galut and were not about to pack up and move to Israel.

Ten years later, in 1960, Ben Gurion reneged on the deal. In a speech to the World Jewish Congress, he quoted from the Talmud, "Whoever dwells outside the land of Israel is considered to have no God," (Ketubot 100b) and warned that in America, "Judaism faces death by a kiss—a slow and imperceptible decline into the abyss of assimilation." Golah might be comfortable, but assimilation was dangerous: indeed, too much comfort would bring an end to Jewishness altogether. If Zionism offered Jews a redemption from exile, Jews had to feel they were in exile and not in a secure and tolerant diaspora.

For Ben Gurion, diaspora was Zionism's enemy because it was seductive. Although Ben Gurion was avidly secular, he echoed the warnings of Rabbi Isaiah Horowitz, of seventeenth-century Tiberias, who wrote, "When I saw in this world the children of Israel building for their own use houses like princely palaces, building permanent houses made of stones in a land of impurity [...] it was as if they had renounced redemption."

Freedom in America

Most striking is the swift identification of Jews in America with white people and with the freedom America accorded white privilege. They spoke of having left behind the galut of Europe and arrived in a "A New Promised Land" of safety and equality, not recognizing that to Native Americans, Asians, Mexican Americans, and, above all, African Americans, America was a biblical Egypt of racism and slavery.[22] In dedicating a new synagogue in Charleston, South Carolina in 1841, Gustav Poznanski proclaimed, "This country is our Palestine, this city our Jerusalem, this house of God our temple."[23] Poznanski spoke these words, seemingly oblivious that he had arrived in a slave holding state and a slave trading city. Yet for him, the Other was Europe and European Judaism – oppressive, backward, and authoritarian – and America was the land of freedom. Reform Rabbi Samuel Adler, who arrived in New York from Germany in 1857, was equally unconcerned with the slavery in America and also compared Europe to Egypt, America to freedom: "Behind us lies Egypt, the Middle Ages, before us the sea of Talmudic legalism [...]. The spirit indwelling here in the West, the spirit of freedom, is the newly-born Messiah."[24] Poznanski spoke in Charleston, a slave-trading city, and Adler spoke in New York, which was also pro-slavery at the time.

The problem is whether Jews can claim they have left exile when they have entered a slave state. Moreover, in their eagerness to identify as white, Jews were also identifying themselves with the oppressors. While Jews stand as models of how to preserve identity in diaspora and reclaim homeland, for African Americans, whose time in exile was enslavement, torture, and rape, followed by Jim

22 Hasia Diner, *A New Promised Land: A History of Jews in America* (New York: Oxford University Press, 2002).

23 David Philipson, *The Reform Movement in Judaism* (New York: Macmillan, 1907), 467.

24 Philipson, *Reform Movement*, 483.

Crow, segregation, mass incarceration, and murder by the police, America as homeland is no refuge. Africans were dragged onto slave ships under horrific conditions and were transformed into slaves, whereas Jews came to America to escape oppression and economic stultification and were transformed into free citizens. For African American Jews, the problem has even greater complexity, disrupting and experiencing both. Whiteness in America, for Jews as well as other Europeans, was facilitated, if not guaranteed, by the existence of Black African slaves. The end of the exile of Europe and its antisemitism could take place for Jews in the United States precisely because the country was too busy enslaving Africans to create a state of exile for Jews.

Claims to have brought exile to an end with the immigration to the United States brought with it an abandonment of a Jewish ethical mandate. To speak of freedom in the context of legalized enslavement also makes it clear that Jews identified themselves as white. If America meant an end to exile for Jews, and even an end to diaspora, it also meant an end of the position of the prophetic, critical of societal injustice and hopeful for redemption. If America meant that redemption had already arrived, the biblical narrative of Heilsgeschichte was no longer relevant.

Yet while America of the nineteenth century meant freedom to Jews, it was a hopeless exile to Black slaves. The Hebrew Bible's central narrative promises liberation from enslavement, protest against injustice, and an ultimate redemption from suffering. That narrative, which formed the backbone of Western culture, shifted in America to Black slaves. The voice of Israelite exile, expressed with such passion in Psalm 137, was now spoken in a Black register. The distinguished freed slave Fredrick Douglass, in a famous address he delivered on July 4, 1852, "What to the Slave is the Fourth of July?," quoted Psalm 137 and stated:

> Fellow-citizens; above your national, tumultuous joy, I hear the mournful wail of millions! Whose chains, heavy and grievous yesterday, are, to-day, rendered more intolerable by the jubilee shouts that reach them. If I do forget, if I do not faithfully remember those bleeding children of sorrow this day, "may my right hand forget her cunning, and may my tongue cleave to the roof of my mouth!" To forget them, to pass lightly over their wrongs, and to chime in with the popular theme, would be treason most scandalous and shocking, and would make me a reproach before God and the world. My subject, then fellow-citizens, is AMERICAN SLAVERY. ... Whether we turn to the declarations of the past, or to the professions of the present, the conduct of the nation seems equally hideous and revolting. America is false to the past, false to the present, and solemnly binds herself to be false to the future. Standing with God and the crushed and bleeding slave on this occasion, I will, in the name of humanity which is outraged, in the name of liberty which is fettered, in the name of the constitution and the Bible, which are disregarded and trampled upon, dare to call in question and to denounce, with all the emphasis I can command, everything that serves to perpetuate slavery – the great sin and shame of America!

America was long been valorized by Jews as their redemption from exile. As a land of economic opportunity, freedom of religion, and democracy that has seen very little overt antisemitism compared to Europe, it remains the greatest challenge to Zionism. Yet the America of Jews is not America. Returning to the image offered by Simone Luzzatto, who compared Jews to a river passing through changing sediments, we cannot simply celebrate America as the land of freedom and liberty and ignore its genocide of Native Americans, its history of slavery its claim of Manifest Destiny, and the ongoing racist aftermath of slavery. For Jews to claim their exile has been overcome in American is for Jews to be in exile from Judaism and live as squatters within America, not a presence invested in its history and culture.

Yet hope for redemption in America also stirs hope for the redemption of America, most prominently by African American theologians, who are the greatest allies of prophetic Jews. Once again, the river is the key metaphor; the African American theologian Vincent Harding strikingly entitled his history of the Black struggle for freedom from slavery in nineteenth-century America, *There is a River,* not after Psalm 137, but after Psalm 46:4: "There is a river, the streams make glad the city of God, the holy habitation of the most high." Although writing about enslavement and Black liberation, he did not invoke the psalm of sorrow, suffering, and vengeance, but a psalm in the prophetic tradition, calling for human action against oppression. His point is that "the river of black struggle" consists of people and of hope that flows through the United States as "the active black struggle for freedom and justice."[25] Neither a metaphor for exile nor the carrier of human pain and suffering, as in Psalm 137, the "cascading river" for Harding consists of human beings in a quest for transformation, integrity and a society of "justice, equity and compassion."[26] Perhaps the most powerful evocation of the river metaphor is found in the famous early poem of inspiration by the great African American poet Langston Hughes (1902–1967), *The Negro Speaks of Rivers:*

> I've known rivers:
> I've known rivers ancient as the world and older than the
> flow of human blood in human veins.
>
> My soul has grown deep like the rivers.
>
> I bathed in the Euphrates when dawns were young.
> I built my hut near the Congo and it lulled me to sleep.
> I looked upon the Nile and raised the pyramids above it.

25 Vincent Harding, *There Is a River: The Black Struggle for Freedom in America* (New York: Harcourt Brace Jovanovich, 1981), xx.
26 Harding, xxiv.

I heard the singing of the Mississippi when Abe Lincoln
went down to New Orleans, and I've seen its muddy
bosom turn all golden in the sunset.

I've known rivers:
Ancient, dusky rivers.

My soul has grown deep like the rivers.

Conclusion: Against the Valorization of Exile

To live with the consciousness of exile is to live at a crossroads: either to turn inward and nurture one's sorrows or to turn outward and recognize that our sorrows are echoed by people all around us. To live today at the verge of the dismemberment of society by elected leaders who are increasingly authoritarian, anti-democratic, racist, and corrupt makes the challenge of exile particularly intense. Too often exile can be an excuse for failing to participate in society's political troubles, for a turn inward, with concern only for Jewish issues, abandoning the prophetic position that derives its loyalties not from either side of a conflict, but from transcendent principles.

In the contemporary world, exile has come to be a choice for most Jews, as it was for the many Israelites in sixth century Babylonia who were offered the opportunity to return to Jerusalem but chose to remain, turning exile into diaspora. The choice to remain in Babylonia ultimately resulted in a vibrant, cosmopolitan Jewish society and the creation of Judaism and the Talmud. By contrast, the insularity of Jews from the wider society, the concern only with what directly affects Jews and a rejection of involvement in the causes of fellow citizens: that is exile. The repudiation of exile in favor of diaspora brings Jewish engagement with the larger society and gives rise to a Jewish voice of prophetic justice, an inner drive to address the tensions and atrocities of the wider society even if Jews are not directly implicated. During the Civil Rights era, Jews were active and courageous on behalf of African Americans; Jews were beaten, arrested and even murdered for their efforts to register Black voters, campaign for voting rights, desegregate schools, shops, restaurants and other public venues, and insist that federal laws guaranteeing integration be enforced. Jewish activism was based on a repudiation of being in exile in America and they acted as an expression of Jewish identity and faith.

But exile is not a political condition – Jews were not exiled by the Romans from the land of Israel – it is an existential state, cultivated as such in Jewish thought. Is it possible to leave that existential state of exile while remaining in diaspora? In his critique of Zionism, Daniel Boyarin has upheld the Talmud as Judaism's portable homeland and, along with others, has reclaimed diaspora "as a theoretical and historical model to replace national self-determination."[27] But the Talmud, a text authored by men over the course of five hundred years, cannot alone bring Jews, including Jewish women, out of homelessness to overcome the melancholy of the existential experience of exile and inspire engagement in movements of social justice. In recent years an unfortunate valorization of exile has been invoked by some critics of Zionism, including Boyarin. Instead of Zionism redeeming Jews from exile, exile is said to redeem Jews from Zionism.

Yet if exile denotes a position of alterity, what will overcome the alterity to engage Jews in a political program of action, especially now that the politics of the State of Israel has driven a wedge between the ethical and the Jewish? Alterity is not a guarantor of political engagement; what is needed is to shed the sensibility of being in exile. The challenges are great, and a moral imperative demands our attention to lift others out of their exile. Perhaps Zionism will come to be understood and enacted not as a redemption from exile, but as a new form of Jewish diasporic existence in the State of Israel.

"Who am I without exile," asks the Palestinian poet Mahmoud Darwish in the title of a poem, echoing the Hasidic understanding of existential exile.[28] "A stranger on the riverbank, like the river...water binds me to your name." "What will we do without exile?" Indeed, if twenty-first century Jews have finally escaped the theology of exile and the existential burden of being exilic, what is the purpose of being a Jew? In recent years, the Argentinian Jewish thinker Santiago Slabodsky has proposed a path: to produce a decolonial Judaism.[29] During the course of diaspora, he argues, Judaism was colonized by the hegemonic Christian West in which Jews lived; now it is time for Jews to forge alliances with those displaced and dispossessed by European colonialism, those labeled by European imperialists as "barbarians," that is, standing outside the framework of "the speech community, the community of selves."[30]

If a Jewish declaration of being in exile arose in response to Christian claims in antiquity, as Yuval argues, Slabodsky's challenge would demand a return to that moment of exilic birth to imagine a very different Jewish path through the course of history. In a similarly suggestive way, Amnon Raz-Krakotzkin writes that "the

27 Daniel Boyarin, "Diaspora: Generation and the Ground of Jewish Identity," *Critical Inquiry* 19:4 (1993), 711.

28 Mahmoud Darwish, *Unfortunately, It Was Paradise*, trans. and ed. by Munir Akash and Carolyn Forche (with Sinan Antoon and Amira El-Zein) (University of California Press, 2003), 113.

29 Santiago Slabodsky, *Decolonial Judaism* (New York: Palgrave Macmillan, 2014).

30 Sidra Ezrahi, "Acts of Impersonation: Barbaric Space as Theater," in *Mirroring Evil: Nazi Imagery/Recent Art*, ed. Norman L. Kleeblatt (East Brunswick, NJ: Rutgers University Press, 2002), 18.

Jew must be part of the dominant culture but maintain a critical relationship to this dominant culture…basing Jewish existence in Israel on the concept of exile means removing the land 'as place' and turning it instead into a spiritual concept, thus separating the concrete land from the idea of redemption."[31] Turning the place of Israel into a spiritual concept would mean replacing an exilic consciousness with a consciousness that Israel is, in fact, within us: there is no exile, home is within, or as yet another place of diasporic possibilities, Jews living in diaspora among Israelis. Such transformation offers the possibility of an ethics of transcultural encounter that links Raz-Krakotzkin with Slabodsky into a political project. Exilic Judaism has meant two thousand years of Jewish history, theology, and religious practices that have left Jews standing on the margins; some would say outside the framework of history altogether.

I would argue that it is neither exile nor its overcoming that will provide the conditions for Jews to act on the ethical mandate intrinsic to Judaism. Exile is isolating, melancholic, often paralyzing in its sense of homelessness, both in its political and existential state, while full assimilation fails to offer the marginal positionality that fosters the necessary critique of social injustice. It is rather the in-between state of diaspora, with awareness of exile yet committed to the present condition, that represents the possibility of the prophetic stance of the critic who identifies with Slabodsky's "barbarians" and offers a constructive jeremiad of "moral chemotherapy."[32] For Judith Butler, for example, diaspora is the key "to locate Jewishness in the moment of its encounter with the non-Jewish, in the dispersing of the self that follows from that encounter."[33] If Jews in diaspora are rivers, as Luzzatto suggests, perhaps they can turn the land of diaspora, in Harding's words, into a "holy habitation," if not a holy land.

A decolonial Judaism would no longer need to respond to Christian supersessionism with a theology of exile. Indeed, the political decolonization of the twentieth century is no doubt an additional reason for Christian questioning or even withdrawal from its supersessionist theology. In exile the souls of Jews are melancholy. In Babylon, "we lay down and wept," but today there is no time for weeping when we are surrounded by injustice. What the prophets accomplish is a transformation of exilic mentality into a position of marginality within diaspora: the lonely

---

31 Amnon Raz-Krakotzkin, "Galut betokh ribonut: Le-bikoret 'shlilat ha-galut' ba-tarbut ha-israelit" ("Exile within Sovereignty: A Critique of the 'Negation of Exile' in Israeli Culture"), *Teoria u-Bikoret* 4 (1993): 23–55. Hebrew.

32 Cathleen Kaveny, *Prophecy without Contempt: Religious Discourse in the Public Square* (Cambridge: Harvard University Press, 2016), 287.

33 Judith Butler, *The Parting of the Ways: Jewishness and the Critique of Zionism* (New York: Columbia University Press, 2012), 26.

but very loud voice of justice, compassion and hope that constitutes the promised redemption:

> "They know no bounds in deeds of wickedness; they judge not with justice the cause of the fatherless, the rights of the needy. Shall I not punish them for these things, says the Lord, and shall I not avenge myself on a nation such as this? An appalling and horrible thing has happened in the land: the prophets prophesy falsely and the priests rule at their direction; my people love to have it so, but what will you do when the end comes?" (Jeremiah 5:28–31)
>
> "I hate, I despise your feasts, and I take no delight in your solemn assemblies. [22] Even though you offer me your burnt offerings and cereal offerings, I will not accept them, and the peace offerings of your fatted beasts I will not look upon. Take away from me the noise of your songs; to the melody of your harps I will not listen. But let justice roll down like waters, and righteousness like an ever-flowing stream." (Amos 5:21–24)
>
> "Thou art the man!" (2 Samuel 12:7)
>
> "O LORD, I have heard the report of thee, and thy work, O LORD, do I fear. In the midst of the years renew it; in the midst of the years make it known; in wrath remember mercy." (Habakuk 3:1–2).
>
> "Your wounds I will heal, because they have called you an outcast." (Jeremiah 30:17)
>
> "Not by might but by spirit, says the Lord of hosts." (Zechariah 4:6)

Can the existential sense of exile that has pervaded Jewish identity over the centuries be transformed into diaspora to awaken the prophetic voice for social justice and hope for redemption? As prophetic, the diasporic Jew is never at home, never content or complacent in a world of injustice. Perhaps the glass that is smashed at the end of a wedding ceremony can be interpreted anew as the new couple's commitment to eradicate injustice.

Diaspora can transform exile into Jewish creativity, as has happened at times during the course of the past two millennia. The prophet is a diasporic exemplar, leaving home and journeying to the urban seat of the political, military, and economic power to demand an end to corruption, exploitation, cruelty, and indifference. The prophetic position cannot exist by trying to end exile with statehood or by embracing exile as the essential mentality of Jewishness. To insist on a consciousness of exile is to walk away from the prophetic; to reject exile and embrace diaspora is to affirm the prophetic passion for justice by identifying as Jews with the "barbarians" whose suffering demands redemption.

Works Cited

Boyarin, Daniel. "Diaspora: Generation and the Ground of Jewish Identity." *Critical Inquiry* 19:4 (1993): 693–725.

Burg, Avrum. "A Zionist Changes His Mind." *Tikkun* 22:6 (2007), 53–57.

Butler, Judith. *The Parting of the Ways: Jewishness and the Critique of Zionism.* New York: Columbia University Press, 2012.

Darwish, Mahmoud. *Unfortunately, It Was Paradise.* Translated and edited by Munir Akash and Carolyn Forche (with Sinan Antoon and Amira El-Zein). University of California Press, 2003.

Davidovich Eshed, Avital. "'How then could I gaze at a virgin?' The Concept of Virginity in Medieval Ashkenazi-Jewish Culture in Christendom." [Hebrew] PhD diss., Tel Aviv University, 2014.

Diner, Hasia. *A New Promised Land: A History of Jews in America.* New York: Oxford University Press, 2002.

Elkins, Caroline and Susan Pedersen. "Settler Colonialism: A Concept and Its Uses." In *Settler Colonialism in the Twentieth Century: Projects, Practices, Legacies*, edited by Caroline Elkins and Susan Pedersen, 1–20. New York: Routledge, 2005.

Ezrahi, Sidra. "Acts of Impersonation: Barbaric Space as Theater." In *Mirroring Evil: Nazi Imagery/Recent Art*, edited by Norman L. Kleeblatt. East Brunswick, NJ: Rutgers University Press, 2002.

Geiger, Abraham. *Das Judentum und seine Geschichte.* Breslau: Schlettersche Buchhandlung, 1864.

Gruen, Eric. *Diaspora: Jews amidst Greeks and Romans.* Cambridge: Harvard University Press, 2002.

Harding, Vincent. *There Is a River: The Black Struggle for Freedom in America.* New York: Harcourt Brace Jovanovich, 1981.

Johnston, Anna and Alan Lawson, "Settler Colonies." In *A Companion to Postcolonial Studies*, edited by Henry Schwarz and Sangeeta Ray. Malden, MA: Blackwell, 2000.

Kahane, Meir. *The Jewish Idea.* Institute for Publication of the Writings of Rabbi Meir Kahane, 1998. Vol. 1.

Kaveny, Cathleen. *Prophecy without Contempt: Religious Discourse in the Public Square.* Cambridge: Harvard University Press, 2016.

Magid, Shaul. *Meir Kahane: An American Jewish Radical.* Princeton: Princeton University Press, forthcoming.

Meyer, Michael. *Response to Modernity: A History of the Reform Movement in Judaism.* Detroit: Wayne State University Press, 1995.

Moltmann, Jürgen. *Experiences of God.* Translated by Margaret Kohl. Philadelphia: Fortress Press, 1980.

Philipson, David. *The Reform Movement in Judaism.* New York: Macmillan, 1907.

Raz-Krakotzkin, Amnon. "Galut betokh ribonut: Le-bikoret 'shlilat ha-galut' ba-tarbut
ha-israelit" ("Exile within Sovereignty: A Critique of the 'Negation of Exile' in Israeli Culture"), *Teoria u-Bikoret* 4 (1993): 23–55. Hebrew.

Scholem, Gershom. *On Jews and Judaism in Crisis.* New York: Schocken Books, 1976.

Scholem, Gershom. *Major Trends in Jewish Mysticism.* Translated by George Lichtheim. Jerusalem: Schocken Publishing House, 1941.

Slabodsky, Santiago. *Decolonial Judaism.* New York: Palgrave Macmillan, 2014.

Wessely, Herz. *Divrei Torah v'Emet.* Berlin, 1782.

Yuval, Israel. "Christianity in Talmud and Midrash: Parallelomania or Parallelophobia?" In *Transforming Relation: Essays on Jews and Christians throughout History in Honor of Michael A. Signer*, edited by Franklin T. Harkins and John van Engen. South Bend, IN: University of Notre Dame Press, 2010.

Yuval, Israel. "The Myth of the Jewish Exile from the Land of Israel" *Common Knowledge* 12:1 (2006): 16–33.

Ino Augsberg

Diaspomenos: Hermeneutics of Exile

I

"I get it" is a colloquial expression, widely used especially in the US, which means that the speaker understands what another person has said or meant to say. The metaphorical expressions of "capturing," "catching," or "grasping" a particular meaning obviously point in the same direction, as they try to catch the same aspect. According to the common understanding as captured in these expressions, understanding means to get a hold of something, that is, to acquire a certain knowledge. In this view, to understand something means that it no longer appears strange, foreign, or alien to those who understand, since its particularities have been successfully integrated in the broader horizon of our pre-existing worldview. Everything is put back in its place, right where it belongs. Nothing is left aside and thus nothing remains disturbing or even irritating. Understanding, then, is complete once we have become familiar with what is to be understood. Yet this familiarity cannot be created anew. It refers to a concept that already has to exist before. In consequence, cognition is basically a process of recognition, a peculiar variant of *anamnesis.* It takes us back to the place where we have always been.

Understood in this way, a successful understanding works precisely like a successful translation from one language to another, for instance from Greek to English or from German to French. However, the question remains if a translation can ever be entirely successful in this sense or if, by contrast, any translation conceived of in this manner just reveals that the only thing that can really be translated, that is, transferred from one linguistic context into another, is the meaning of a given text of speech, but not this speech or text itself.[1] Thus, if we want to understand not only the meaning of understanding, but also the limits of an understanding constituted by meaning only, we have to ask whether there is an alternative understanding of understanding, an understanding of understanding that might be connected with the concept of *diaspora.* This is what I intend to do in the following.

1 Georges-Arthur Goldschmidt, *Freud wartet auf das Wort. Freud und die deutsche Sprache II* (Zürich: Ammann, 2006), 9. In this preface to the German translation of his book, Goldschmidt briefly summarizes his book's topic – which deals with the reverse problem, namely, the difficulty of translating Freud's texts into French – for a German audience.

https://doi.org/10.1515/9783111062631-003

II

In chapter 24 of his "Dialogues of the Gods," Lucian of Samosata lets the messenger of the gods, Hermes, lament his own sufferings towards his mother Maia. In the English translation by Henry Watson Fowler and his brother Francis George Fowler, the passage reads as follows:

> HERMES: Mother, I am the most miserable god in Heaven.
> MAIA: Don't say such things, child.
> HERMES: Am I to do all the work of Heaven with my own hands, to be hurried from one piece of drudgery to another, and never say a word? I have to get up early, sweep the dining-room, lay the cushions and put all to rights; then I have to wait on Zeus, and take his messages, up and down, all day long; and I am no sooner back again (no time for a wash) than I have to lay the table; and there was the nectar to pour out, too, till this new cup-bearer was bought. And it really is too bad, that when every one else is in bed, I should have to go off to Pluto with the Shades, and play the usher in Rhadamanthus's court. It is not enough that I must be busy all day in the wrestling-ground and the Assembly and the schools of rhetoric, the dead must have their share in me too.[2]

At first glance, the use of the expression "to be hurried from one to another" in the first sentence seems perfectly in line with the general narrative. Accordingly, Hermes' trouble is simply a lack of time. Although one might be a little distracted by the fact that this lack of time is caused by the double occupation with the business of both the living and the dead, the general experience thus seems to be a fairly well-known, if not a typically modern one. Hermes is simply stressed out because he is so super busy. On this account, he might be taken as a role model for contemporary academics who will find no difficulty in joining his lamentations.

Yet a second, closer look at the original text reveals a more disturbing aspect of the description. The original expression translated as "hurried from one to another" is the Greek word *diaspomenos.* Once again, at first the word seems rather innocuous. It has a literal or material meaning that comes to the fore very clearly in a combination like *aer diaspomenos* which we find, for instance, in Aristotle's work on the soul.[3] In this context, it refers to a specific process of distribution, namely, the evenly distributed air in a certain room. Thus, it presupposes an object of distribution already subdivided into a countless number of small elements that can easily be distributed in a specific area. As such, it designates a natural process

2 Lucian of Samosata, "Dialogues of the Gods," in *The Works of Lucian of Samosata*, trans. H. W. Fowler and F. G. Fowler, vol. 1 (Oxford: Oxford University Press, 1905), 62–89.

3 See Aristotle, *De anima*, 411a, 20.

leading to an equilibrated state of affairs, a *homeostasis.* Thus, one might regard it as a peaceful, harmonious movement. However, Hermes does not use the word in such a context. He uses it in order to describe his own personal situation. In this way, applied as an attribute to a person, the movement reveals a different, rather uncanny aspect. According to this description, the *per definitionem* undividable individual is nevertheless divided, that is to say, torn into bits and pieces. Thus conceived, the word enshrines a certain traumatic core. No wonder, then, that *diaspomenos* refers to a linguistic root which has another, much better-known offspring, which also indicates a certain process of disrupture and self-alienation: diaspora.

The question, then, is whether the process of distribution or fragmentation that Hermes attributes to himself is opposed to the specific art or technique bearing his name, hermeneutics, or if this activity, by contrast, partakes in that very business, indicating indeed its very nature. Is hermeneutics rather a process of dispersion or of re-collecting the shattered pieces? Is it an endeavour to re-construct a certain unity or a procedure which constantly decomposes any pre-given entity? Is it a struggle for (re-)gaining and defending identity, or a process of learning to live with and indeed even of multiplying differences?

III

The first position is taken by those claiming that understanding is basically a process of homecoming. Thus, to understand something properly means to leave the state of diaspora, returning from a foreign, possibly even hostile environment into one's own home (country). What is more, the proper understanding not only includes this negative dimension of turning away from a strange and thus incomprehensible surrounding. It actually claims to be bringing something home that used to belong to a foreign sphere, but which is now, by the very process of understanding, transferred to the person who understands it. Conceived of in this way, the movement has a quasi-legal (and also economic) dimension, since the process of returning is by the same token characterised as a process of appropriation.[4] Understanding means, at least according to Schleiermacher's understanding, the process which turns something that used to be strange or foreign into something of one's own.[5] Thus, by the same movement, the strange and foreign are described

4 Jacques Derrida, *Spurs. Nietzsche's Styles / Éperons. Les Styles de Nietzsche* (Chicago and London: The Chicago University Press, 1979), 110.

5 Friedrich Schleiermacher, "Über den Begriff der Hermeneutik mit Bezug auf F. A. Wolfs Andeutungen und Asts Lehrbuch," in Schleiermacher, *Hermeneutik und Kritik*, ed. Manfred Frank (Frankfurt am Main: Suhrkamp, 1977), 315.

not only as a sphere in which one does not belong, but also as a sphere which does not belong to oneself. Understanding alters this situation. To understand something properly, therefore, means to understand something as one's property.

The remaining question, then, is who is typically already in that privileged position from which it is possible to take possession of those things we intend to understand. In the classical Platonic tradition, this privileged position is ascribed to the reader, for no author of a text can hold onto his possession. By the time he publishes his text, he can no longer be called the owner of the text and its meaning. On the contrary, from then on, the author must be aware of the fact that any reader can take advantage of the text, reading and understanding it in his or her very own way.[6]

Yet in the Greek and Latin debates on the topic, we also find an opposite concept of the relationship between an author and his readers. In this perspective, the author remains the master or owner of his text. In contrast to the Platonic scheme, it is now the author taking advantage of the reader, and not the other way round. This relationship is expressed in a Greek saying which has a very explicitly sexual, or more precisely homosexual connotation. It presents the said relationship as a process of sodomy. In its slightly less explicit Latin translation, this proverbial understanding of understanding reads as follows: *amat qui scribet, qui leget pedicatur.*[7] In this perspective, the *stilus* of the writer is no longer only an instrument used to create certain traces on the surface of the *tabula cerata.* It is also a symbol of the unavoidable penetrating force that every reader must endure.

Notwithstanding the differences, the general approach of both positions is identical. Both assume not only that knowledge is power but that understanding is a process in which a certain subject tries to get a hold of something, claiming to have a right to use it exclusively according to its own will, and for its own pleasure. Along the lines of understanding as ownership, the process of understanding presupposes a quasi-majestic, sovereign subject that is able to determine meaning by commanding and controlling its referential relations, allowing for some, and setting limits and prohibitions for others.

Language obviously bears witness to this kind of understanding, if it speaks of understanding as grasping something, that is to say, to take things literally into one's own hands, or of conceiving, thus referring back to the Latin *capere*, to catch. Along the same lines, one might read the Latin verb *legere* in the sense of collecting, of putting together the dispersed elements of, for instance – which of

6 Plato, *Phaidros*, 275d f.

7 See Jesper Svenbro, *Phrasikleia: An Anthropology of Reading in Ancient Greece* (Ithaca: Cornell University Press, 1993), 187.

course is more than just an example – a text. Indeed, the German verb *lesen* resonates this double meaning of both reading and collecting; furthermore, the even more outspoken the noun *Lese* explicitly points to the second aspect. In a parallel movement, the notion of "comprehending" indicates a movement of taking or putting things together. In both cases, the functional necessity of this understanding is based on the idea that meaning can only be derived from certain units (namely, words or syntactical structures), but never from the smaller fragments themselves (namely, the individual letters). This is, once again, the position held by Schleiermacher, who explicitly rejects such a "kabbalistic" way of reading texts. In order for something to be possessed, it has to be a real object, a given entity, not just a disturbing multitude of fragments.[8]

Against this twofold background of a certain understanding of understanding, one might take another step, claiming that the common ground for both perspectives is a specifically legal concept of understanding. This categorisation – which itself, traced back to its origins as *kategoresthai*, points back to a juristic origin – seems fairly evident with regard to hermeneutics as appropriation, since this process is obviously based on juristic categories. Yet it also holds true for the fundamental movement of understanding as gathering or collecting. Read in this way, it refers to an idea of *lex* as *legere*, in the above-mentioned sense, as well as of *ligare*. Elaborating on the specific character of this legal movement, one might add another aspect that seems to be intertwined with the general concept. On both accounts, we find at the center of the conception a subject capable of gathering and collecting the fragmented elements of both a normative text and the factual circumstances, tying them together into a form which is said to be correct and thus normatively powerful: a binding decision. It is obvious that this concept is at least strengthened, if not enabled as such by a legal system that embodies this kind of idea, in the sense that it concentrates the power of law- and decision-making – and thus the determination of legal meaning – in one central authority figure, namely, an emperor or the pope. In any case, the appropriation model appears to be based on the conception of a subject which is the master in its own home and thus, normatively speaking, autonomous.

IV

If in this way the first model of understanding can be characterized as this kind of appropriation, then, by contrast, the opposing view must emphasize the herme-

8 Schleiermacher, *Hermeneutik und Kritik*, 129.

neutical procedure as a process of ex-appropriation.[9] Yet this ex-appropriation should not be confused with the two-step movement of an ex- and re-appropriation, for this would be nothing else than just another, though slightly more complicated, variation of the first movement. In order to fulfil its role as a real counterpart, the second understanding cannot simply be interested in a different distribution of ownership. It has to aim at and attack property as a central category. Accordingly, ex-appropriation cannot just point to a distribution in the sense of a pluralization of possible meanings. It has to insist on a position which – since it itself can never be appropriated – by its very existence subverts the fundamental role of the appropriation approach in hermeneutic understanding. Thus, the insistence on the decisive role of each and every single element in the hermeneutic process – in particular of the individual letter, the instance of the letter – cannot be conceived of as a perspective which is now willing to accept and admit that even the smallest linguistic elements may be regarded as possible meaningful units. Once again, this kind of approach would remain in the same general line of argument, merely broadening the focus instead of changing the perspective entirely.

By contrast, to understand hermeneutics in the context of ex-appropriation means to conceive of language not only as a sphere of certain smaller and bigger elements which, like in a puzzle, have to be collected and put together in order to grasp the general picture. There is no longer such a picture, since no element is conceived of as an *atomos* in the strict sense, but is continuously subdivided, cut into other pieces. Reading, then, can no longer mean simply collecting. It must be understood – a relationship explicitly marked, for instance, by Jacob Grimm in his essay on poetry within the law, "Von der Poesie im Recht" – as partaking in the permanent process of parting and dividing, which we call language.[10]

Obviously, this process can hardly be reconciled with the position of a majestic, sovereign subject claiming to be the owner and master of its own home. What is more, this subversive movement seems, at least at first glance, also completely opposed to the legal view, which evidently aims at securing order and stability. If the law and the hermeneutics of appropriation are inseparably intertwined, then the loss of a functioning hierarchical legal system and the loss of the hermeneutic ability to guarantee stable meaning are two corresponding sides of the same coin.

9 See on this concept Jacques Derrida, "'Eating Well,' or the Calculation of the Subject," in Derrida, *Points... Interviews 1974–1994* (Stanford: Stanford University Press, 1995), 255–287.

10 Jacob Grimm, "Von der Poesie im Recht," in *Zeitschrift für geschichtliche Rechtswissenschaft* (1815) in *Kleinere Schriften, Band 6: Recensionen und vermischte Aufsätze. Dritter Theil* (repr., Hildesheim/Zürich/New York: Olms – Weidmann, 1991), 152–191; Thomas Schestag, *Parerga: Friedrich Hölderlin/Carl Schmitt/Franz Kafka/Platon/Friedrich Schleiermacher/Walter Benjamin/Jacques Derrida. Zur literarischen Hermeneutik* (Munich: Boer, 1991), 51.

In this context, one might, referring to Jewish history and tradition, point to Robert Cover's statement that, since "the Temple *has* been destroyed – meaning *is* no longer unitary; any hermeneutic implies another."[11] Obviously, this statement itself has to be understood as a narrative. Yet it is against this background that we must take into view and understand the contemporary discussion in Israel, in which some claim that the Sanhedrin should be re-established.

One may ask, however, if this is the only story that can be told. For as the Talmud states, even though the temple was destroyed, Jewish law continues to exist. Hence there apparently is a possibility of law in the diaspora, and, by the same token, a possibility of a hermeneutics of exile. In consequence, there appears to be some empirical evidence that neither law nor hermeneutics are categorically connected to the appropriation model. Yet of course, the same holds true for the ex-appropriation model, as this model does not, and indeed cannot, *per definitionem*, belong to one specific tradition.

From this perspective, one might take another view on the so-called Western legal tradition, too. In doing so, we could note, for example, a certain characteristic of legal operations which Rudolf von Jhering, the most famous German legal scholar of the nineteenth century, presented in his seminal work on the "Geist des römischen Rechts auf den verschiedenen Stufen seiner Entwicklung." According to Jhering's own analysis, the main achievement in the development of Roman law is its capacity for analytical thinking, that is to say, a thinking which dissects a problem into its separate elements. Interestingly, Jhering calls this procedure by its Greek name, *analysis*, but he also uses a German word to describe this operation: *Zersetzung.*[12] He thus uses a word that indicates the precise opposite to the typical expression for law-making, *Rechtssetzung.* What is more, Jhering uses a word that in German usually has a peculiar, rather negative connotation. *Zersetzung*, in this understanding, is not a process which stops at a certain point, presenting us with some neatly arranged elements that later can be used to construct something new. Rather than referring to anything similar to a logical (or, in Jhering's use of the concept, chemical) analysis, or a *lösen* conceived of as the *Lösung eines Rätsels*, the solving of a puzzle (as in Goethe's *Faust*, where Faust, in the scene "Walpurgisnacht", states: "Da muß sich manches Rätsel lösen," and Mephistopheles replies: "Doch manches Rätsel knüpft sich auch."), the movement indi-

11 Robert Cover, "Nomos and Narrative," in *Narrative, Violence, and the Law. The Essays of Robert Cover*, ed. Martha Minow, et. al. (Ann Arbor: University of Michigan Press, 1993), 163.

12 Rudolf von Jhering, *Geist des römischen Rechts auf den verschiedenen Stufen seiner Entwicklung. Dritter Teil, Bd. 1* (Leipzig: Breitkopf und Härtel, 1865), 12; See also Jhering, *Geist des römischen Rechts auf den verschiedenen Stufen seiner Entwicklung, Zweiter Teil, Bd. 2* (Leipzig: Breitkopf und Härtel, 1858), 361.

cates a process of decomposition, even decay. Thus, conceived of as *Zersetzung*, the legal mechanisms will eventually turn against themselves, decomposing the classical idea of a legal system built on clear-cut categories. Hermes is leading the way to the realm of the dead.

Obviously, one may easily object to this kind of reading, claiming that this is but an over-interpretation of a certain word which, in order to be understood in this peculiar way, must be isolated from its original specific context and its specific function within it. Moreover, the interpretation is evidently closely linked to the German word as such. One may be able to explain what is happening here for an English-speaking audience; but the movement itself, this peculiar *Zersetzung* of concepts, is untranslatable.

However, this may lead us to just another aspect. On the one hand, the untranslatability bears witness to the fact that no language, not even the so-called mother tongue, can ever be considered the property of those who use it. That no expression can ever be completely transferred, translated from one language to another, is due to the fact that no language can ever be appropriated. It slips away from every attempt to grasp and take possession of it, thus eluding a translation fixed on the determination of meaning.

Yet on the other hand, a certain translation is not only possible but indeed takes place all the time. On this account, we may be able to connect Jhering's *Zersetzung* with a certain understanding of the Greek concepts of *nemein* and *nomos*. In this context, these expressions no longer refer only to the separation and distribution of a given entity, namely, a newly conquered land. Rather, they indicate something like a self-distribution of the law. Normativity thus appears as a form of operationalizing differences, which cannot stop at a certain point but continues to analyze and part or split its own differences. In this perspective, the *nomos* itself is something that we can never fully grasp or understand, and thus never allows for a situation where the *autos* has taken complete control. Within the *nomos*, there remains something uncanny, or, to use the German translation, *unheimlich*. Hence, even if someone should indeed manage to pass the doorkeeper and get access to the law, that does not mean that inside the legal system he or she will ever feel at home. Quite the opposite.

V

The last question that may be asked, though not (for reasons that by now should have become sufficiently clear) properly answered, is whether this contrast, the presentation of two seemingly contradictory approaches, the alternative of hermeneutics being either a process of appropriation or of ex-appropriation, of *legere*, *logos* and *lex* on the one side and *nemein*, *nomos* and *Zersetzung* on the other, is itself rather a process of ongoing disrupture or of re-collection. Which one of the said alternatives should we prefer?

Yet perhaps it is wrong to formulate the question in this way in the first place. We cannot conceive of the ex-appropriation as the proper form of hermeneutics without falling into the common trap of self-contradiction. Thus, if for instance Theodor Adorno states that "only those thoughts are true that do not understand themselves," one may ask if Adorno's thought expressed in this way is actually meant to be true.[13] The difference between the two perspectives is asymmetrical, as the very principle of a thinking in alternatives already belongs to one side of the distinction.

Thus, rather than presenting one hermeneutical perspective as the alternative view to the other, we may ask whether there is a possibility to combine things in a way that simultaneously works as a resistance against the mere accumulative appropriation. In his work "Jerusalem," which itself combines two fairly distinct if not even almost irreconcilable sections,[14] Moses Mendelssohn refers to a famous Rabbinic saying, stating that "although the one solves and the other binds, both are teaching the words of the living God."[15] Mendelssohn comments on this saying (whose apparently clear-cut distinction one might be tempted to associate with the difference between *nemein* and *legein/legere/ligare*) and on the accusation by some Christian scholars that it must be read as a statement against logic, or more precisely, against the necessity of binary logic to exclude the third option. Mendelssohn's tactic in his comment on this critique is remarkable. He does not openly contradict this law of logic, since such a statement would have to use the very notion that is to be questioned at the same time. Rather, he affirms this law. Yet in the same movement, he shifts the debate from the field of logic to the field of ethics, thereby formulating a supposedly very strict exception from the general rule – from a rule, however, which of course allows for no exception whatsoever. Thus, in supporting the rule and merely adding or supplementing a new perspective, Mendelssohn also undermines it.

---

13 Theodor W. Adorno, *Minima Moralia. Reflexionen aus dem beschädigten Leben*, in *Gesammelte Schriften*, vol. 4, 2nd ed., ed. Rolf Tiedemann (Frankfurt am Main.: Suhrkamp, sec. ed. 1995), 218.

14 See on this often-noted aspect of the work Alexander Altmann, "Moses Mendelssohn's Concept of Judaism Reexamined," in Altmann, *Von der mittelalterlichen zur modernen Aufklärung. Studien zur jüdischen Geistesgeschichte* (Tübingen: Mohr Siebeck, 1987), 234–248.

15 Moses Mendelssohn, "Jerusalem oder über religiöse Macht und Judentum" in *Gesammelte Schriften. Jubiläumsausgabe, vol. 8: Schriften zum Judentum*, ed. Alexander Altmann (Stuttgart: Frommann [Holzboog], 1983), 168.

> I have seen so many pedants use this saying to prove that the rabbis do not believe the sentence of contradiction. I wish to live the days when all the peoples of the earth will accept this exception to the general law of contradiction: *the fast day of the Fourth Month and the fast day of the Tenth Month may be transformed into joy and gladness, only love truth and peace* (Zachar. 8, 19.).[16]

Maybe this kind of strategy could also be a suitable role model for the hermeneutic difficulty: a form of collection which is at the same time, *zugleich*, a process of disjuncture, and vice versa. On this account, nothing, not even diaspora itself, can serve as a stable point of reference. It may not even suffice to stabilize the concept by confronting a rather positive connotation of diaspora in the sense of *t'futsoth* with its negative counterpart *galut.*[17] By contrast, it might be necessary to turn the concept of diaspora against itself, i.e., to insist on the diaspora within (or from) the diaspora. One might be tempted to see such a strangely twisted movement in a letter which Paul Celan writes to Max Frisch, explaining why he could not accept an invitation by Frisch and Ingeborg Bachmann:

> I have just been reminded of a duty from which I do not know how to escape, of my promise made months ago to go to London for the Jewish Easter, and now, although I do not remember ever having left Egypt, I will celebrate it in England.[18]

In this perspective, the diasporic turn within the diaspora means to celebrate *pesach* in Egypt.[19]

References

Adorno, Theodor W. *Minima Moralia. Reflexionen aus dem beschädigten Leben.* In *Gesammelte Schriften,* edited by Rolf Tiedemann. Vol. 4, 2nd ed. Frankfurt am Main: Suhrkamp, 1995.

Agamben, Giorgio. "Easter in Egypt." In *The Fire and the Tale.* Stanford: Stanford University Press, 2017.

Altmann, Alexander. "Moses Mendelssohn's Concept of Judaism Reexamined." In *Von der mittelalterlichen zur modernen Aufklärung. Studien zur jüdischen Geistesgeschichte.* Tübingen: Mohr Siebeck, 1987.

16 Mendelssohn, "Jerusalem," 168.

17 See on this difference Michael Galchinsky, "Scattered Seeds: A Dialogue of Diaspora," in *Insider/ Outsider: American Jews and Multiculturalism*, ed. David Biale, et. al. (Berkeley: University of California Press, 1998), 195.

18 Paul Celan, "Letter to Max Frisch from 18 April 1959," in Ingeborg Bachmann/Paul Celan, *Herzzeit Der Briefwechsel*, ed. Bertrand Badiou et al. (Frankfurt am Main: Suhrkamp, 2008), 165.

19 See Giorgio Agamben, "Easter in Egypt," in *The Fire and the Tale* (Stanford: Stanford University Press, 2017), who, however, combines this idea with a highly problematic and dubious political association, confronting Celan's statement with the "Zionist ideal."

Aristotle, *De anima. Leiden: Brill, 1994.*

Celan, Paul. "Letter to Max Frisch from 18 April 1959." In *Herzzeit. Der Briefwechsel. Mit den Briefwechseln von Paul Celan und Max Frisch sowie zwischen Ingeborg Bachmann und Gisèle Celan-Lestrange*, edited by Bertrand Badiou et al. Frankfurt am Main: Suhrkamp, 2008.

Cover, Robert. "Nomos and Narrative." In *Narrative, Violence, and the Law. The Essays of Robert Cover*, edited by Martha Minow, Michael Ryan, and Austin Sarat. Ann Arbor: University of Michigan Press, 1993.

Derrida, Jacques. *Spurs. Nietzsche's Styles/Éperons. Les Styles de Nietzsche.* Chicago and London: The Chicago University Press, 1979.

Derrida, Jacques. "'Eating Well,' or the Calculation of the Subject." In *Points... Interviews 1974–1994.* Stanford: Stanford University Press, 1995.

Galchinsky, Michael. "Scattered Seeds: A Dialogue of Diaspora." In *Insider/Outsider: American Jews and Multiculturalism*, edited by David Biale, Michael Galchinsky, and Susannah Heschel. Berkeley: University of California Press, 1998.

Goldschmidt, Georges-Arthur. *Freud wartet auf das Wort. Freud und die deutsche Sprache II.* Zürich: Ammann, 2006.

Grimm, Jacob. "Von der Poesie im Recht." *Zeitschrift für geschichtliche Rechtswissenschaft* 2, no. 1 (1815): 25–99. Reprint in *Kleinere Schriften, Band 6: Recensionen und vermischte Aufsätze. Dritter Theil.* Hildesheim: Olms - Weidmann, 1991.

Jhering, Rudolf von. *Geist des römischen Rechts auf den verschiedenen Stufen seiner Entwicklung. Dritter Teil.* Vol. 1–2. Leipzig: Breitkopf und Härtel, 1865.

Jhering, Rudolf von. *Geist des römischen Rechts auf den verschiedenen Stufen seiner Entwicklung, Zweiter Teil.* Vol. 2. Leipzig: Breitkopf und Härtel, 1858.

Lucian of Samosata, "Dialogues of the Gods." In Vol. 1 of *The Works of Lucian of Samosata.* Translated by H. W. Fowler and F. G. Fowler. Oxford: Oxford University Press, 1905.

Mendelssohn, Moses. "Jerusalem oder über religiöse Macht und Judentum." In *Gesammelte Schriften. Jubiläumsausgabe: Schriften zum Judentum*, edited by Alexander Altmann. Vol. 8. Stuttgart: Frommann (Holzboog), 1983.

Plato. *Phaidros.* Vol. 9 of *Plato in Twelve Volumes*, translated by Harold N. Fowler. Cambridge, MA: Harvard University Press, 1925.

Schestag, Thomas. *Parerga: Friedrich Hölderlin/Carl Schmitt/Franz Kafka/Platon/Friedrich Schleiermacher/ Walter Benjamin/Jacques Derrida. Zur literarischen Hermeneutik.* Munich: Boer, 1991.

Schleiermacher, Friedrich. "Über den Begriff der Hermeneutik mit Bezug auf F. A. Wolfs Andeutungen und Asts Lehrbuch." In *Hermeneutik und Kritik*, edited by Manfred Frank. Frankfurt am Main: Suhrkamp, 1977.

Svenbro, Jesper. *Phrasikleia: An Anthropology of Reading in Ancient Greece.* Ithaca: Cornell University Press, 1993.

II. Traditions of Plurality

Suzanne Last Stone

Law without Nation? The Ongoing Jewish Discussion

I Introduction

In his preface to *Law and Revolution*, Harold Berman urged us "to overcome ... the identification of all our law with national law and all our legal history with national legal history."[1] He penned these words in 1983 when, he claimed, an age was coming to an end: the age of the Western legal tradition. By the mid-twentieth century, that tradition, born in revolution, was itself facing a revolutionary crisis—the disintegration of community. "Bonds of race, religion, soil, family, class, neighborhood and work community" had "dissolved into abstract and superficial nationalisms," concomitant with "the decline of unity and common purpose in Western civilization as a whole."[2] Religion and law, Berman noted, are the traditional symbols of community in the West, yet religion became a private matter and law a matter of practical expediency." Neither expresses any longer the community's vision of its future and its past; neither commands any longer its passionate loyalty."[3] Berman was engaged in an intellectual retrieval project. He hoped to cure the ills of the twentieth century by looking backward at the Western legal tradition and resuscitating the integration of religion and law—at least, at the metaphoric level in order to restore to law a transcendent or utopian cast—along with an integrative jurisprudence that did not reduce law to a set of rules or technical devices nor merely identify it with the positive command of the national sovereign.

Although Berman mentions vaguely some countersigns to the nationalist idea —increased economic, cultural, and scientific interdependence on a regional and worldwide basis—he could hardly anticipate the immense transformations of the

Note: This essay was published originally in *Law Without Nations*, edited by Austin Sarat, Lawrence Douglas, and Martha Merrill Umphrey, (Stanford: Stanford University Press 2010). Reprint with kind permission by the Board of Trustees of the Leland Stanford Jr. University.

For a more detailed piece of the section *From the bible to the state of Israel*, and an earlier version of the section *The Cosmopolitan Halakha*, see Suzanne Last Stone, *"Religion and State: Models of Separation from within Jewish Law,"* International Journal of Constitutional Law 6 (2008):631.

1 Harold Berman, *Law and Revolution* (Cambridge, MA: Harvard University Press, 1999), vi.
2 Ibid.
3 Ibid.

https://doi.org/10.1515/9783111062631-004

last thirty years as the nation-state yielded to the market-state and the twin phenomena of globalization and privatization took wing. On the heels of these transformations, law, too, is changing dramatically as it develops new mechanisms to support this interdependence. The existence of the European Union, together with the globalization of the commercial world, has propelled the search for transnational law—general principles of law that transcend the law of any nation-state —and that can be applied to purely internal and not only international cases.[4] Talk of a global constitutionalism, over and above divisions of nationalism and ethnicity, of a *ius humanitatis*, a transnational humanitarian and human rights law, is now commonplace. Thus, Europeans are debating the need for a new *ius commune*, a common legal tradition that transcends the law of any nation-state, and even the United States is engaging the community of nations by resorting to foreign law in constitutional interpretation.

The new alliances across the globe and a growing cosmopolitanism, however, have not yet produced a genuine world legal community nor restored a common sense of the transcendent purpose of law. If anything, law has become more technical, more bureaucratic, and more mass-produced. Instead, in answer to the social disintegration and loss of community Berman identified, increased globalization has been accompanied by the countervailing fragmentation of national identities into local identities and by a resurgence of religious belief. Indeed, if the last five hundred years of Western history were marked by the emergence of utopian political movements aimed at creating perfection in the immanent reality of this world —Jacobinism, communism, the Enlightenment, the American and French revolutions, and National Socialism—today we are witnessing the rise of trans-state, transnational utopian religious movements. These movements, by and large, aim to achieve this perfection through the construction of new collectivities and reconstruction of collective boundaries.[5] Even apart from any utopian aim, world historical religions are being constituted for the first time as "de-territorialized, transna-

4 See, generally, H. Patrick Glenn, "Transnational Common Laws," *Fordham International l Law Journal* 29 (2006): 457.

5 These religious movements often depict themselves as anti-modern, of course. Indeed, they portray themselves as attempts to recover the lost, original ideal of a unified religious polity. But this is not traditionalism; it is a modern reaction to modern themes. If one problem of modernity is fragmentation and the splintering of social life into multiple and separate domains, unity is the way to overcome it, which is often depicted as a return to origins. As we know, the reconstruction of a tradition far more traditional than the original one ever was is one of the defining characteristics of modernity. See Haym Soloveitchik, "Rupture and Reconstruction: The Transformation of Contemporary Orthodoxy," *Tradition* 28 (1994): 64; Eric Hobsbawm, "Introduction: Inventing Tradition," in *The Invention of Tradition*, ed. Eric Hobsbawm and Terence Ranger (Cambridge: Cambridge University Press, 1983), 1.

tional global imagined communities, detached from the societal settings in which they were traditionally embedded."[6]

The simultaneous globalization and fragmentation of political life has led many theorists to conclude that we are in a period of "paradigmatic transition,"[7] in which the decline of the significance of national boundaries and of nationstates as the privileged unit of analysis is merely the most visible sign. While the decline of nation-states, and their loss of charisma, has been a large topic in the academy, it is only recently that attention has been given to the challenge of globalization for the project of jurisprudence and legal theory. The new division of social life into global and local units puts into question, as Berman foresaw, two fundamental premises of modern understandings of law: the identification of law with the political agency of the state and the idea of law as a scientific inquiry, divorced from the subjective systems of religion and morality. Yet the major jurisprudential theories dominating twentieth-century Continental European and Anglo-American legal thought, particularly positivist models such as the one put forward by H. L. A. Hart, are inextricably entangled with these premises.

> A central task of jurisprudence *is* to give a picture of law adequate to sustain a legal culture, but what picture of law can coherently explain contemporary legal practices? While no new cosmopolitan jurisprudential theory has yet emerged, many legal theorists grappling with this question cite legal pluralism as central to any new descriptive project.[8] As Brian Tamanaha points out, it has been heralded as the "key concept in a post-modern view of law,"[9] and "capable of identifying authentic legal phenomena operating on a global level."[10] This new turn to legal pluralism comes, paradoxically, just as that descriptive project seemed to have fallen apart due to deep division over the foundational question of what is the concept of law.[11] Nonetheless, as Tamanaha has recently argued, if one adopts a nonessentialist view of law as the social practices to which people conventionally attach the label "law," such as religious law, international law, or natural law,[12] the focus shifts to the ways these "legal" systems coexist and interact, which has the potential to yield a richer picture of law.

---

6 José Casanova, "Public Religions Revisited," in *Religion: Beyond a Concept*, ed. Hent De Vries (New York: Fordham University Press, 2008), 101.

7 Scott Veitch, Emilios A. Christodoulidis, and Lindsay Farmer, *Jurisprudence: Themes and Concepts* (London: Routledge-Cavendish, 2007), 199.

8 See William Twining, *Globalization and Legal Theory* (New York: Cambridge University Press, 2000), 82–88.

9 B. de Sousa Santos, "Law: A Map of Misreading. Toward a Postmodern Conception of Law," *Journal of Law and Society 14* (1987): 279, 297.

10 Gunther Teubner, "Legal Pluralism in World Society," in *Global Law without a State*, ed. Gunther Teubner (Aldershot: Dartmouth, 1997).

11 Brian Z. Tamanaha, "A Non-Essentialist Version of Legal Pluralism," *Journal of Law and Society* 27, no. 2 (June 2000): 296, 297.

12 Ibid., 313.

I want to single out two recent accounts of how plural legal orders interact, especially as it relates to globalization. First, the emergence of the local and the global, in contrast to the nation-state, as the potentially privileged units of analysis in the postmodern world, has provided an opportunity to resuscitate an older intellectual category: the particular and the universal. Thus, Patrick Glenn, like Berman before him, argues that the rise of transnational law returns us to jurisprudential models long obscured by the dominance of contemporary positivism, the jurisprudential conception that accompanied the rise of national or municipal legal systems. Transnational law, Glenn urges, is the old system of a common law, a universal law in relation to its "inescapable intellectual companion," the particular law.[13] This universal law, although it may originate outside of the particular legal community, can be drawn on even in an internal context. Thus, for Glenn as for Berman, the coexistence of universal and particular legal systems within a single complex legal order, was a longstanding conceptual instrument of the Western legal tradition, and is at the heart of the new transnational turn.

If Glenn emphasizes a return to premodern law, a thinker such as Boaventura de Sousa Santos sees in the contests between the global and the local—between state and nonstate law—opportunities to return to law a utopian dimension. Santos argues against the artificial intellectual distinction between state and civil society, which confines politics to the state while excluding it from other sites of social power.[14] Instead, nonstate, local forms of law embedded in society, which oppose state law, have for him emancipatory potential. Islamic law, he argues, is one example of a local law embedded in society that is used to counter the dominant law of the modern nation-state.[15] Thus, Santos revives in new form Berman's project of resuscitating the connection between law and religion. For Santos, however, that connection is one of dynamic interlegality, in which each legal system challenges the other.

I intend to explore these two themes—the relationship of the universal and the particular as well as the utopian use of nonstate law—in the context of investigating the Jewish legal tradition's complex relationship today to the nation-state of Israel. This legal tradition constituted, from the beginning, a revolution against the idea of identifying law with territory or state. While the Bible tells the story of origin of a legal system intended for a sovereign Jewish nation—that is, a national law for Jews living in their land and pursuing a political life—the rabbis transformed the biblical conception and created a transnational legal culture known

13 H. Patrick Glenn, *On Common Laws* (New York: Oxford University Press, 2004), vii.

14 Santos, "Law: A Map of Misreading," 313.

15 Ibid., 314.

as the halakha. The ordinary features of statehood—political structures—and the ordinary features of collective identity so apparent in the Bible—from land to language—were largely subsumed into the halakha, which claimed to be both a portable political entity[16] and the new, exclusive definition of national identity. The rise of a new Jewish national center and site of national identity in the State of Israel is profoundly challenging this exilic pattern. Indeed, it is prompting halakhic thinkers to re-envision the law, either by retrieving a new version of the older biblical model of a national law or by carving out new roles for halakha vis-à-vis the nation-state.

The contemporary emergence of new conceptions of halakha along nationalist lines, and the counter-responses it has evoked, provides a fascinating opportunity to re-examine the conceptions of law that underlay halakha and supported it as a transnational legal culture. In contrast to the usual depiction of halakha today as comprehensive, self-sufficient, and unified[17]—aspiring to create a total, sacred society—I offer an alternative picture of halakha as the coexistence of universal and particular legal systems within a complex legal order. These systems are conceptually and normatively distinct, although they interact within the overarching halakhic framework. The universal is not the domain of the transcendent, however, as moderns have come to think. Instead, the universal is that part of halakha shared with all conventional societies. The particular is over and above the universal; it is the domain of true justice or the sacred and, to the extent it is embedded in civil society, is available to critique and counter the dominant law of the nation-state.

In the next section, I offer some necessary historical background by tracing the transformation of the biblical view of a national, collective law to the classical rabbinic transnational model, and then outlining the tensions inaugurated within Jewish legal thought with the rise of the modern nation-state and especially the State of Israel.

---

16 Eliezer Schweid, "The Attitude toward the State in Modern Jewish Thought before Zionism," in *Kinship and Consent: The Jewish Political Tradition and Its Contemporary Uses*, ed. Daniel J. Elazar. (Washington, DC: University Press of America, 1983), 134.

17 For this classic description of Jewish law, see Menahem Elon, *Jewish Law: History, Sources, Principles = Ha-Mishpat Ha-Ivri* (Philadelphia: Jewish Publication Society, 1994): 111–122. See also Gidon Sapir, "Can an Orthodox Jew Participate in the Public Life of the State of Israel?," *Shofar* 20 (2002): 85.

II The Return of the Repressed: From the Bible to the State of Israel

According to its story of origin, the Jewish legal system came into being by way of a historical covenant at Sinai. The covenant was made with a particular people, orienting Jewish collective life in a particularist direction. Moreover, the story tells of the founding of a nation organized for political action. Not only is biblical law concerned with issues pertaining to the land of Israel and to the establishment of political structures, it also addresses the rights of citizens and resident strangers within the nation-state. In short, the Hebrew Bible presents law for national, political life. This is religious nationalism: the religious law is the national law of the people of Israel. The biblical metaphors of intentional disobedience to the law revolve around treason and betrayal no less than sin.[18]

This national, political, and religious order came to an end with the destruction of the Second Temple in 70 C.E. An alternative concept of collective identity emerged: a collective dedicated to the observance of the law, which, in turn, was conceived of as transnational in scope. The Bible became Judaism's canonical national history yet it is only part of the Jewish legal system (halakha), which is composed of the written law (the first five books of the Bible describing the law received by Moses) and the oral law (recorded in the Mishna and Talmud). Indeed, the biblical picture of a religious polity was, to a large extent, simply transferred over to the halakha even though it was developed in exile without a state, or official institutions such as a Supreme Court, or national center. It was believed that halakha created all the political institutions necessary for continued self-governance across the globe. As Eliezer Schweid put it, the halakha functioned as "a portable political entity."[19] This conception of the law reverses the biblical image: the law itself constitutes the nation, and without the law there would be no nation. This notion only solidified with the gradual transformation of the Talmud from a scholastic document into a devotional object—a new site of divine space taking the place of the Temple or the arena of history.[20] The law book—that is, the Talmud—became the new embodiment of the nation.

18 The nationalist idea is ordinarily dated to the eighteenth century; yet the biblical commonwealth has been cited as a singular exception. See, generally, Anthony D. Smith, *Theories of Nationalism* (New York: Harper and Row, 1971).

19 Schweid, "The Attitude toward the State," 134.

20 See Moshe Halbertal, *People of the Book: Canon, Meaning and Authority* (Cambridge: Harvard University Press, 1997).

This was a revolutionary transformation, and one can catch many glimpses of the early rabbinic struggle with the biblical conception of Torah as national law. Perhaps the most dramatic concerns the issue of what Paul Kahn has termed law's space—its borders and jurisdiction.[21] Spinoza, more than anyone else, articulated the problem. From the perspective of the Bible, as well as good political theory, the law was obligatory only in the land under conditions of sovereignty.[22] Halakha can have no authority in the diaspora and is not binding on the Jewish community. The talmudic rabbis raised this very problem, questioning whether God had authority to punish violations of the law in the diaspora and sought to resolve it by positing a theory of tacit consent by the people during exile.[23]

The national-collective orientation of the Bible also was transformed. The biblical conception of national law portrays rewards and punishments for performing the law in national-collective terms: the nation as a whole performs the law and reaps material blessings or punishment. In late antiquity, however, religious orientations arose that were more focused on the individual and on individual salvation. Paul's famous critique of "the law as death" transforms the biblical focus on collective performance into one of individual performance. Viewed from this new individualist perspective, no individual can adequately perform the law, and hence, it is a snare. The rabbis, too, transformed the national-collective orientation of the law into a far more individualized system. As Shlomo Fischer points out, "[O]bservance of Jewish law in exile became incumbent on the individual Jew, or in regard to a number of cases, on the local community, which was conceived as being constituted by individual Jews."[24] While "the obligations upon the individual Jew derived from his membership in the primordial community, nonetheless, "the legal-behavioral implications of this membership are worked out in regard to the individual."[25] The rabbinic abolition of collective punishment, despite its biblical pedigree, is but one example of how deep the new individualist orientation ran.

The rabbinic conception of the law as the sole locus of national identity and as a fully functional, albeit portable, political entity succeeded in no small part because the imperial corporatist models in which Jews were situated cooperated. Contrary to what Salo Baron labeled the lachrymose view of Jewish history, the legal and po-

---

21 See Paul W. Kahn, *The Cultural Study of Law: Reconstructing Legal Scholarship* (Chicago: University of Chicago Press, 1999).

22 Schweid, "The Attitude Toward the State," 183.

23 Babylonian Talmud, Tractate Sabbath 88a.

24 Shlomo Fischer, "Excursus: Concerning the Rulings of R. Ovadiah Yosef Pertaining to the Thanksgiving Prayer, the Settlement of the Land of Israel, and Middle East Peace," *Cardozo Law Review* 28 (2006): 229, 236.

25 Fischer, "Excursus: Concerning the Rulings," 229.

litical autonomy Judaism enjoyed under Roman rule, feudal Europe, and the Ottoman Empire was remarkable. Jews maintained their own court systems throughout this time and possessed sufficient legal autonomy to enforce traditional Jewish law. Enforcement was effected by means of a range of sanctions from corporal punishments to excommunication and while they were ordinarily deprived of the power to execute criminals, the state's execution of Jewish offenders was sometimes a joint affair, in consultation with the rabbinic authorities. To be sure, foreign rule occasionally intruded on autonomy, and the tradition developed early on, in the fourth century, a Jewish version of "render under Caesar, what is Caesar's." The Babylonian *amora* Samuel is credited with formulating the principle that "the law of the kingdom is the law." In terms of duties owed to foreign rulers, the principle originally had limited practical application.

The rise of the modern nation-state put an abrupt end to this era. Large parts of the halakha fell under the nation-state's commitment to the unity of law and its monopolization of legal subjects formerly left to subgroup elaboration and enforcement. The standard history of Jewish legal transition to the new political formation of the modern nation-state tells a story of modern rupture and pragmatic accommodation. These accounts emphasize the post facto legitimization of the ideology of the modern nation-state, made possible because the halakha, like any rich legal tradition, had something available "to hang necessity and opportunity on."[26] According to this standard history, at the dawn of the Jewish emancipation, the old principle "the law of the kingdom is the law" was seized in order to justify the trading of Jewish sovereignty over governmental, communal, civil, and domestic matters for equal citizenship rights. The principle thus facilitated and legitimated the reorganization of Judaism from a semisovereign entity into a voluntary organization. The principle figured prominently in the responses of the Assembly of Notables to Napoleon I's questions about the suitability of Jews to fulfill the obligations incumbent upon them as French citizens. From then on, Judaism took its shape as a private religious faith, concentrating mainly on the performance of private rituals, with the retention of overlapping sovereignty with state only on issues relating to marriage and divorce. Again, according to the standard history, the principle became Judaism's corollary for the division of the secular and religious realms of life, and in the process, was responsible for the modern demise of the halakha from a distinctive system governing all aspects of life—the social, civil, communal, political, and religious—to a manual for ritual performance.

26 Bernard Susser and Eliezer Don Yihyeh,"Prolegomena to Jewish Political Theory," in *Kinship and Consent*, ed. Daniel J. Elazar (Washington, DC: University Press of America, 1983), 91.

The rabbinic responses to Napoleon's questions were cunningly framed, and "historians often regarded the answers as evasive and not truly representative of contemporary Jewish opinion."[27] One answer, directly responsive to Compte Clermont-Tonnere's famous challenge,[28] included the statement that "Jews no longer constitute a separate nation and they regard their incorporation into the great Nation as a privilege and a political redemption." This answer was probably a compromise to satisfy both the traditionalist and reformer camps that composed the Assembly.[29] Yet, despite the social upheavals and pace the historians, the conceptual basis for life as citizen within a host-nation already had been laid down by the talmudic abandonment of the biblical national-collectivist conception of identity in favor of an individualist orientation. Debate over the value of religious coercion as opposed to freely chosen observance could, indeed, be found within the talmudic tradition. So too the contraction of the sphere of halakha to ritual matters, as we will see later, had genuine halakhic purchase.

From Moses Mendelssohn on through the rise of Zionism, modern Jewish thought engaged in a rich dialogue about the changes that needed to be made in the traditional Jewish vision of halakha to adjust to the new reality of the modern nation-state and, with it, the new phenomenon of a secular Jewish identity. With the modern separation of domains of life into separate spheres, argument centered for the first time on whether halakha was a political theory, a law, a religion, or an ethic. Mendelssohn himself followed Spinoza, although he arrived at a different conclusion. He, too, agreed that enforcement of the religious law was justified only when God Himself was the actual sovereign.[30] Thus, the commandments of the Torah had no obligatory validity from the institutional viewpoint of the diaspora. However unlike Spinoza, Mendelssohn believed that all Jews were obliged to perform the Torah's commandments, which were moral obligations of the individual Jew to his creator, not legal obligations.[31] Therefore, Mendelssohn called for the abolishment of the portable political institutions of the halakha, such as the excommunicative authority of the Jewish community.[32] This was, for Mendelssohn, the true Jewish view—the culmination of the individualist orientation of the talmudic revolution.

27 Jacob Katz, *Exclusiveness and Tolerance: Studies in Jewish-Gentile Relations in Medieval and Modern Times* (New York: Behrman House, 1961), 183.

28 "The Jew should be denied everything as a nation, but granted everything as individuals …"; and "[It] should not be tolerated that the Jews become a separate political formation or class in the country."

29 Katz, "Exclusiveness and Tolerance,"183.

30 Schweid, "The Attitude toward the State," 186.

31 Ibid.

32 Ibid., 188.

If Mendelssohn moved from politics to ethics, neo-orthodoxy moved from politics to law, insisting that the halakha was an autonomous legal system or "pure theory of law," an argument parallel to the rise of modern legal positivism.[33]

Intertwined with this argument was renewed attention to an age-old question about the relationship of the universal and particular elements of Judaism. The prophetic writings proclaimed a universal message of peace and social harmony when the nations of the world worship the one God. Rabbinic thought elaborated on the universal dimension by positing social laws that were shared obligations of all legal societies in contradistinction to the primarily ritual laws particular to Jews. And underlying both was the persistent issue of a national-collective Jewish identity apart from halakha. The participants in this debate differed primarily over whether the Jewish community should give up its collective national identity, retaining only the sacral, only its universal parts, or whether it should seek to retain a national identity by trying to "find a way to achieve a compromise with the state."[34] While the reformers took the position that what is primary for Judaism is ethical monotheism, the more traditionally minded Jews continued to insist that the exclusive organizing principle of Jewish collective identity was obedience to halakha. No other Jewish national expression was required.

But looking backward after the passage of a century, even some non-orthodox thinkers such as Mordechai Kaplan located one of the major ills of contemporary Judaism in its capitulation to the modern political order. In *Judaism as a Civilization*, Kaplan begins his list of the factors of Jewish disintegration with the political factor. For Judaism, the idea of citizenship in the nation-state is more pernicious, Kaplan writes, than for other religious groups, because Judaism was intended as a total society. Whereas before Judaism was conceived as a nation and as politically and culturally autonomous, and the halakha was conceived as a comprehensive Jewish national law, Judaism is now reduced to a private religion. He indicts neo-orthodoxy in particular for its abandonment of much of the former subject matter of the halakha. Quoting from the Vilna preface to an edition of the sixteenth-century code of Jewish Law, the Shulkhan Aruch, which states that much of the laws contained therein are no longer operable because of the principle "the law of the land is the law," Kaplan states: "We are amazed to find that the most important elements of Jewish law are as obsolete in neo-orthodoxy as they are in Reformism."[35] These

---

33 See Leora Batnitzky, "From Politics to Law: Modern Jewish Thought and the Invention of Jewish Law," *Harvard Theological Review* 102, no. 3 (2009): 279.

34 Schweid, "The Attitude toward the State," 135.

35 Mordechai Kaplan, *Judaism as a Civilization* (Philadelphia: Jewish Publication Society of America, 1994), 157.

eighteenthand nineteenth-century debates set the stage for the contemporary contests over modern Jewish nationalism.

Zionism, even before the establishment of the State of Israel, posed a major crisis to the traditional mindset. One issue was its identification as a secular, modern movement—a title that made it automatically inimical to religion. The issue I wish to focus on, however, is its wish to reactivate, in the present, the biblical national-collective worldview, such as territorial sovereignty and national-collective institutions of military and state. Most of the Jewish religious movements current in Israel are modern utopian movements. However they differ markedly in how they interpret the meaning of history. The ultra-religious do not relate to the state as a religious vehicle or as any means for perpetuating Jewish collective national identity. For them,"Jewish collective identity has become 'bracketed'-relegated to the distant biblical past or messianic future" and perpetuated in the present only through the community of the faithful.[36] The religious Zionist movement, however, understands the establishment of the State of Israel both as religiously significant and a vehicle for reviving halakha as national law in the nation. Some wings of this movement see it in vivid messianic terms, as the beginning of the fulfillment of the redemption. For them, the state provides the opportunity to resuscitate the original biblical ideal of law in the nation and to re-sacralize the secular. The more sober, non-messianically oriented wings also see it as an opportunity to revive halakha as a religio-national law and Jewish national-cultural expression by developing the nascent democratic strains within it.[37] Both wings of this movement have produced a remarkably large body of distinctive law that deals with subjects unaddressed for nearly two millennia, creatively fashioned out of sparse indigenous sources.

This is not the place to linger on the fascinating question of whether the halakha could, indeed, be brought up to date through creative reinterpretation to address the needs of a fully functioning modern democratic state. Instead, I would like to concentrate on the different models of halakha that have emerged in reaction to the establishment of the Israeli State. The impact of Zionism on contemporary halakhic methodology has been extensively addressed, especially by Arye Edrei, whose

36 Fischer, "Excursus: Concerning the Rulings," 236. Fischer identifies their utopian orientation in terms of the wish to recapture the transhistorical, objectively true divine law "as it exists in the mind of God." For this reason, they base their rulings on the most stringent interpretation, lest actual practice fail to conform to divine halakhic truth. This is a departure from the more modest and skeptical epistemology of the Talmud, which emphasizes procedural validity rather than metaphysical truth.

37 See, generally, Arye Edrei, "Law, Interpretation, and Ideology: The Renewal of the Jewish Laws of War in the State of Israel," *Cardozo Law Review* 28 (2006): 187.

work I draw on here.[38] Less attention has been paid, however, to the relationship of contemporary models of halakha to long-standing debates about the very nature of the halakha. Is it an ethic, a political theory, or an autonomous law? Is it addressed to individuals or collectives? Is it comprehensive or does it have gaps? What is the relationship of the universal domain it posits to the particular? My aim here is to show how contemporary responses of halakhic jurists to the establishment of the State of Israel are related to these numerous long-standing arguments within the Jewish legal tradition over the proper description of halakha itself.

III Three Contemporary Models of Halakha

Among modern and contemporary halakhic thinkers and decisors in Israel, at least three different models of halakha have emerged that I have variously termed: the traditional transnational model (or "law as the nation"), the national-organic model ("law in the nation"), and the cosmopolitanism model ("law interacting with the nation").

The traditional transnational or "law as the nation" school of thought attempts to perpetuate a distinct post-talmudic conception of halakha as autonomous, pure transnational law: a normative framework independent of any philosophic, political, or mystical ideologies, whether religious or secular. This approach essentially treats the nation-state, and its institutions and policies, whether a host-state or the State of Israel, as external conditions or circumstances, to which the transnational halakha is objectively applied.[39] Thus, the Jewish State is, at best, a neutral phenomenon like any other nation-state—a new political formation to be assessed under the traditional, autonomous legal categories of the transnational halakha. Pursuant to this approach, a variety of halakhic principles and doctrines are canvassed and marshaled to assess whether discrete and particular acts of statecraft, from war to secular legislation to a secular court system, are compatible with pre-existing halakhic rules. This school continues to reject a Jewish national identity apart from the transnational halakha itself.

In contrast, the nationalist ("law in the nation") model revives the original biblical conception of law as the law of a sovereign nation whose identity is defined in collective, national terms. The law is conceived in terms of organic models, and the

38 Ibid.

39 For a theoretical overview of this method, see Suzanne Last Stone, "Formulating Responses to Egalitarianism," in *Halakha in an Egalitarian Age*, ed. Marc D. Stern (Lanham, MD: Rowman and Littlefield, 2005), 53.

elaboration of norms concerning statecraft, such as the norms of war, proceeds from a collective point of view. The nation is a collective entity with rights and duties and not merely a bundle of individuals bound by individual halakhic obligations. Halakha, in this vision, is decidedly a politics—a means to achieve the spiritual and political perfection of the nation. Thus, the school harks back to Maimonides's conception of the halakha as a politics aimed at perfection of the body and the intellect.[40]

The chief jurisprudential division between the nationalists and the transnationalists, as Shlomo Fischer has astutely observed, is the question whether the law recognizes only the rights and duties of individuals or also recognizes the Jewish state as a separate corporate embodiment of the nation, with collective rights. The latter entails a marked shift away from the individualist orientation of the talmudic revolution. Nowhere is this shift more evident than as applied to the issue of war, which exposes acutely the tension between a collectivist versus an individualist framework. For example, as Arye Edrei has analyzed at length, one of the key representatives of the nationalist school, Rabbi Goren, argued that there are "two planes to Jewish law: that of individual conduct, which is governed by classic halakhic norms such as saving lives wherever possible unless the right of self-defense is immediately activated, and that of national existence and institutions, bound by national-collective obligations as well as rights, including the right to conduct war and peace in the national interest without regard to the lives of its individual citizens."[41] It is this construction, at the normative level, of a national-collective plane in which different halakhic rules apply that the more traditional adherents of the transnationalist school of thought is at pains to deny. Instead, they are intent on preserving the traditional construction of halakha as a set of obligations addressing only individuals, whose adherence to these norms is the exclusive legitimate national expression.

What both schools of thought have in common, however, is a commitment to a total halakhic society and to preserving a transcendent element in the law in both the domestic and international arena. Traditionalists have often asserted that halakha is seamless and has no gaps; there is a halakhic answer to every question. And, for the traditionalists, halakha is comprehensive, addressing every facet of life and human experience from the private to the public to the economic. A supposed gap in the law—such as rules of war—is merely apparent, not real. The gap either signals that the conduct is forbidden to the individual or the rule must be extrapolated by analogy from other, developed areas of Jewish law, such as the criminal

---

40 Maimonides, *The Guide for the Perplexed,* 3:31; 26—27.

41 Edrei, "Law, Interpretation, and Ideology," 217.

law. It is precisely by reasoning through the spiral of precedent that the transcendent dimension of halakha, embedded in the tradition, is retained.[42] A commitment to halakha as total way of life is the position of the collectivist school, as well. Rabbi Goren, for example, rejected the idea of halakhic indifference to any area of life; rather, as a normative system, halakha is able and required to relate to all areas of life including areas such as war, which it had no experience of for two thousand years. Indeed, as Edrei explains, he claimed this was merely the logical extension of the traditional idea that Jewish nationalism is defined by its law rather than by territory or other sociological categories. He fashioned a separate normative system for war from biblical sources and even non-canonical ones, rather than rely on the developed criminal law precedents, because he was himself a military man who viewed the criminal law as an inadequate analogy for war. He hoped to retain a transcendent dimension to the newly fashioned rules by joining law with ethics and a sensitivity to a uniquely "Jewish worldview."[43] It is precisely this idea that the halakha is all-encompassing, covering every aspect of human life under a single, unified sacred framework and forming a total society governed by Torah law, that is ultimately disputed by the cosmopolitan school, which is the primary subject of this essay.

I will address two distinct versions of what I have termed the "cosmopolitan model." Indeed, they differ radically in motivation, content, and goal. They share, however, a jurisprudential picture of halakha with deep roots in the tradition, which until now has been largely overlooked and deserves genealogical attention. In the first school of thought, the nation-state is seen as essentially profane, either because nationalism demands that religious conceptions of holiness be extended to mundane—or even evil—acts of statecraft, such as war and international confrontation, or because nationalism fails to give precedence to the individual as an autonomous human being, subordinating the human being to society. The immediate impetus for this school of thought was the excesses of modern nationalism, including those of the Israeli state, and the cult of statism that surrounded it. At the same time, this school of thought is an intensification of the individualist orientation of the transnational halakha as a collective of individuals with society as secondary. In this view, the halakha is first and foremost a sacred religion, defining the essence of divine worship, or an ethics guarding the status of the individual as against society, the state, or other collective ideologies. The mundane aspects of statehood, and nationalist law occasionally and obliquely addressed by the halakha, are not particular to halakha nor its essence; they reflect its universal, conventional,

---

42 Ibid., 219.
43 Ibid., 221–222.

and therefore peripheral and profane aspect. Perhaps the best known proponent of this view was the late Yeshayahu Leibowitz, who initially thought the revival of the halakha in areas of public, national life was of deep religious significance and then changed his mind and became the foremost proponent for the radical separation of halakha from the state.[44] In short, the role of halakha vis-à-vis the modern nation-state is ethical critique.

The second version also attempts to overcome the modern nation-state formation by identifying the Jewish nation as such as merely one member of the global community of nations. In this view, all questions of national existence and statecraft involving the obligations of Jews vis-à-vis the international community, in contradistinction to domestic matters between Jews inter se, should be resolved by resorting to international law or a common law of nations. This position is most clearly articulated by Shaul Yisraeli in the context of discussing the laws of war.[45] The actual impetus for this viewpoint is precisely the opposite of the one described above. In his analysis, Yisraeli makes clear that halakhic norms per se could not countenance the manner of conducting warfare acceptable within the international community. But rather than view halakha as a ground for ethical critique, Yisraeli sees halakha as allowing the incorporation of looser standards of behavior when the nation acts beyond its border.[46]

Both versions of the cosmopolitan school are dependent on essentially emptying the nation-state of concrete and particular halakhic rules. Instead, matters of statecraft and public order are viewed either as a realm of discretion—a halakhic gap where legal rules have run out—or as a sphere conceptually subject to a different set of legal rules from halakha proper. The most critical issue separating the two versions of cosmopolitans, then, is the role of the halakha as an ethics embedded in civil society that can serve as a counter to the law of the state.

The Cosmopolitan Halakha

I want to draw on my earlier work on Jewish law and legal pluralism,[47] as well as on Jewish law and the conceptual distinction between state and religion,[48] to show how the cosmopolitan school, along with its distinctive jurisprudential picture of

44 See discussion in ibid., 203.

45 See discussion in ibid.

46 Ibid., 214.

47 See Suzanne Last Stone, "Sinaitic and Noahide Law: Legal Pluralism in Jewish Law," *Cardozo Law Review* 12 (1991): 1157.

48 Stone, "Religion and State," 631.

halakha, emerges from earlier traditions within Jewish legal culture about the legitimacy of political structures. The contemporary critique of nationalism as subordinating the individual to society can be conceptually traced to ancient discussions about the role of the Jewish king, while the contemporary attempt to link halakha with a global community advancing common law for humanity can be conceptually traced to ancient discussions about the non Jewish kingdom. Both of these ancient discourses, the one around the image of the Jewish king and the second around the image of the non-Jewish kingdom, are fascinating, as I have explored at greater length elsewhere, precisely because they change the paradigmatic picture of the halakha from one that is comprehensive and unified to one that is interstitial, pluralist, and composed of different jurisdictions generating law in accordance with fundamentally different principles.[49] Each radically limits the ambit of the halakha: the first because it views political structures enforcing law for the sake of society as necessary but ultimately profane; the second because it views them as necessary and commanded and, as such, ultimately sanctified. The first identifies the essence of halakha with sacred ritual and the rights of the individual, and the second views large parts of halakha as replaceable by the law of other societies.

Both of these approaches ultimately can be traced back to the tense coexistence within Judaism of the universal and the particular—of two normative systems, the one consisting of universal obligations binding all humanity and the other of commandments particular to Jews. The Bible first launched this complex internal structure by describing the pre-Sinai world as one filled with law given to humanity, including Israel's forefathers. This account is transformed in the Talmud into a full-fledged description of two normative orders. The Talmud focused on the universal law primarily as an explanatory model for the law that existed before "the law"—the law given at Sinai—and used the model as a contrasting image of a conventional society, unlike the covenantal one forged at Sinai, in order to explore the differences between the two and construct identity.[50] Although it left open the relationship between the two legal orders, it largely presented that relationship as a historic progression, with the universal law superseded for Jews by the particular obligations revealed at Sinai. It was left to the medieval period to construct a far more complex relationship between the two, with the universal law serving in the eyes of some jurists, as I have claimed,[51] essentially as an alternative source of norms even in a national Jewish context. This is a fascinating case illustration of the universal or

49 Ibid., 643.

50 I explore this at length in Stone, "Sinaitic and Noahide Law," 1157.

51 See discussion in ibid. See also recent rabbinic opinion by the High Rabbinic Court of Jerusalem (Case No. 4276, November 11, 2003) (on file with the author) (Heb.).

common law existing, or even generated, outside of the particular legal system but available to it even in an internal context.

A. The Jewish King in the Halakhic Imagination

Deuteronomy 16:18 through 18:22 lists the officials of the polity—judge, king, priest, prophet—and assigns each a role, although there is considerable overlap of functions. In Deuteronomy 17, the king has only one positive duty: to write out a scroll of the law, read it every day of his life, and obey its commands. At the same time, the king is described as a monarch "like all the other nations."[52] The text thus immediately sets up a tension between a model of kingship that is culturally specific and one that is universal. Moreover, elsewhere in the Hebrew Bible, kings are portrayed as unfettered by the law or, at least, exercising a variety of powers, especially that of dispensing royal justice—and royal adjudication, even by good kings, is unhedged by the due process requirement, in Deuteronomy 17, that no defendant may be convicted except on the testimony of two conforming witnesses.[53]

Juristic reconciliation could take a variety of forms: that lawless kings reigned in Israel for much of the monarchy but that this did not sever the relationship of ruler to subjects or give rise to a right of resistance; that kings held legally defined emergency powers to administer royal courts or that they had political discretion to depart from Torah law in times of need, to name a few solutions that later emerged. A far more radical reading views the textual phrase "like all the nations" as a warrant for interpreting the powers of the Jewish king in light of a universal and not a particular concept of kingship.

Maimonides seems to pursue this more radical reading, even though he couched his approach in the language of emergency powers. According to Maimonides, the Torah in its entirety is a divine political structure because all its laws have a purpose: the perfection of the body or the soul. The Torah's commandments addressed to governmental structures are part of the perfection of the body because they aim at securing social order, which is a necessary condition for achieving perfection of the soul.[54] Although, from a technical perspective, Maimonides gives the king (and the court) emergency powers to depart from Torah law,[55] these emergency powers are only theoretically temporary. They include power to punish free of

52 Deuteronomy 17:4.

53 Later jurists imported further requirements, such as forewarning the defendant that he is about to transgress.

54 Maimonides, *The Guide for the Perplexed,* 3:31; 26–27.

55 See Maimonides, *Mishneh Torah,* Laws of Kings 3:8–10; Laws of Killing 2:4.

the biblical procedural restrictions of two witnesses and forewarning.[56] Maimonides seems to be the first among rabbinic jurists to view the biblically ordained two-witness rule as essentially formal and, thus, an obstacle to pursuing a rational system of procedure designed to ensure social order.[57]

On closer inspection, however, as Gerald Blidstein points out, Maimonides's king, unlike the jurist-sage, has very little discretion. This is not a realm of politics or wisdom but of law. As Blidstein shows, Maimonides has transferred over to the Jewish king a separate body of talmudic law about the universal "Noahide" laws that bind non-Jewish societies.[58] In addition to six substantive commands, Noahide law includes a command of justice, *dinin*,[59] which Maimonides codifies as a duty to preserve social order by establishing a judiciary that will enforce the other substantive commands. The Talmud had already noted that "Noahides" punish in accordance with the testimony of one witness and without forewarning.[60] In Maimonides' Code, the Jewish king, like non-Jewish government, is authorized to punish on the basis of the testimony of one witness and no forewarning."Maimonides' entire edi-

56 Maimonides purports to be codifying talmudic law, and there are scattered statements in the Talmud reporting a tradition that the court meted out punishments not according to law "in order to safeguard the law." Babylonian Talmud, Tractate Sanhedrin 46a and parallels. The two cases attached to the statement tell of impositions of the death penalty by the court for highly public violations of the law. These cases emerge as rare exercises of judicial discretion to depart from biblical rules, although they do attest to a talmudic distinction between law as an aspect of individual justice, entitling the individual to full due process of the law, and law as an aspect of political or social governance, which may require relaxation of the rigors of the law in times of extreme breakdown of social order. See the discussion in Gerald Blidstein, "'Ideal' and 'Real' in Classical Jewish Political Theory," *Jewish Political Studies Review* 2 (1990): 43–66. But compare Hanina Ben-Menahem, *Judicial Deviation from Talmudic Law: Governed by Men, Not by Rules* (New York: Hardwood Academic, 1991) (arguing that talmudic judges had power to disregard norms and exercised broad judicial discretion). The Talmud also depicts the court as authorized to "correct" the law, by relaxing or tightening it, through rabbinic legislation addressing social needs, applicable to everyone.

57 A century later, another member of the Spanish royalist school, Ibn Adret, invoked similar ideas to legitimate medieval punishment practice. Thus, Adret in a series of responsa dealing with handing over informers to the Spanish government for capital punishment, draws on a variety of precedents for departing from the criminal law strictures: citing the powers of the community (acting in lieu of king) and of the rabbinic courts exercising emergency jurisdiction. Adret remarks that the Torah's procedural laws are not aimed at discerning the truth of guilt or innocence, unlike that of the king, which is aimed at discerning the truth and punishing. And "if you issue decisions based exclusively on the law as given in the Torah, why then society would be destroyed." Cited in Joseph Karo, Commentary to Tur, Hoshen Mishpat, Rules of Judges, Section 2.

58 Blidstein, "'Ideal' and 'Real,'" 53.

59 Stone, "Sinaitic and Noahide Law," 1157.

60 Babylonian Talmud, Tractate Sanhedrin 56a-58b.

fice of monarchic powers identified Jewish and gentile governance as a single structure possessing similar goals and utilizing similar instruments."[61] The biblical language to appoint a king "like all the other nations" now becomes a warrant for resorting to universal norms of governance to define the powers of the Jewish king. Of course, these "non-Jewish" norms of governance are themselves off-shoots of talmudic jurisprudence.[62] Nevertheless, they are universal and not particular norms (from the Jewish point of view). They operate, however, as a kind of indigenously "Jewish" universalist fall-back or residual law, which can be drawn on when the particular law requires supplementation or adjustment.

While Maimonides paved the way for equating the Jewish king with a universal conception of kingship, he nonetheless stitched the Jewish king into the religious fabric and integrated political structures with particular religious norms, thereby creating a cohesive whole. Other medieval thinkers, however, more decisively split the two domains—universal Noahide law and particularist halakhic obligations—exposing a deep and creative tension between the two. Attention was turned not only outward but also inward. If the universal Noahide law is God-sanctioned, a reflection of the divine plan for moral political societies—and, indeed, a part of the halakha itself—what is the purpose of the particular obligations given to Jews at Sinai, especially those that seem, at first blush, to address political and social order? Already in the Talmud and midrash, rabbinic discussion of Noahide law evidences a tacit theory about the distinction between aspirational and conventional societies and concomitantly the different duties members of covenantal as opposed to merely political societies bear. Indeed, the two-witness rule itself was thought to symbolize the covenantal community.[63] This line of thought intersected with another longstanding debate about the "metaphysics of judging" in accordance with halakhic norms. As Haim Shapiro has shown, judging in the Talmud is deeply connected with the theme of God's presence. Nevertheless, in the talmudic period, neither the notion of God's presence in judgment nor the religious weight of God's law seems to be an obstacle to the actual administration of justice. By the medieval period, however, adjudication in accordance with Torah law came

61 Blidstein, "'Ideal' and 'Real,'" 53. Traditional jurists commenting on Maimonides note this connection. See Meir Simhah Cohen, Ohr Sameah, Laws of Kings 3:10.

62 Indeed, as a historical matter, their real origin may well lie in talmudic observation of Roman practice just as much as in legal dissection of the Genesis narratives "attesting" to the universal law God commanded. For Maimonides, surely, it didn't matter. He most likely thought the whole topic of universal Noahide law was based on natural law thinking on the part of the jurists from the beginning.

63 Stone, "Sinaitic and Noahide Law," 1157.

to be seen by many thinkers as too fraught with holiness for this worldly enforcement.[64]

These two themes come together in the fascinating sermon of Rabbi Nissim Gerondi, a renowned talmudic commentator and physician in the royal court of Spain in the fourteenth century. This sermon, which over time became transmuted into a legal source, has become increasingly influential in halakhic circles in Israel, serving as a precedent for separating religious halakha from conventional state functions. In so doing, a structure has been created for the religious halakha to serve as a site of protest within civil society against the nation-state. Whether Gerondi's sermon was motivated by practical concerns—"to provide a defense for allowing deviations from biblical-talmudic law in the workings of the contemporary Jewish polity"[65]—or theoretical ones—to offer a new conception of halakha—is open to debate. As I note elsewhere in more detail, Gerondi points to a central gap in the halakha. Torah law, with its requirements of judging in accordance with the testimony of two witnesses and forewarning, cannot enforce social order. Thus, it is deficient in comparison to conventional political systems. According to Gerondi, the Torah itself provides the means for correcting this deficiency. The king, who is concerned only with guilt or innocence, may punish without resort to the Torah method's of criminal adjudication. Like Maimonides, Gerondi links the king's authority to a general religious command to preserve social order: *tikkun olam*. This term cannot be found in the Pentateuch and is cited by the early rabbis, not as a rule but as an explanation for enacting a variety of social legislation. But both Maimonides and Gerondi are using the talmudic term as a generative legal "principle." Gerondi, at least, takes the Bible's instruction about kingship as the source of this command.

Gerondi's discourse on kingship occupies a central place in contemporary conceptions of halakha in Israel because, for him, kingship is not an institution but, rather, a power that must always be embedded somewhere in the Jewish polity.[66] The monarch is merely the site of social order historically chosen by the people, who may consent to another institutional form if they so desire, such as the Israeli Parliament. Second, the language about the need for public order and social welfare is so broad that it is virtually impossible to confine the "power" Gerondi is describing to punishment.[67] Third, Gerondi does not place the king's powers within the more

---

64 See Haim Shapira, "For the Judgment Is God's"—On the Metaphysics of Judging in Jewish Law," *Bar Ilan Law Review* (2009).

65 Gerald Blidstein, "On Political Structures—Four Medieval Comments," *Jewish Journal of Sociology* 22 (1980): 52.

66 Blidstein, "On Political Structures," 47–58.

67 Gerald Blidstein, "On Lay Legislation in Halakha: The King as Instance," in *Rabbinic and Lay Communal Authority*, ed. Suzanne Last Stone (New York: Yeshiva University Press, 2006), 1.

conventional emergency jurisdiction model, although he cites the phrase once or twice. Moreover, the political domain is stripped of any aura of the sacred. Although there is a vague bow to the Jewish king upholding the religion, there is no attempt to integrate the king within the rest of the system, as Maimonides labored to do, nor is there any attempt to coordinate state power with religious law and institutions. This is a separate and theoretically permanent jurisdiction legitimately operating under its own rules.

At first blush, one might interpret Gerondi as merely extending the Maimonidean thrust in new directions shaped by his halakhic predecessors living in Christian Spain and by the surrounding culture. His emphasis on monarchy as the product of the people's consent and the opening he provides for legislative powers are all tied to the new theory of the self-governing Jewish community, the *kahal*, as a corporate form endowed with legislative, judicial, and administrative powers, forged by Nachmanides and Adret a century before.[68] Medieval developments in canon law —the emergence of criminal law as public law, arguments about social deterrence, and relaxation in standards of proof—also date from this period. Where formerly, criminal conviction could be secured solely on the basis of two conforming eyewitnesses (or else by torture), there slowly developed in the twelfth and thirteenth centuries a sense of the need to convict on the basis of circumstantial evidence.[69] Thus, across traditions, a new perception of a "public sphere," having both powers and need for new forms of social regulation, came into being.

Yet, in the course of elaborating the purpose of the king's law, Gerondi reconceives the very purpose of the halakha altogether and decisively parts company with Maimonides. In contrast to Maimonides's naturalist, rationalist defense of the Torah, Gerondi saw the divine law as a means to "transcend the natural" by delivering the community from the rule of nature.[70] He did not share Maimonides's basic

68 Blidstein, "On Lay Legislation," 1; Menachem Lorberbaum, *Politics and the Limits of Law: Secularizing the Political in Medieval Jewish Thought* (Stanford: Stanford University Press, 2001).

69 Richard M. Fraher, "Conviction According to Conscience: The Medieval Jurists' Debate Concerning Judicial Discretion and the Law of Proof," *Law and History Review* 7 (1989): 23; Richard M. Fraher, "'Ut nullus describatur reus prius quam convincatur': Presumption of Innocence in Medieval Canon Law?," in *Proceedings of the 6th International Congress of Medieval Canon Law*, ed. S. Kuttner and K. Pennington (1985): 483–506; Richard M. Fraher, "The Theoretical Justification for the New Criminal Law of the High Middle Ages: Rei Publicae Interest, ne Crimina Remaneant Impunita," *University of Illinois Law Review* (1984): 557; Richard M. Fraher, "Preventing Crime in the High Middle Ages: The Medieval Lawyers' Search for Deterrence," in *Law and the Sacred*, ed. Austin Sarat, Lawrence Douglas, and Martha Merrill Umphrey (Stanford: Stanford University Press, 2007); Nomi Stolzenberg, "The Profanity of Law," in *Law and the Sacred*, ed. Austin Sarat, Lawrence Douglas, and Martha Merrill Umphrey (Stanford: Stanford University Press, 2007).

70 On his antirationalism, see Lorberbaum, "Politics and the Limits of Law."

framework, which assigns a rational and comprehensible purpose to each commandment. Instead, the sphere of Sinai law is the sacred and the numinous. Judging in accordance with biblical law was never intended as a practical means to govern society, he writes. Rather, its purpose is to bring on the divine effluence.

Here, Gerondi can be interpreted in two ways, but these two readings are deeply interconnected in terms of their contemporary political implications. According to the less radical reading, judging in accordance with biblical procedural and substantive law is true justice because the law is exceedingly sensitive to the rights of the individual accused. True justice cannot take into account the needs of society and remain faithful to the rights of the individual. The Sanhedrin judged the people "according to that which is truly just in itself . . . according to the laws of the Torah alone, which are just in themselves."[71] Thus, Gerondi rejects out of hand Maimonides' entire project of embedding divine law in society and integrating the two. According to the more radical reading, religious law, or, more precisely that part of the halakha that is particular, is a mysterious ritual. Thus, he writes, even the *mishpatim* (the social laws of the Torah whose purpose is evident), including evidentiary and procedural rules, are designed primarily to bring down the divine effluence. Indeed, Gerondi suggests, perhaps some of the social laws are, in reality, *hukim* (ritual laws whose purpose is not immediately evident to reason and may or may not be discoverable), and he goes on to include in this category the entire system of biblical procedure. Perhaps Gerondi intended to limit this notion to biblical penal law, but the logic of his argument and its intellectual roots is not confined to this subject.

If we speak of Christian influences, by far the most important here is the Gelasian doctrine of two powers—pope and king. Yet Gerondi is certainly working off earlier rabbinic sources as well as extending the doctrine of Noahide law to one logical conclusion. He is following, as Gerald Blidstein pointed out, Yehuda HaLevi, who wrote about "the social—ethical law given to humanity (Noahide law) to which the spiritual-ceremonial law is added at Sinai," and decisively splitting the two into the realm of the sacred and particular, where true justice is possible, as opposed to the realm of the profane and universal, where the needs of society are irreconcilable with the rights of individuals.[72]

---

71 Rabbi Isaac Herzog, "The Rights of Minorities in Jewish Law," in *Constitution and Law in a Jewish State According to the Halakha*, ed. Itamar Warhaftig (Jerusalem: Mossad HaRav Kook, 1989), reprinted in *The Jewish Political Tradition*, ed. Michael Walzer et al. (New Haven: Yale University Press 2000), 471—476.

72 HaLevi also speculated whether certain social laws were really religious commands with no social function except to bring on the divine overflow.

The intellectual line I want to draw, however, extends back to a certain conception of priestly religion, and of criminal adjudication as a ritual service, and then forward again to the twentieth-century criticism of excessive nationalism by Yeshayahu Leibowitz and others. According to one biblical conception of priesthood, their ritualized worship of God has no practical, this-worldly, political, or social function. Instead, "[T]he focus is solely on the encounter between a numinous God and a serving priest,"[73] who is confined to the sacral realm—the Temple—and isolated from the social and political order. The reason to mark off the sacred from all other realms is connected to the idea of a wholly other God who transcends morality and politics and is uninvolved in human affairs. "Uncovering the hidden dimensions of divinity, bringing on the divine effluence, requires a set of rituals unrelated to human concerns."[74] Temple service in this view is divine worship "out of love" and not for instrumental purposes. Thus, secular space may emerge out of a certain conception of the deity rather than from external critique and opposition to religion.[75]

Gerondi's picture of halakha as mysterious ritual and of criminal adjudication in accordance with divine laws that have no social purpose except to bring on the divine effluence reflects this conception. It is ritual observance, which must, of necessity, be divorced from social or political concerns in order to reveal the divine. Gerondi extends the priestly role to the judiciary, especially to the High Court, which was located in the Temple, and he writes elsewhere that its judges ideally should be priests.[76] But, in retrospect, we can see how the judiciary and this priestly role were collapsed already in the Mishna, the formative text of Jewish law, which describes the polity as ruled by two agencies: judge and king.[77] One may speculate whether the two are separated not only to secure the court's independence but also in order to relocate in the judiciary and their rabbinic successors the sacral power formerly

73 Yair Lorberbaum,"The Place of the Priest," in *The Jewish Political Tradition,* vol. I, ed. Michael Walzer (New Haven: Yale University Press, 2000): 179; see also Israel Knohl, *The Sanctuary of Silence: The Priestly Torah and the Holiness School* (Minneapolis: Fortress Press, 1995).

74 Lorberbaum, "The Place of the Priest," 179.

75 For a fascinating discussion of the link between transcendent conceptions of the divine and the rise of secularism on the world-historical stage, see Maurice Gauchet, *The Disenchantment of the World: A Political History of Religion* (Princeton: Princeton University Press, 1997).

76 Sifre Deut., cited in Hiddushe HaRan on Sanhedrin. The judicial function and priestly role are already coupled in Deuteronomy 17 and continued in Philo.

77 See Mishna Sanhedrin; David Flatto, "It's Good to Be King: The Monarch's Role in the Mishna's Political and Legal System," *Hebraic Political Studies* 2 (2007): 255; David Flatto, "The King and I: The Separation of Powers in Early Hebraic Political Theory," *Yale Journal of Law and Humanity* 20 (2008): 61.

found in the Temple.[78] Already in this early layer, judging is depicted as a sacral site, a site of the divine overflow,[79] and judicial execution which is also depicted as a form of atoning sacrifice or ritual killing possible only while the court sat in the Temple.[80]

These theological conceptions have profound contemporary political implications. Gerondi's intellectual successor is precisely that segment of the cosmopolitan school which perceives certain totalizing characteristics of political nationalism as idolatry.[81] The nation-state is essentially seen as idolatrous, either because nationalism demands that religious conceptions of holiness be extended to mundane—or even evil—acts of statecraft, such as war and international confrontation, or because nationalism fails to give precedence to the individual as an autonomous human being, subordinating the human being to society. The immediate impetus for this school of thought was the excesses of modern nationalism, including that of the Israeli state, and the cult of statism that surrounded it. At the same time, this school of thought is merely an intensification of the individualist orientation of the transnational halakha as a collective of individuals with society as secondary. Thus, as in Gerondi, the halakha is first and foremost a sacred religion, defining the essence of divine worship, or an ethics guarding the status of the individual as against society, state, or other collective ideologies. The mundane aspects of statehood, and nationalist law occasionally and obliquely addressed by the halakha, such as war, are not particular to halakha nor its essence; they reflect its universal, conventional, and therefore peripheral and profane aspect.

Perhaps the best known proponent of this view was the late Yeshayahu Leibowitz, who initially thought the revival of the halakha in areas of public, national life was of deep religious significance and then changed his mind and became the foremost proponent for the radical separation of halakha from state.[82] For Liebowitz too, Jewish religion is worship of God through observance of commandments that are divorced from human concerns and thus transcend the social

78 I pursue this theme in a different context in Suzanne Last Stone, "Rabbinic Legal Magic: A New Look at Honi's Circle as the Construction of Legal Space," *Yale Journal of Law and the Humanities* 17 (March 2005): 97.

79 See Shapira, "For the Judgment Is God's."

80 Thus the Mishna reports that in order to strip itself of authority to execute, the court relocated itself to the marketplace. Babylonian Talmud, Tractate Avodah Zara 8b. See also Beth A. Berkowitz, "Execution and Invention: Death Penalty Discourse," in *Early Rabbinic and Christian Cultures* (New York: Oxford University Press, 2006).

81 See, generally, Ellie Holzer, "Attitudes toward the Use of Military Force in Ideological Currents in Religious Zionism," in *War and Peace in the Jewish Tradition*, ed. Lawrence H. Schiffman and Joel B. Wolowelsky (New York: Yeshiva University Press, 2007), 341.

82 Edrei, "Law, Interpretation, and Ideology," 203.

and political. This is the realm of the sacred, and to preserve it, the state must be desacralized and stripped of any religious component, because vesting sanctity outside its proper place is idolatry. At the same time, however, the state is necessary from the perspective of the political and social, as Gerondi held. Hence, the role of halakha vis-à-vis the state in Liebowitz's system is critique. Halakha becomes a source of criticism of nationalist-political ideology when the latter becomes total and radical, and tramples the status of the individual. Thus, this position is sharply distinguishable from that of the collectivists who seek precisely to re-sacralize the body politic and for whom the concept of Jewish kingship should be culturally specific, not universal.

B. The Global Community in the Halakhic Imagination

The halakha has long recognized the legitimacy of the non-Jewish state over certain domains. The principle *dina de-malkhuta dina* ("the law of the land is the [legitimate] law," henceforward DDM), as noted, played a seminal role in the adjustment of Jewish law to the then new formation of the nation-state. Now it is playing a central role in adjusting Jewish law to the reality of a new globalized community. On the face of it, no principle would seem to symbolize more visibly the loss of Jewish sovereignty than this one, which appears four times in the Babylonian Talmud. Several scholars have already noted how far this appearance is from reality,[83] once one focuses closely on how the principle is actually deployed in the talmudic discussion. In none of these cases is it operating as a concession to foreign rule or an expression of powerlessness. On the contrary, in its original uses the principle serves to make the halakha fully functional in exile. Yet the internal logic of doctrinal progression has led to precisely the opposite result. The principle "the law of the kingdom is the law" is first articulated because it is necessary to enable Jews to fully comply with their halakhic obligations in exile. This postulate took on a life of its own as the jurists began to theorize in the Middle Ages about the conceptual basis for the principle. And, in a chain of logical progression, these conceptual bases begin to undermine the conception of halakha as an all-encompassing system. Instead, the sphere of halakha became more and more contracted.

The locus classicus is a talmudic text[84] that poses the question whether the kingdom is robbing Jews or Jews are robbing the kingdom. The legal question is

83 See Shmuel Shiloh, *Dina De-Malkhuta Dina* [*The Law of the State Is Law*] (Heb.) (Jewish Academic Press, 1974).
84 Babylonian Talmud, Tractate Baba Kamma 113a–b.

whether Jews may utter a false vow in order to evade the king's taxes. Samuel's maxim is not questioned; rather, it is raised as an objection: if the king's laws are valid, then evading the kings' collectors through the artifice of uttering a false vow is robbery under Jewish law.[85] The second example poses the legal question more starkly: Jews cross bridges built from palm trees expropriated from their Jewish owner by the king. The king's act must be classified as legal or illegal in order to serve as a premise for further halakhic reasoning about the duties owed between Jew and Jew. If the king's act is illegal, the property expropriated cannot be classified as abandoned. In such cases, Jews will be evading their own religiolegal obligations vis-à-vis the Jewish tree owners, who should be compensated for use of their property each time a Jew crosses the bridge. The Talmud does not define the prerogatives of kingship, other than citing examples of taxation and expropriation, but it does define what monarchical actions are "law" as opposed to tyranny. Taxes that have no limit and the unequal imposition of obligations—for example, precluding the tree owners from arranging equal distribution of their obligations—are robbery and not law of the kingdom. These two limits—lack of arbitrariness and equality in framing the law—are definitional of the word "law," whether Jewish or non-Jewish, and function as internal conditions of legality.[86] In the medieval period, as Shmuel Shiloh elucidates in his magisterial study, further rationales for this principle were explored. The Talmud already hints at a close association between the principle and the custom of the people,[87] and many

85 Side by side with the ethical impulse, one might also see a self-serving aim here. With respect to vows, passive civil disobedience is being advocated, with the locution of Gentile legitimacy almost a kind of subterfuge. This is hardly surprising, as the social reality is almost certainly confiscatory taxes aimed at Jews—the fiscus Judaicus—which may explain why the Mishna and Talmud begin with a presumption that tax collection is robbery. Later sources tend to mute this presumption, reflecting a different social reality.

86 This point is driven home by Jacob b. Meir Tam, Responsa of the Tosafists 12, and Isaac Or Zarua Tractate Bava Kamma 47. A law may be wrongful under Jewish law—cutting down the palm trees that belong to the owner—and still deserve the name law. Such a Gentile law is still perfectly valid law because, unlike the Jewish king, the Gentile king owns the land.

87 The Talmud notes that Jews are consistently using the bridges without paying the owners. This practice is taken as evidence of a pre-existing halakhic norm known to the populace, later given legal expression by the talmudic jurists as DDM. One of the more radical extensions of this mode of reasoning is in a contemporary responsum on the authority of the State of Israel. It begins with the observation that Jews are granting legitimacy to the legislation of the state and then seeks a rationale for this practice in DDM. Ovadiah Hedaya; compare the contemporary responsum of Rabbi Moses Feinstein on the permissibility of using secular wills. He cites the familiar expression: "If the children of Israel are not prophets, they are the sons of prophets." The instinct of the people must be given weight, and it is the task of the rabbinic decisor to comb the sources to ascertain the

of the medieval theories revolve around one or another form of popular consent or social contract theory. As Shiloh notes, the theories also attest to the rich interpenetration of the medieval discussions of the rights of kings taking place in the European Middle Ages.[88] Unlike in the case of Gerondi, the very definition of halakha does not change, but portions of halakha become theoretically optional and not mandatory as the principle is extended through a series of logical progressions and in tandem with the extension of the rights of kings in Europe far beyond the concrete context from which it sprang—taxes and land—and far beyond what is necessary to resolve actual, rather than theoretical, cases.

The twelfth-century talmudic commentator Rashi potentially shifts the paradigm, however, by building a bridge between the principle and the by now familiar idea of a universal divinely ordained law, which played so critical a role in the discussion of the Jewish monarchy in the preceding section. Rashi focuses on the one instance in the Babylonian Talmud where DDM functions not as a duty-imposing rule but as a power-conferring rule to Jewish litigants in an intra-Jewish dispute to take advantage of non-Jewish validation of deeds even though the signatories are non-Jews and the method contrary to Jewish law.[89] Here, DDM is allowing non-Jewish law to penetrate into Jewish law as an alternative norm.[90] Rashi draws on the familiar Jewish legal principle that only one who is himself under a divine obligation to perform an action can be an effective legal agent for others. He explains the talmudic permission as resting on the notion that non-Jews are commanded to "institute justice"—citing the Noahide norm of *dinin.* Accordingly, they can be effective agents for all matters subsumed under that command. Recall that, from the internal perspective of rabbinic Judaism, this command obligates humanity to pre-

legal basis that underlies Jewish customary practice. See Jeffrey Roth, "Crossing the Bridge: A Reply to Professor Shmuel Shiloh," *Cardozo Law Review* 12 (1991): 753.

88 Thus one sees DDM as a subspecies of personal contract law in that Jews are assumed to have implicitly contracted to obey the kingdom's customary, established laws and to have waived their rights under Jewish law. From the thirteenth century onward, the distinction between custom and new legislation begins to disappear, probably under the influence of the rise of positive law in Latin Europe. See Amos Funkenstein, *Perceptions of Jewish History* (Berkeley: University of California Press, 1993), 158. The subject is fully explored by Shmuel Shiloh, see "Equity as a Bridge between Jewish State and Secular Law," *Cardozo Law Review* 12 (1991).

89 Babylonian Talmud, Tractate Gittin 9b.

90 This usage of DDM may reflect the general predisposition of the Babylonian Talmud toward legal pluralism and decentralized law, which Rashi's localized comments illuminate. See Ben-Menahem, "Judicial Deviation," 93.

serve social order by enacting systems of law.[91] The kingdom's law is rooted ultimately in divine command and therefore has legal and moral legitimacy equal to that of Jewish law. As the product of divine command, it is, in a sense, sanctified. Accordingly, non-Jewish legal activity can serve here as an alternative norm even for Jews and even when it is at variance with Jewish law. Conversely, with respect to matters not subsumed under the command of *dinim*—Jewish marriage and divorce bills—DDM cannot be invoked as a power-conferring rule to utilize alternative norms. The implication of Rashi's rationale is that large portions of the halakha are in fact replaceable by the law of other civilizations, thus shrinking the scope of halakha to matters of ritual and religious prohibition.[92]

I want to pause for a moment on the picture of halakha that can be extrapolated from Rashi's comment here and in several other places. In my view, Rashi consistently understands halakha as composed of overlapping jurisdictions that legitimately generate law pursuant to divine command. Rashi's position on Jewish lay legislation is consistent. He equates lay legislation with Torah law and the transgression of lay legislation as the abrogation of a commandment.[93] The lay communal body has direct legal agency to bind others. This is a pluralistic, bottom-up picture of law, in which law emanates from a variety of potentially authoritative jurisdictions. Non-Jewish legal orders are one jurisdiction, comparable to law-generating institutions such as that of the Jewish king, the lay communal bodies, and the rabbinic courts. Discretion can exist only so long as law doesn't exist to fill the space. And pursuant to Rashi's interactive model, gaps in halakha disappear once law appears, whether the law is generated by the nonJewish state, the Jewish state, or even the international community.[94] According to the pluralist conception, the function

---

91 Exactly what is included in this command—whether to institute criminal enforcement jurisdiction alone or to develop a legal system—is, as one would expect, a subject of juristic debate. See Stone, "Sinaitic and Noahide Law," 1157.

92 Jewish law maintains that with respect to financial matters, as opposed to religious matters, it is possible for parties to contract out of the law in any event, despite the fact that these norms originate in Divine law. But the rationale that links the validity of Gentile law to the Noahide command of *dinim* would suggest that it could extend to all laws subsumed under the Noahide command, including criminal law and punishment, traditionally categorized as "religious." Rashi elsewhere assumes that it is permissible to hand Jews over to the criminal processes of the non-Jewish government, despite bypassing of Jewish evidentiary and penal law. Babylonian Talmud, Tractate Niddah 61a. Rashi's theory has very few internal limits, except that subjects unique to Jewish law cannot be displaced.

93 Rashi, Responsa 247.

94 See Stone,"Sinaitic and Noahide Law," 1157; and Jeremy Wieder,"International Law and Halakhah," in *War and Peace in the Jewish Tradition*, applying this idea to the question whether the halakhic polity is bound by international law.

of DDM is to arbitrate which norms generated by diffuse jurisdictions are relevant in different circumstances. In this light, Rabbi Yisraeli ruled that the Jewish state was obligated by, and only by, international standards of war.[95] From a technical perspective he relies on the talmudic dictum "the law of the kingdom is the law," but he gives it an innovative meaning. Where formerly the dictum governed the obligations and privileges of individual Jews to their host-states, it now, in the elaboration by Rabbi Yisraeli, governs the obligations and privileges of the Jewish nation acting in the international context. And where formerly, the dictum extended only to the laws of a sovereign ruler, such as king or state, it now, in the elaboration of Rabbi Yisraeli, extends to international law on the theory that the non-Jewish kingdom could be defined in global terms, so long as the collective will of the world's citizens ratified the global kingdom's law. Rabbi Yisraeli's opinion, moreover, seems to blend the underlying rationales of the DDM consent school and of Rashi's turn to Noahide law. Jews can consent to be governed by international norms, just as they can consent to be governed by the civil laws of hoststates. Consent to laws pertaining to war is legitimate even though war is a far cry from monetary matters. War, however, is a chosen means to settle disputes in contemporary life and, as such, fulfills the goal of civilizing the world and securing social order—even if such wars are not undertaken solely for the sake of enforcing Noahide norms.[96]

The upshot of this innovative use of DDM is the treatment of the modern Jewish state as merely one member of the global community of nations. International codes of war, treaties, and so forth govern the State of Israel—from the halakhic perspective—and not indigenous, national-collective norms, nor particular, aspirational norms developed to govern relations of members within a covenantal community. In his analysis, Rabbi Yisraeli makes clear that halakhic norms pertaining to use of force developed within the context of individual selfdefense could not countenance the manner of conducting warfare acceptable within the international community. But rather than view halakha as a ground for ethical critique, Yisraeli sees halakha as allowing the incorporation of looser standards of behavior when the nation acts beyond its border.[97] Should international society adopt more stringent norms than halakha, these too would be binding on the nation acting in the international arena. The Jewish nation-state is no longer modeled on a

95 Rabbi Shaul Yisraeli, "Military Action in Defense of the State," in Amuda Ha-Yemini, discussed extensively in Edrei, "Law, Interpretation, and Ideology," 187.

96 For additional discussion of the halakhic issues surrounding the incorporation of international laws of war, see Weider, "International Law and Halakhah."

97 Edrei, "Law, Interpretation, and Ideology," 214.

concept of exceptionalism. Instead, it is merely a member of international society whose norms should therefore converge.

IV Transnational versus Cosmopolitan Law

As should be clear by now, there is an interesting parallel between the new transnational law and the relationship between universal and particular law within halakha that I have sought to describe. In both cases, universal, international, or global norms developed from outside are deemed capable of importation into national, particularistic, internal contexts. This is hardly surprising, as legal historians have been quick to point out that transnational law rests on a picture of law with a long pedigree stretching back not only to the eighteenth century but also to the medieval period and even before. It is a picture of law based on a conception of a universal or common law that is in constant relation to a particular law—a picture of law obscured by the nineteenth-century rise of exclusive nationalism and, with it, analytic positivism and the historical school. The debate this transition to transnationalism has engendered in U.S. constitutional circles parallels the Jewish discussion. Vicki Jackson recently proposed that the debate over constitutional transnationalism could be charted across three models: resistance (by national constitutions to outside influence or foreign practice); convergence (national constitutions as sites for implementation of international or transnational law so the two converge); or engagement (universal and particular, national law as relational with each the interlocutor of the other).[98] The long halakhic discussion over the relationship of the universal law to the particular law also divides over models of resistance, convergence, and engagement.

Resistance is the familiar problem of the loss of national distinctiveness, which many medieval jurists raised as an objection to expanding the range of DDM.[99] Yet, other rabbinic authorities, especially in the modern age, saw application of non-

98 Vicki C. Jackson, "The Supreme Court, 2004 Term: Comment: Constitutional Comparisons: Convergence, Resistance, Engagement," *Harvard Law Review*119 (2005): 109.

99 The thirteenth-century Provencal jurist Menahem Ha-Meiri placed the issue squarely on the table. Meiri held that non-Jewish society was an enlightened civilization and, singularly among rabbinic thinkers, argued that they were brothers within the meaning of scripture to whom full legal and juridical equality under Jewish law was owed. Yet he vigorously opposed the conclusion that Jews can use non-Jewish law when the two conflict. "The laws of their ancient sages, which oppose our laws, are not included in the scope of DDM. For, if they were, all the laws of Israel would be cancelled." Various consent advocates also tried to limit what is properly deemed a law of "the kingdom" to core governmental functions such as taxes or matters pertaining to land, in order to keep the doctrine confined.

Jewish law within an internal halakhic context, through the mediating principle of DDM or Noahide law, not as a threat to Jewish distinctiveness and particularity but, rather, as a method of correcting the halakha. The assumption that drives this approach, already found in the Talmud, is that one of the purposes of the universal law preceding Sinai must be to set a floor on ethical obligations, and this notion, as Shiloh put it,"became incorporated into the discussion of DDM."[100] If Jewish law allows ethically inferior conduct that other legal systems forbid, the ethically superior norm should displace Jewish law so that the two converge. Thus, as Shiloh points out, the progress forward in the self-correction of the halakha in light of the laws of other civilizations was made in the modern era with exposure of halakha to democratic systems.[101]

However the idea of convergence is a two-edged sword. As we saw, Rabbi Yisraeli takes it as permission to turn to international law—to have the halakha converge with international standards when operating in an international context—even if the particularist norms of halakha embody an ethically stricter standard of behavior. This view leaves no room for halakha to function as an aspirational set of norms—as a ground for protest from within civil society. This is precisely the issue separating the two versions of cosmopolitanism. The first school insists that the relationship between the universal or common norm outside and the particular, now needs to be reversed with the particularist halakha serving as a resource for ethical critique of nationalist, state law. While some argue that the State of Israel should view the halakha as setting a floor on acceptable conduct in all domains of public life, others insist that they do not aim to genuinely bind the state. Rather, they aim to engage the state.[102]

Conclusion

As I write, the predicted demise of nation-states as privileged units of analysis in law is in increasing question. National sovereignty and regulation on a national scale has gained power in order to meet economic turmoil on the global front. Law without nation is still unthinkable. What is finally thinkable, however, is the complex interaction among the national state and its law, global law, and local laws. "Our legal life," Santos writes, "is constituted by an intersection of different legal orders, that is by *in-*

100 Shiloh, "Dina De-Malkhuta" (Heb.).
101 Shiloh, "Equity as a Bridge," 753.
102 See discussion in Edrei, "Law, Interpretation, and Ideology," 187.

terlegality."[103] The contemporary Jewish discussion about the role of halakha in the nation-state of Israel within the context of an increasingly globalized world offers a window onto how these complex interactions are conceptualized from the perspective of one local law—the halakha—as the interaction of multiple legal orders that are both outside of and a part of itself.

103 Boaventura de Sousa Santos, "Toward a New Legal Common Sense: Law, Globalization, and Emancipation," in *Law in Context* (London: Butterworths LexisNexis, 2002), 437.

Charlotte Elisheva Fonrobert

Dina de-malkhuta dina and Talmudic Divorce Law: A Challenge for Rabbinic Law in Diaspora

> The world exists for the sake of three things – for the sake of judgement (*din*), and for the sake of truth (*emeth*), and for the sake of peace (*shalom*), as it is said: 'Truth, justice (*mishpat*), and peace shall establish you in your gates.'
>
> *Mishnah Avot* 1:18[1]

> Jeremias und Mar-Samuel verdankt das Judentum die Möglichkeit seines Bestandes in der Fremde.
>
> Heinrich Graetz, Geschichte der Juden IV[2]

The Historical Context for *dina de-malkhuta dina*

From the earliest manifestations of their legal scholarship in the Mishnah (second and early third century C.E.) and onwards, the rabbinic scholars of Late Antiquity had to contend with political structures and empires (Hebr., *malkhuyot*) not of their own making. Emerging initially within a political context of gradually increasing hegemony of Roman imperial legislation, early rabbinic law, at least not in its classical formulation, is thus not a derivative of, or connected to political hegemony. Rather, we might say, it is formulated and produced *in spite of* the absence thereof.[3] If anything, it is a derivative of scholarship, of legal scholarship, of

1 Quoted from Martin Jaffee's translation of Mishnah *Avot* in *The Oxford Annotated Mishnah: A New Translation of the Mishnah* (Oxford University Press, 2022). Jaffee annotates his translation of *din* as "judgement" here with "judicial impartiality" (p. 718). The verse from Zechariah has *mishpat* (rendered as "justice") rather than *din*.

2 Graetz here has in mind Jeremiah 29:5–11 and his famous call to the (biblical) people of Israel to "seek the peace and prosperity of the city to which I (i.e., God) have carried you into exile" (Verse 7), along with the slogan *dina de-malkhuta dina* attributed to the Babylonian rabbinic sage (Mar) Samuel, in this paper rendered as Shmu'el.

3 As Amnon Linder and others have pointed out, some leading Jewish communities, including the Jewish population in the world of the Roman Empire, were granted various degrees of legal autonomy, with institutional structures underwriting such autonomy, such as for instance the Jewish ethnarch in Alexandria, the *nassi* or patriarch in the land of Israel, and – beyond the Roman world – the ethnarch or *resh galuta* in Sasanian Persia. This is to say, that there is no simple binary between political hegemony and absence thereof. The Mishnah may not have been formulated completely in a rabbinic jurisdictional vacuum. However, since the catastrophic Roman – Jewish wars

https://doi.org/10.1515/9783111062631-005

turning biblical legal teachings, or Torah, into a web of commandments (Hebr. *mitzvot*), however aspirationally seeking to bind together a community even in the absence of the structure of a state to support it. In short, the earliest rabbinic effort at articulating Jewish norms and laws after the loss of Jewish sovereignty can be read as an effort to underwrite the diasporic existence of a post-war Jewish community. Whether within the rapidly Romanizing province of Syria Palaestina, or within the realm of the Sasanian Empire, both political super-structures of governance that drew on a variety of legal traditions to establish, maintain, and manage their respective imperial hegemonies, the rabbinic scholars promoted their learning of Torah as *halakhah*, their vision of a normative "path" for Jews, in the context of political and state structures to which they themselves were subject. Rabbinic law, one might say, is born from negotiating a potential rule of rabbinic law for Jews with the state or sub-state (provincial) rule of law of others. After the disastrous Jewish-Roman wars of the first two centuries C.E., this situation applied *even within* the territory that bore the heritage of former Jewish sovereignty, i.e., in the area of ancient Israel, or – as some moderns would have it, the Jewish homeland.

Traces of this political reality of negotiating one's political existence with the other can be found scattered around the Mishnah already, and even more so in the later Talmudic discussions of Mishnaic law. The maxim of *dina de-malkhuta dina*, arguably one of the better-known Talmudic locutions, is one such trace and captures this reality in the most shorthand of (Babylonian) Aramaic formulations: "the 'law' of the kingdom is (the) 'law.'"[4] It might seem from this shorthand formulation, that when all is said and done, it is in the end "the law of the kingdom," of the empire or of the state, the political super-structure of whomever, that rules the day. The talmudic maxim, that is, expresses first and foremost acquiescence to the political circumstance of dwelling in someone else's sovereign state, kingdom, or empire. However, what precisely the maxim entails, and how it is to be applied, is a more complex question, one that has occupied the minds of rabbinic scholars

in the first and second centuries CE , the implementability of rabbinic law depended mostly on sufferance only. As Amnon Linder writes: Rabbinic law in the early period "was, so to speak, on parole, always liable to be overruled and invalidated" by Roman legislative powers at any moment, "The Legal Status…" (132).

4 The magisterial collection and discussion of the sources is Shmuel Shilo's *Dina de-Malkhuta Dina: The Law of the State is Law* (Jerusalem: Jerusalem Academic Press 1974, Hebrew). Another collection, less comprehensive and geared towards a broader audience, can be found in Chapter 9, "The Gentile State," of *The Jewish Political Tradition*, Vol. 1 (edited by Michael Walzer, Menachem Lorberbaum, Noam J. Zohar (Yale University Press 2000, 430–463). The more recent Cambridge Companion to *Judaism and Law* (2017) edited by Christine Hayes, discusses the origin and implementation of the principle in various chapters. For further literature see below.

from the early post-Talmudic, i.e., medieval period onwards, and into the early modern and modern period: if it is a legal maxim, how might it operate as a jurisdictional principle and in what contexts? Is it a theoretical principle, and if so for which theoretical discourse?[5] Is it a political principle, and therefore to be read as an "accommodationist" principle, ceding jurisdictional hegemony to whichever state power?[6] Or does it suggest a principle of resistance, in that it insists that in fact *only* when the state's hegemony operates as "law," i.e., lawfully, is it to be considered legitimate (*dina*), by rabbinic account?[7] What, in fact, is *dina* (Aramaic),[8] the *dina* of the state that is lawful or legitimate (*dina* or "law for Jews subject to the kingdom"), as opposed to, say, *halakhah*, or other concepts of law (*mishpat, hok*) that the late antique rabbinic scholars work with? And finally, what areas of rabbinic or Jewish law are meant (perhaps) to be included with, respectively excluded from, declaring the "law of the state" to be *the* law, and therefore

5 For instance, Beth Berkowitz, in "Approaches to Foreign Law in Biblical Israel and Classical Judaism through the Medieval Period," in *Cambridge Companion to Judaism and Law* (2017), discusses the maxim as a statement of *legal* theory, and one that counters tendencies of legal isolationism in rabbinic literature (146).

6 For comparison's sake one might think of a similar saying attributed – much earlier – to Jesus in the gospels: "Render unto the emperor the things that are the emperor's, and unto God the things that are God's" (Matthew 22:21, cp. Mark 12:13–17; Luke 20:20–26). This maxim has invariably been read as a theo-political statement of sorts. The rabbinic maxim obviously is missing the second half of the Christian maxim recorded in the gospels. I am not aware of any study comparing the intellectual histories of Matthew 22:21 and *dina de malkhuta dina* comparatively. Interestingly, in my opinion, the enlightenment Jewish philosopher Moses Mendelssohn in his famous treatise *Jerusalem* cites the gospels' principle rather than the rabbinic one (p. 104). See Gil Graff, Separation of Church and State: Dina de-Malkhuta Dina in Jewish Law, 1750–1848 (University of Alabama Press,1985), 80.

7 See Amos Funkenstein, "Law, Philosophy, and Historical Awareness," in *Perceptions of Jewish History* (University of California Press, 1993): "The principle DMD, far from demanding blind obedience, entails even a law of resistance of sorts – not active perhaps (taking arms against the ruler) but certainly passive. It is as much a principle of disobedience, as it is a principle of obedience" (157). Also Beth Berkowitz, "Approaches to Foreign Law" (155). For a different political reading of the invocation of the maxim in medieval rabbinic literature in Central Europe (Ashkenaz), see Joseph Isaac Lifshitz, *Rabbi Meir of Rothenburg and the Foundation of Jewish Political Thought* (Cambridge University Press 2016), especially pp. 101–105. See also L. Landman, *Jewish Law in the Diaspora: Confrontation and Accommodations* (Philadelphia, 1968).

8 For a discussion of the usage and meanings of the Hebrew term *din* in the earlier rabbinic texts see Ephraim Urbach's "The Term 'Din' and Its Implications" in his *The Halakhah: Its Sources and Development* (trans. Tel Aviva: Modan 1996), 88–92. Urbach claims that in tannaitic Hebrew *din* refers to the judicial act rather than law more broadly, such that the epigraph above from mAvot 1:18 would stand to mean: "The world stands on three things: on *din* (in the sense of the act of performing justice), on truth and on peace."

perhaps legitimate and authoritative for rabbinic communities as well? What could be ceded to the rule of the kingdom's hegemonic law, and what needs to be protected from it? Any and all of these questions have been discussed in various forms, from the medieval rabbinic legal literature to contemporary academic scholarship.

For our purposes here I am particularly interested in the last question. That is, what drives this essay is the question about the interpretative and theorical efforts to understand and reign in the reach of the Talmudic maxim, with an eye towards the rabbinic normative claims over marriage in general and divorce in particular.

In general, the history of the interpretation of the maxim can be described as an argument over the limitations of its claim. That is, surely the Talmudic maxim could not have meant that the "law" of the state/kingdom could or even should have jurisdictional force in place of rabbinic law in its entirety.[9] Certainly, no post-Talmudic interpreter and rabbinic *posek* (legal decisor) ascertained *that* possibility. The medieval Talmudic commentator Menachem ben Salomon HaMeiri (in rabbinic shorthand, the Meiri; 1249–1315) makes this point succinctly: "(Anything that the king introduces arbitrarily, and) the laws that the [non-Jewish] nations maintain according to the teaching of *their* books or the laws of *their* ancients sages which *oppose our* laws, are not to be included" under the maxim.[10] Virtually everyone for most of the history of rabbinic discussions of *dina de-malkhuta dina* has assumed that some exclusionary or boundary principle has had to be implied in its very formulation, to be determined to some degree by the original contexts in which the Talmudic discussions themselves deploy it.

Scholars and intellectual historians have assumed that, aside from what they sometimes deem to be "ritual" or more generally "religious" law,[11] the area of rab-

9 In the chapter on "The Gentile State" in *The Jewish Political Tradition*, Menachem Lorberbaum writes with regards to the reach of the maxim that "the limits of gentile authority were fixed, *of course*, by whatever was taken to be central as crucial in halakhah" (432, my emphasis). However, since what is central to *halakhah* is by no means obvious, those limits started to be debated almost the moment the maxim was first articulated.

10 *Bet ha-Behirah* on bBava Kamma 113b, cited from the translation in "The Gentile State," 446.

11 Any of these second-order categories for mapping rabbinic law into various other epistemic mappings remain problematic. Rabbinic halakhah does not distinguish between "religious" and "secular" law. This is not to say that the Talmudic rabbis themselves, and even more so the medieval codifiers, did not try to categorize areas of law. Lorberbaum puts this most succinctly when he writes: "... the rabbis distinguished between *mamona*, civil and economic matters, where *dina de-malkhuta* was legitimately dominant even over Torah law, and *isura*, literally, "forbidden" that is, religious matters, where the Torah could not be superseded." This mapping one may follow with lesser hesitation, albeit "religious" does not map easily onto "forbidden." However, when he continues to suggest that "we may read this as a more or less straightforward distinction between sec-

binic law-making circumscribing and institutionalizing Jewish marriage and especially divorce has been understood as being variously excluded from *dina de-malkhuta dina,* from any legal accommodation of the rule of the state's law, at least until early modernity, and the confrontation with the rise of the European nation-states towards the end of the imperial order.[12] However, it may be worthwhile to revisit and consider the reasons for the dominant insistence in Jewish rabbinic, intellectual, and interpretive tradition on excluding rabbinic *marital* law from *dina de-malkhuta dina.* A mere insistence on the obviousness of that limitation of the maxim's claim lacks explanatory potential. Opening the question, on the other hand, on why Jewish marital law, and particularly divorce law, is not and could or should not be ceded to the jurisdiction of the kingdom/state *(malkhut),* might allow us to think more carefully about the gender-politics of Jewish diaspora. Nothing in Jewish or rabbinic legal tradition is ever set in stone, although some things have incredible staying power. *Dina de-malkhuta dina* by all accounts appears as a fundamental strategy of diaspora, even when in so many respects it appears as merely stating the obvious. Of course, the *din* or jurisdiction of the empire/state *din* is so because it has the means of enforcing it. At the same time, the maxim enables a reflective collective diaspora existence that in the best scenario can work to enable a minority community (Jews) to evaluate the legitimacy of laws and norms of collective co-existence to which they are subjected.[13] But the gender-politics entailed in thinking about what diaspora might and should be are by no means self-evident. Vice versa, we may ask what can be learned about diaspora politics when trying to make sense of the legal aspiration to control the institution of marriage.

ular and religious regulation, *mamona* representing but not necessarily exhausting the secular interest" (434), one wonders about such equations of different epistemic maps, especially in light of the recent discussions of the category of the "secular" in the aftermath of Talal Asad's genealogical critique in *Formations of the Secular: Christianity, Islam, Modernity* (Stanford University Press 2003).

12 On the confrontation of French Jewry with Napoleon and his demands on them in order to turn them into decent French citizens, see especially Gil Graff, *Separation of Church and State: Dina de-Malkhuta Dina in Jewish Law, 1750–1848* (University of Alabama Press, 1985), but also Menachem Lorberbaum in *The Jewish Political Tradition.* For the Austria-Hungarian Empire Kaiser Joseph II instituted his *Ehepatent* in 1783, putting the institution of marriage the state's authority and norm, under thereby challenging the rabbinic courts of his time.

13 On mobilizing *dina de malkhuta dina* to theorize diaspora, see also Sylvie Anne Goldberg, "Common Law and Jewish Law: The Diasporic Principle of dina de-malkhuta dina," *Behemoth: A Journal on Civilisation* 2 (2008), 39–53.

For the purposes of the following discussion, the basic historical contexts of the classical rabbinic formulation of *dina de-malkhuta dina* can be briefly summarized:[14]

In the precise articulation of the maxim, *dina de malkhuta* appears only in the later *Talmudic* discussions of the earlier Mishnah, although the Mishnah at least touches upon the relationship between rabbinic and non-Jewish legal institutions implied by it in a precursory form, as we will have opportunity to discuss further below.

a) In the Talmudic discussions, the maxim appears in the *Babylonian* Talmud only, the Talmud of the Jewish and, more precisely, of the rabbinic diaspora, and by some accounts rabbinic Judaism's diaspora manifesto *per definitionem.*[15] In terms of original context, then, *dina de-malkhuta dina* is a concept of diaspora, a concept born from diaspora, and thereby underwriting at least to some degree diaspora politics. In the Babylonian Talmud it is attributed consistently to Shmu'el (third century CE), one of the most famous Babylonian rabbinic scholars of the earliest generations of Mishnah interpreters and one of the founding figures of rabbinic scholarship in the Sasanian empire. Whether or not he *historically* articulated the maxim, the consistent *attribution* to Shmu'el writes it into the earliest memory of the Babylonian diaspora.[16]
b) Without ever being defined with conceptual and theoretical precision as to its scope of legal applicability,[17] *dina de-malkhuta dina* is mentioned on four occasions in the Babylonian Talmud. As most scholars have noted, it is invoked

14 Any and all discussions of the Jewish intellectual history of *dina de-malkhuta dina* rely on Shilo's magisterial study *Dina de-Malkhuta Dina: The Law of the State is Law* (Jerusalem: Jerusalem Academic Press, 1974).

15 See Daniel Boyarin, *A Traveling Homeland: The Babylonian Talmud as Diaspora* (2015).

16 Geoffrey Herman has argued that greater historiographical weight should be put on the transmission of the maxim rather than its non-verifiable original formulation, since Shmu'el is always only reported to have done so originally. Herman attributed the transmission to one of the reigning Jewish exilarchs (*resh galuta*) of the Babylonians Jewish community in the fourth century CE, based on a passage in the Babylonian Talmud (bBava Batra 55a). The exilarch's interest in accommodating Persian imperial law is self-evident. See G. Herman, *A Prince without a Kingdom: The Exilarch in the Sasanian Era* (Texts and Studies in Ancient Judaism 150; Mohr Siebeck 2012), 203–207. Regardless, at the very least as an act of memory Talmudic teaching attributes the maxim to one of the founding scholars of the rabbinic diaspora.

17 In the words of Salo Baron: "*Dina de-malkhuta dina* was more frequently invoked than clarified" (Graff, 144, n.23).

mostly in contexts of discussing fiscal matters and contract law: taxation,[18] public works,[19] and property law.[20] The one exception seems to be the invocation of the maxim in the context of divorce law, in connection with an early rabbinic dispute about the reliance on non-Jewish institutions of law for divorce documentation, recorded in the Mishnah. Below we will examine this context more carefully. Even here the Talmudic discussion seems to turn to questions of financial matters and transfer of property,[21] but, after all, marital law intersects with property law in fundamental ways.

c) From the late antique Talmudic discussions, therefore, we can only second-guess from those contexts a more limited, jurisdictional application of the maxim matters in the minds of the makers of the Talmud; namely, in the context of property and finance/taxation law. These would, of course, have been of urgent economical interest to any imperial power.

The contextual limitation and its conceptual clarification will become important for post-talmudic rabbinic discussions, especially in the contexts of the medieval European kingdoms and empires. The Talmud itself does not provide us with such conceptual clarification for categorizations of law for which areas of rabbinic law *dina de-malkhuta dina* may or may not be invoked or applied, hence allowing its diverse invocations later on.

---

18 bNedarim 27b-28a: one may lie to a tax collector, theoretically a representative of the 'kingdom,' in spite of Shmu'el's maxim. That is, a Jewish person does *not* have to accept the *din* of the kingdom as *din,* if the tax collector comes up with arbitrary requests. In post-talmudic discussions, Jewish scholars of law and codifiers associate tax collectors with robbers, if they are 'unruly,' i.e., if a tax-collector is self-appointed, or if there is no general tax-code in a manner of speaking, or if the king's taxation law itself is arbitrary. See, e.g., Maimonides' *Mishneh Torah,* "Laws of Robbery and Lost Property" 5:11. Lorberbaum (433) suggests that "taxation is the standard example not only because it was the most common practical issue, but also because it suggested the range of issues to which the maxim was meant to apply" (413), in short, the economic life of diaspora communities. Even more, taxation is the primary tool (other than violence) that secures subjection to or participation in hegemonic rule.

19 bBava Kamma 113 b, on "public" works like bridges. Here the Shmu'el's maxim is invoked to explain why a Jew should be allowed to use a bridge built from trees expropriated from a Jewish owner. *Dina de-malkhuta dina* explains why the government might have done an expropriation "legitimately," such as for reasons of eminent domain and equitably.

20 bBava Batra 54–55a, involving the case of a Jew purchasing land from a non-Jew, also involving taxation. Here the statement is part of collection of (three) rulings having to do with Persian civil law, attributed to Shmu'el and transmitted by the exilarch. See Herman (n. 11), 203–204.

21 bGittin 10b, discussing the nature of transactional documents and contracts as either performative (gift) or as receipts.

Early Rabbinic Divorce Law and the (Non-Jewish) Empire's Jurisdiction

As mentioned above, one of the seeming exceptions to the cluster of civic case-law in which *dina de-malkhuta dina* is invoked in the Talmud is rabbinic divorce law (*gittin*).[22] This may seem surprising in light of the post-talmudic focus of the maxim on fiscal and taxation law, although clearly in classic rabbinic legal discourse marriage of course constitutes always an economic as much as a gender relationship. However, it appears that in the earliest texts of rabbinic law the jurisdictional boundaries were *not* drawn quite as tightly around rabbinic divorce proceedings as later halakhists might have preferred. Since this appears as a more surprising moment in rabbinic legal discourse, much as it demonstrates an early flexibility, in rabbinic legal discourse about their own socio-legal project for a community under the hegemony of others, we shall engage in a brief journey of examining the rabbinic source.

Let us briefly and quite generally consider the role of Jewish divorce law in the history of Jewish marriage.[23] The normativization and institutionalization of the severance of marriage presents a quintessential aspect of the history of Jewish marriage. While earliest rabbinic law, as presented in the Mishnah, devotes significant interest in this area of marital law, Biblical law devotes all of five verses to it.[24] Biblical law explicitly enables the severance of a marriage, with an emphasis on the document (*sefer keritut*) that the husband writes for his wife, a document which effects the severance. Subsequently, the five biblical verses and their interpretation as to the production and delivery of the document, or in rabbinic shorthand the *get*, underwrite a significant portion of rabbinic marital law that maintains validity to this day, summarized succinctly by Yair Furstenberg: "The husband unilaterally executes the divorce by writing and delivering (either directly or through a messenger) a signed bill of divorce (get) to his wife in front of two witnesses. This bill declared that only after she received the document will her marriage be dissolved and she be permitted to remarry."[25] Jewish legal tradition therefore allows divorce, considering it a biblical norm, but has made the gendered unilaterality an enduring challenge for contemporary Jews, especial-

22 See bGittin 10b.

23 See also the recent, more historiographically oriented study by Yair Furstenberg, "Provincial Rabbis: Shaping Rabbinic Divorce Procedure in a Roman Legla Environment," *JQR* 109:4 (Fall 2019), 471–499.

24 Deuteronomy 24:1–4.

25 "Rabbinic Divorce Procedure," 476.

ly women, seeking to abide by Jewish law when husband and wife have become more and more equal partners in most contexts of civil marriage.

Like biblical law, rabbinic law does not exactly prescribe divorce, but assumes the practice among the Jews it seeks to speak for, and scholars have uncovered and demonstrated the diverse options Jews – and especially Jewish women – had in the early Roman Empire of the first two centuries C.E. to pursue their divorce proceedings.[26] In contrast to early contemporaneous, emerging Christian traditions rejecting the validity of divorce,[27] but overlapping with Roman legal tradition,[28] the rabbinic Mishnah assumes divorce as a given practice, certainly among Jews but also among (some) others. From the Mishnah onwards, the severance of a marital relationship turns into one of the most fundamental aspects of rabbinic personal status law, especially for women, in terms of their economic security as much as in terms of their ability to maneuver their relationships with men. Like other, biblically inspired areas of rabbinic law, divorce therefore, appears as an area of rabbinic law-making that had the potential to become heavily invested in the rabbinicization of Jewish tradition. To the rabbis, their Torah-based legal tradition clearly provided guidelines for the publicly legitimated divorce of a marriage in such a way as to organize and stabilize social relations within the community. Much of rabbinic divorce law, therefore, is vested in rules and norms that apply to Jews specifically, and Jews only, derived from (interpretations and expansions of) biblical or Torah law. As the medieval Talmudic commentator Rabbi Shlomo ben Yitzhak (Rashi, 1040–1105) emphasizes: non-Jews "are not subject to 'severance' (*keritut*), because the biblical teachings of divorce and marriage (*torat gittin ve-kiddushin*) do not refer to them."[29] Much as the impossibility of divorce marked hegemonic Christian-Catholic marital law for so long, divorce, therefore, always had the potential to turn into an identitarian legal area, especially under Christian hegemony.

26 Tal Ilan, "Notes and Observations on a Newly Published Divorce Bill from the Judean Desert," *Harvard Theological Review* 89 (1996): 195–202. The archive of the Babatha documents (second century C.E.) constitutes the most famous evidence for a woman having sought legal restitution from Roman courts, although her cases are not divorce cases. See especially Hannah M. Cotton, "The Guardianship of Jesus son of Babatha: Roman and Local Law in the Province of Arabia," *Journal of Roman Studies* 83 (1993): 393–420.

27 1 Cor 7:10–13 and Mark 10:11–12 (with the synoptic parallels in Matt 19:9 and Luke 16:18).

28 Susan Treggiari, *Roman Marriage: Iusti Coniuges from the Time of Cicero to the Time of Ulpian* (Oxford: Clarendon Press, 1991), Chapter IV: Separation/ Divorce, 435–483. Yair Furstenberg has carefully shown how much of the "milieu" of Roman marital and especially divorce law was absorbed by the rabbis of the Mishnah, "Provincial Rabbis: Shaping Rabbinic Divorce Procedure in a Roman Legal Environment" *JQR* 109:4 (Fall 2019), 471–499.

29 bGittin 9a-b. The Talmudic text is offered as an early tradition (*baraita*), but invoked also in the Mishnah at 1:5.

Remarkably, however, European Christian rulers did not interfere with Jewish divorce practices until the formation of the European nation-state and the inclusion of divorce law in the aspects of rabbinic law was to be questioned and negotiated with the emerging French nation-state under Napoleon.

It is all the more noteworthy then, that the Mishnah's treatise on divorce law (*Gittin*) includes comparatively more references to Roman institutions and power, and not always negative ones.[30] An important such reference, much discussed in scholarship on rabbinic law, can be found with a rabbinic dispute regarding the role of non-Jewish institutions and witnesses in production of divorce bills. The dispute between the anonymous normative voice of the Mishnah and an early sage appears like this:

> All documents[31] entered in the *arka'ot*[32] of non-Jews, even though their signatories are non-Jews, are valid (*kesherim*); **except for** bills of divorce (*gittei nashim*) and documents of manumission of slaves (*shihrure avadim*).
>
> *Rabbi Shim'on said: These also are valid.*
>
> They only mentioned this regarding when they were issued by laymen. (Mishnah Gittin, 1:5).[33]

This rabbinic dispute presents a remarkable moment the Mishnah's discussion of divorce law. While the first anonymous and therefore dominant halakhic voice is not surprising, Rabbi Shimon's opinion and the fact that it is recorded are all the more so. To clarify, the Mishnah's (anonymous) voice of law insists on a fundamental distinction between every other (fiscal?) contract/document/bill and between personal status documents, in which either a woman or a slave is released from

30 Furstenberg, 472, n. 4

31 *shetarot.* The Mishnah uses the term *shtar* in a vast diversity of contexts, for contracts, bills, receipts, and proof of debt or *credit*, and here apparently as an umbrella term for documents of personal status law.

32 *arka'ot:* Krauss suggests the Greek etymology of ἀρχή = ἀρχεῖον and renders as *Rathaus, Archiv* (city-hall or city archive). Marcus Jastrow renders *arka'ot* as 'recorder's office,' presumably something like Archiv. Medieval commentators, such as Rashi, read the *arka'ot* as "their courts" (bGittin 9b). It is questionable whether in the Mishnah the *arka'ot* are quintessentially "non-Jewish" institutions or offices. Here the Mishnah feels compelled to qualify the *arka'ot* as those of 'non-Jews,' implying that they are not always non-Jewish. Elsewhere the Mishnah refers to the "old *archë* of Sepphoris" (mKid 4:5), where Jews worked as witnesses, and leaving it open whether this is understood to be a "Jewish" institution. See also Tosefta Bava Batra 8:2, loc. cit. See below.

33 My emphasis; cf. the parallel tradition in Tosefta *Gittin* 1:4 which frames the dispute as taking place between Rabbi Akiva and the collective sages.

the legal relationships that bind them to another person.[34] Accordingly, the former can be signed off by non-Jews and can be presented to non-Jewish "legal" institutions, whatever precisely the Mishnah has in mind with the Greek term (*arka'ot*) it introduces here to represent those.[35] Non-Jewish interference with legal documents involving Jewish persons is recognized as valid, *except for* divorce and manumission. That is, a jurisdictional boundary is drawn between personal status documents and fiscal documents. The Mishnah, earlier fundament to the Talmud that it is, of course does not have (or present) the conceptual vocabulary of *dina de-malkhuta dina* here. But is seems clear that the Mishnah's voice of law foreshadows Shmu'el's maxim: the jurisdiction of the (Roman) state "generally," here in the form of non-Jewish signatories and non-Jewish courts or legal institutions, is granted legitimacy, except that is for personal status documents (divorce/manumission). The jurisdiction of the empire is not to apply to the latter.

However, and that needs to be emphasized, the Mishnah records the minority legal dissent. According to the second-century sage Rabbi Shim'on "these" documents, that is, the documents that change the (bounded) personal status of women and (Jewish) slaves *also* can be ceded in whichever limited ways to non-Jewish hegemony.[36] According to this sage, then, such documents should also be regarded as valid when signed off by non-Jews, and presented to non-Jewish institutions, thereby allowing non-Jews a certain jurisdictional role. His position appears to make the boundary between rabbinic and non-Jewish legal institutions (the state/*malkhut*) significantly more porous, depending on what kind of importance in either procedure (divorce or manumission) would be attributed to such certification. When it comes to intersecting the authoritativeness of legal institutions, according to Rabbi Shimon, *non-Jewish* institutions – at the very least with respect to the process of their legal *documentation*, would have equal standing to *Jewish* ones. In terms of the later Talmudic maxim, Rabbi Shimon might hold that in some respects the "jurisdiction of the state" (even when non-Jewish) does indeed apply, however circumscribed, even to Jewish divorce proceedings.

Which leaves the last clause of the Mishnaic paragraph and its enigmatic phrasing, that "they" (referring to the Mishnah's voice of law in the first clause) mentioned "this" (referring to the exclusion of divorce documents from non-Jewish interference) when such documents were issued by laymen and not legal profes-

34 For the purposes of this essay I focus on divorce law and not manumission, much as the linkage between the two in rabbinic law requires much more careful thinking.

35 See Saul J. Berman, "The Boundaries of Loyalty: Testimony Against Fellow Jews in Non-Jewish Courts," Tikvah Working Paper 09/2011 (http://www.law.nyu.edu/sites/default/files/TikvahWorkingPapersArchive/WP9Berman.pdf), 6.

36 In the parallel tradition recorded in Tosefta Gittin 1:4 this is Rabbi Akiva's opinion.

sionals.[37] Divorce documents are to be invalidated only when the non-Jews handling them are laymen, but not otherwise.

To summarize then the import of the early Mishnaic dispute for our discussion: for the historical context of the Mishnaic formulation of rabbinic law during the second century C.E., we have documented evidence of a Jewish practice of turning to Roman courts to record or perhaps even adjudicate divorce cases. Even women (Babatha) would seek the legal counsel that might suit their economic need. The rabbis would have been well aware that Jews did so when push came to shove, and we have evidence within the Mishnah of a (again limited) rabbinic acknowledgment of Roman jurisdiction (Rabbi Shim'on),[38] perhaps even as a compromise with what was then still Jewish practice. Even within the ranks of early rabbinic legal scholarship, therefore, such a practice was not entirely dismissed and remained in dispute. After all, the dispute was recorded as such in the Mishnah. A sense of the dispute around *dina de-malkhuta dina* is therefore reflected in the earliest layers of rabbinic divorce law.

Talmudic Restriction of *Dina de-Malkhuta Dina*

However, the window that let in potential trouble was quickly thrown shut. The Mishnaic dispute and its possible trajectories were quickly contained as early as in the Talmudic discussion and the jurisdiction of the empire/state shut out of divorce proceedings.

A cursory study of the Talmudic discussion of our Mishnaic dispute will quickly reveal the analytic strategies to sideline the potential implications of the expansive minority opinion attributed to Rabbi Shimon in the Mishnah. That is, by its own discursive rules the Talmud can never simply give credence to one position in a mishnaic dispute and dismiss the other. Rather, it must explain minority opinions once they are part of the textual tradition and thereby highlight and direct the stakes of the dispute.

---

37 I am following here the glossing of David Brodsky, as per *The Oxford Annotated Mishnah: A New Translation of the Mishnah*, ed. by Shaye J.D. Cohen, Robert Goldenberg and Hayim Lapin (2022), vol. II, 263. Brodsky bases his gloss on bGittin 11b. From the Mishnaic formulation it is not entirely clear whether the last clause is part of Rabbi Shim'on's dissent, or a gloss to limit it.

38 Or, more significantly, Rabbi Akiva in the parallel tradition recorded in the Tosefta (tGittin 1:4), reference in the Talmud also at bGittin 11a.

In our case the Talmud's anonymous editorial voice,[39] attributed in textual scholarship of the Talmud to the latest layer of the Talmud and therefore shaping the discussion, challenges Rabbi Shimon's opinion by pointing out that non-Jews who are not subject to the biblical laws of divorcing should most obviously not have any role in its documentation, neither as witnesses nor as courts.[40] Another legal tradition is introduced as a principle to frame Rabbi Shimon troubling openness to non-Jewish jurisdiction. That tradition holds that the witnesses on the divorce document are potentially insignificant to the process of divorcing by biblical law, whereas the witnesses of the *delivery* of the document to the wife are what matters most to the process of severance. As the later medieval codifier Maimonides (died 1204) would have it: "... the essence of divorcing is with the witnesses to the delivery (of the *get).*"[41] The witnesses to the delivery of the *get* are, after all, what provides publicity of the severance within the Jewish community, while the signatories to the document testify only to the validity of the document itself.

This differentiation of documentary certification (the signatures on the get) and social certification ("public" knowledge of the divorce) therefore allows the Talmudic discussion to keep the process of divorcing potentially under Jewish supervision, in a manner of speaking, even for the mishnaic minority opinion of Rabbi Shimon, while the non-Jewish signatories are reduced to some sort of sidekicks in the process.[42]

Meanwhile, the analysis of the first anonymous and authoritative opinion of the Mishnah is moved entirely out of the sphere of divorce law since the Talmudic analysis expresses surprise merely about its implication for laws of property transfer. That is, the Talmudic discussant asks how the mishnaic law could declare any and all documentation of Jewish property transfer, produced in non-Jewish *ar-*

---

39 In the scholarship on the textual evolution of the Talmud the anonymous voice in Talmudic discussions is usually attributed to the latest layer of the Talmud and therefore considered to be shaping them altogether. See Moulie Vidas, *The Making of the Talmud.* For simplicity's sake, many scholars resort to the shorthand of "the Talmud" for this voice.

40 Held up also by the medieval commentator Rashi, on which see above.

41 Maimonides, Mishneh Torah. Nashim: *Hilkhot Gerushin* 1:15. The validity of the document is by no means a simple matter in rabbinic law, and even here the Talmudic analysis points in that direction when considering how the ethnicity of the signatories as either Jewish or not would be recognized, and provides clearly non-Jewish – Persian – names (bGittin 11a). Counterintuitively, such names make the *get* valid, because for sure in such a case the witnesses to the delivery will be relied on to validify the severance. This extended discussion deserves a much more detailed analysis that goes far beyond our current context.

42 On this basis, Maimonides rules non-Jewish signatures on a *get* to be valid, while at the same time excluding non-institutions (*arka'ot*) from jurisdiction in divorcing. See Mishnah Torah. Kinyan: *Hilkhot Avadim* 6:5.

ka'ot/ institution valid for Jewish persons, whether deeds of sale or deeds of gifting. The latter is the source of the Talmudic concern since in the case of a gift it is the deed itself establishes the transfer of the property and not a monetary exchange. If, so the implied reasoning goes, a non-Jewish court were to certify such a deed, it should automatically be invalidated under rabbinic jurisdiction: To the late antique Talmudic legal scholars, Jewish gifting requires rabbinic involvement and supervision. Jewish gifting, a material transaction, but quintessentially one dependent on the social rather than merely economic bond of the parties involved remains subject to rabbinic jurisdiction. It is this analysis and not divorce proceedings per se that triggers the Talmud's citation of Shmuel's maxim: the only way the Mishnah's expansive admission of non-Jewish courts in this dispute, now focused on property law, can be justified in the Talmud's eye is because of *dina demalkhuta dina.* It may just be the case that in all matters of property transfer the state/empire holds the ultimate jurisdiction, and that is why the Talmud can imagine the Mishnah to validate non-Jewish courts in such cases.

So even the one seeming exception of invoking the maxim in the Talmudic discussions in the context of divorce law turns out to fit the rest of the picture. As opposed to the Mishnah's tentative precedent in Rabbi Shimon, the Talmudic editors restrict the role of the state's jurisdiction to the context of fiscal matters. The Talmud thereby launches a process that, over the centuries of the consolidation of rabbinic legal discourse, assumes the form of taking for granted that delete *dina de malkhuta*, the non-Jewish jurisdiction, may be valid exclusively in this context but certainly not in matters of biblically based marital law. The rabbis continued to retain jurisdiction in these matters, revising and rediscussing them in the process. At the same time, the system was hardly ever really subjected to a test. That is, Jewish marital law was of little interest to the empire and state, and was mostly ceded to the internal control of the Jewish communities and the rabbinic jurisdictional system.[43]

What might have happened if indeed the state or whichever governing authority had considered rabbinic divorce proceedings a matter of their jurisdictional reach?

And that is of course what precisely started to happen at the end of the eighteenth century, when the rulers of the fading European empires and their successor nation-states made marriage and the right to dissolve a marriage a matter of the state's jurisdiction rather than subject to any particular tradition. Law and the re-

43 The question of intermarriage raises a whole other set of legal and jurisdictional issues that did of course arise in various contexts and at various times. For the era of the Christianization of the Roman imperial legal system see Amnon Lindner, n.3.

formulation of law as law of the state was an incredibly effective and perhaps even the most effective tool to underwrite the invention of nations as unified social collectives. In the process of redrawing the boundaries on the European map in the name of the unitarian desire of the nation-state, palimpsests, multiple layers of jurisdiction, were simply not possible. The institution of marriage and especially the possibility of divorce ended up in the crossfire of nationhood versus diaspora.

A Sustainable Diaspora? A Speculative Conclusion

In the past two millennia of their diasporic existence, Jewish communities the world over have repeatedly forged tools to enable a collective existence *in* diaspora and *as* diaspora. The last two decades of Jewish diaspora studies have demonstrated this in so many ways. One such "tool," it has been argued already by early modern scholars and intellectuals like Heinrich Graetz, is Shmuel's maxim of *dina de-malkhuta dina*, a maxim that expresses everything ranging from disempowerment to subterranean intellectual paths of resistance. That particular diasporic intellectual tool is forged in the Jewish literature I know best: that is, the great compendia of the late antique movement that we have come to refer to as the rabbinic movement. It guided the delicate dance of the diasporic art of compromise, compromise between aspiration and reality, between tradition and renewal, between pragmatism and resistance. Whether sounding like accommodation, compromise, or like resistance to our ears, in the end its greatest effect perhaps is the fact that it was articulated to begin with. This among so many other aspects of rabbinic intellectuality is a remarkable signal of resilience, of insisting that a diaspora community with limited jurisdictional power gets to articulate and live and think with such a maxim. Historically, it has been one of the tools not just to enable, but to sustain diaspora.

Similarly, the institution of marriage developed along with the process of divorcing as legal institution, and as an institution circumscribed tightly by rabbinic legal thinking and jurisdiction, based on the rabbis' understanding of biblical law, and mostly in the context of other people's and other people's empires' law, including the modern European nation-state. Marital law and the protection of its supposed biblical integrity as much as of its practicability is arguably another central tool of sustaining diaspora. The stability of the social dynamics of the community and their projection into the future is almost self-evidently central to a diasporic community. As we have seen, the early and foundational texts allow the interference of others sometimes, and in limited ways. Is it then the case that the more clearly a collective in diaspora is circumscribed as to its social bonds, the stronger the sustainability of diaspora can be learned from the history of Jewish diaspora?

When all is said and done, the Jewish and feminist ethical conundrum emerging from these reflections is really this: Does whatever we may imagine and articulate as sustainable diaspora still need to put the question of the social cohesion of the community for the sake of its projection into the future at the center? Indeed, can Jewish diaspora be thought and done without worry for our collective future? It may be worth the try.

Serdar Kurnaz

The Transformation of Sharia from a Law-Centered Understanding to Ethics: An Overview

1 Introduction

Since the midst of the nineteenth century, with the tendency of translating Western codified law and implementing it as applied law in Muslim societies, scholars began to discuss the nature of Islamic law. Andrew March points out correctly: "The countries in which Muslim populations have grown in the past fifty years are not merely non-Muslim in culture and political values, but defend their political systems and cultures in terms of *universal values* which make both explicit and implicit demands on the Muslim conscience."[1] With the aforementioned tendency, Islamic law was forced out of the realm of applied law. In addition, Islamic law was not codified until the nineteenth century, during the so-called *Tanẓīmāt* era in the late Ottoman period.[2] Traditionally trained scholars reacted to this development in two different ways:

1. Seeing Islamic law as Ethics more than applied law, especially in societies where Muslims were – or for some scholars even today *are* – a minority.
2. Seeing Islamic law as a source for positive law for example in personal status law and succession or for the sake of regulation of individual religiosity of the society. The latter was possible by issuing fatwas for religious questions of the believers.

In particular with the migration of Muslims to Europe, scholars faced a new problem: Islamic law was not yet designed for societies where Muslims were a minority – only some rulings (*aḥkām*) dealt with Muslims living in non-Muslim countries,[3] especially in the contract law. However, with the twenty-first century, anoth-

1 Andrew F. March, "Sources of Moral Obligation to non-Muslims in the 'Jurisprudence of Muslim Minorities'(*Fiqh al-aqalliyyāt*) Discourse," *Islamic Law and Society* 16, no. 2 (2009), 36.
2 Roderic H. Davison, "Tanẓīmāt," in *Encyclopaedia of Islam, Second Edition*, ed. Peri Bearman, et al. (Brill Reference Online, 2002-), accessed March 11, 2022, http://dx.doi.org/10.1163/1573-3912_islam_COM_1174.
3 The Mālikī and Ḥanafī schools of law for example are famous for their rulings concerning Muslims as minorities. See Nuh Ha Mim Keller, "Which of the Four Orthodox Madhhabs Has the Most

https://doi.org/10.1515/9783111062631-006

er discussion occurred. Although we could use the term diaspora for the migrant Muslims in Europe, with the passage of time, a Muslim-European generation was born. They, however, do not want to define themselves as Muslims in the diaspora, knowing that their situation is significantly different from the situation of their parents and grandparents in their countries of origin. Nevertheless, this generation tries to find "Islamic" solutions for their daily life problems. To tackle this question, scholars started to focus on the use of the so-called "objectives of law" (*maqāṣid al-sharīʿa*), even for their own "Islamic context."[4] Thus, scholars like Yūsuf al-Qaraḍāwī (d. 2022) and Ṭāhā Jābir al-ʿAlwānī (d. 2016) tried to find new ways for solving religious matters of Muslims living as minorities and called their approach "Jurisprudence of Minorities" (*fiqh al-aqalliyyāt*).[5] Both of these approaches place a great emphasis on Islamic law as ethics. On the other hand, we know that this approach, i.e., seeing Islamic law as ethics, was also present in previous centuries.

This paper will therefore elaborate upon Arabic terms, generally understood as Islamic law, in order to discuss whether Islamic law is by definition related to ethics. In a second step, I will try to show how Muslim scholars and jurists argued for Islamic law related to ethics. In a third step, I will present the modern *maqāṣid*-approach and the concept of *fiqh al-aqalliyyāt* with a different ethical argumentation for its validity. My thesis is that each of the modern approaches to deal with Islamic law are influenced by ethical reflections and thoughts. Thus, the ethical character of Islamic law takes more and more the place of its juristic character in contemporary discussions, especially in Europe. This, however, can lead to a loss of its normative character.

Developed Fiqh for Muslims Living as Minorities." *Q News, The Muslim Magazine*, accessed June 8, 2020, www.masud.co.uk/ISLAM/nuh/fiqh.htm.

4 For an overview of the modern understanding of the objectives of the Sharia, see Felicitas Opwis, "New Trends in Islamic Legal Theory: *Maqāṣid al-Sharīʿa* as a New Source of Law?" *Die Welt des Islams*, 57 (2017), 7–32.

5 Some of al-Qaraḍāwī's and al-ʿAlwānī's writings on *fiqh al-aqalliyyāt* were translated. See Yūsuf al-Qaraḍāwī, *Fiqh of Muslim Minorities: Contentions Issues & Recommended Solutions* (Cairo: Al-Falah Foundation, 2003); Ṭāhā Ǧābir al-ʿAlwānī, *Towards a Fiqh for Minorities: Some Basic Reflections*, trans. Ashur A. Shamis (London: International Institute of Islamic Thought, 2003).

2 Islamic Law – Is It Equivalent to *Sharīʿa* [divine law], *Fiqh* [jurists' law] or even *Qānūn* [positive law]?

There are different technical terms in Arabic, as far as Islamic law is concerned. The most prominent term is *sharīʿa*. *Sharīʿa* had different meanings in the course of the Muslim tradition. The most common use, which is also mentioned foremost in the modern discussions in Islamic law, is that *sharīʿa* is an umbrella term for different categories of rulings concerning faith (*aḥkām iʿtiqādiyya*), legal norms (*aḥkām fiqhiyya*), and ethical norms (*aḥkām khuluqiyya*).[6] These are not codified norms; rather, scholars try to find these rulings through rational reasoning and interpretation of the texts of the religious sources Quran and Sunna.[7] Legal norms on the other hand, are divided into ritual actions (*ʿibādāt*) and interpersonal relationships (*muʿāmalāt*). The sum of these norms is called *fiqh* (literally: 'to understand'). *Fiqh*, again, is Islamic law as we use the term law in English.

In some centuries, especially in the post-classical period (from the thirteenth to the early nineteenth century), *sharīʿa* was used interchangeably – and is even today – for *fiqh* and thus for Islamic law. So far, Islamic law was seen as jurists' law and could be applied law if the ruler (e. g. the Sulṭān, Amīr etc.) decided to implement, for example, one of the four schools of law in the Sunni tradition. Even the ruler could enact laws (*qānūn*), a so-called *qānūnnāmah* under the Ottoman Empire.[8] Although ethical norms were and still are seen as a separate category from legal rulings, scholars from different centuries saw a link between Islamic law and ethics, especially philosophers like Abū Naṣr al-Fārābī (Alpharabius, Avenassar, d. 339/950), Abū l-Walīd Ibn Rushd (Averroes, d. 595/1198) and the Sunni theologian Abū Ḥāmid al-Ghazālī (d. 505/1111).

6 Mahmoud Bassiouni, *Menschenrechte zwischen Universalität und islamischer Legitimität* (Frankfurt am Main: Suhrkamp, 2014), 41.

7 For the methods of deriving norms see Serdar Kurnaz, "Who is the Lawgiver? The Hermeneutical Grounds of the Methods of Interpreting Qur'an and Sunna (istinbāṭ al-aḥkām)", *Oxford Journal of Law and Religion*, 6 (2017), 347–371.

8 See Chapter 5 of Hayreddin Karaman, *İslâm Hukuk Tarihi* (Istanbul: İz Yayıncılık, 1999).

3 Relationship Between Law and Ethics in al-Ghazālī's and Ibn Rushd's Works

3.1 Al-Ghazālī on Ethics and Law

Al-Ghazālī is one of the scholars who tried to systematize the categories of sciences. He is one of the first scholars who made a distinction between the religious sciences. For him, Islamic law is a purely juridic discourse on the legitimacy of actions. It is a tool for polity and merely so.[9] However, if we look into his *Revival of the Religious Studies* (*Iḥyā' 'Ulūm ad-Dīn*), we can see that Islamic law has relevance for the concept of his mysticist (*ṣūfī*) ethics. For this purpose, he uses the term *wara'* ('moderation'). The first category of moderation is to be a just human; it is the category of the just (*al-'udūl*). They follow the commands and prohibitions according to Islamic law. If one goes further and tries to avoid problematic actions because of having doubt (*shubha*) of its permissibility, then this is called moderation of the righteous (*aṣ-ṣāliḥūn*). But if one refrains from some permissible actions due to probable damage to society, this, then, is the moderation of the pious (*al-muttaqūn*). The last stage of moderation is the stage of the sincere ones (*aṣ-ṣiddīqūn*): to let aside all the actions that do not lead to God's nearness (*mā lā yufīdu ziyādata qurbin 'inda Allāh*). Al-Ghazālī underlines that only the first dimension of moderation is relevant to the sphere of the jurist (*al-faqīh*). He differentiates this dimension from the rest of the other three categories. Hence, the first category of moderation has no direct consequences for the hereafter. However, Islamic law guarantees happiness for this world, and this can have an impact for the happiness in the hereafter. Although al-Ghazālī knows that ritual prayers have direct ethical implications, he reduces Islamic law to interpersonal relationships and therefore excludes Islamic law from the discourse of ethics. Yet al-Ghazālī did not radically separate ethics from Islamic law, since sticking to the permissible and impermissible actions is, for him, an imperative condition for ethically valuable actions.[10] Later, Muslim jurists also distinguished between actions, which they derived by regarding an ethical viewpoint. Generally, the process of such derivations is subject to *fatwā*; they do not fall under the category of judicial judgements (so-called *qaḍā'*).

---

9 Ulrich Rudolph, "Al-Ghazālī on Philosophy and Jurisprudence." In *Philosophy and Jurisprudence in the Islamic World*, ed. Peter Adamson (Berlin/Boston: Walter de Gruyter, 2019), 67–91.

10 Abū Ḥāmid al-Ghazālī, Iḥyā' 'Ulūm al-Dīn, Beirut: Dār al-Ma'rifa, (n.d.), 1:18.

3.2 Ibn Rushd on Ethics and Law

In contrast to al-Ghazālī, Ibn Rushd links Islamic law directly to ethics, in particular the virtue ethics (*al-faḍā'il*). With this, he follows the tradition of philosophers like al-Fārābī before him.[11] Bouhafa has recently shown that al-Fārābī "identifies practical ethics with *sharī'a*."[12] Al-Fārābī says that laws are not valid universally, but have an ethical content, which should be specified for each particular historical situation by the lawgiver.[13] For this purpose, al-Fārābī defines good actions in Aristotelian terms as "mean" (*mesotēs*, μεσότης),[14] and locates law as part of practical philosophy.[15]

Ibn Rushd sees this direct link between Islamic law and ethics. In order to show this connection, he makes use of the distinction of law in written and unwritten law, as we find this distinction in Aristotle's *Rhetoric*. In this sense, Islamic law contains different practices (*sunan*), which are directly linked to one of the four cardinal virtues: prudence (*'iffa*), courage (*shajā'a*), generosity (*sakhā'*), and justice (*'adl*). These practices fall under the category of unwritten law; they are mostly unspecified principles. Scholars have to specify them, then they become written law, restricted to a specific time and space. Ibn Rushd says:

> It is necessary that you know that the purpose of the legal practices are the spiritual virtues. Some of them refer to praise to whom requires praise and thanks to whom requires gratitude. Under this category fall the ritual worships. These are the noble practices. Some of them are related to the virtue, which is called prudence. This is of two kinds: Practices with respect to food and beverages, and practice with respect to marital affairs. Some of them refer to the requirement of justice and abstention from injustice. These are the categories of legal practices that require justice in financial dealings and require justice related to bodies; related to this category are (the rulings of) retaliation, wars and punishments), because all of them request justice. Among them [i. e. legal practices] are practices laid down for honor. Among them are practices laid down for collecting wealth and its valuation, through which is intended the attainment of the virtue called generosity and the avoidance of the depravity called covetousness.[16]

---

11 Feriel Bouhafa, "Ethics and Fiqh in al-Fārābī's Philosophy." In Philosophy and Jurisprudence in the Islamic World, ed. Peter Adamson (Berlin/Boston: Walter de Gruyter), 2019, 11–27.

12 Bouhafa, 18.

13 Bouhafa, 20.

14 Bouhafa, 25.

15 Bouhafa, 21.

16 Serdar Kurnaz, "Ibn Rushd's Legal Hermeneutics and Moral Theory for a 'Living Sharī'a' – an Alternative Approach to Islamic Law in Ibn Rushd's *Bidāyat al-Mujtahid*," *Oxford Journal of Law and Religion* 8 (2019), 174–205. For this passage, see Abū l-Walīd Ibn Rushd, *Bidāyat al-Muǧtahid wa-Nihāyat al-Muqtaṣid*, ed. Abū Aws Yūsuf b. Aḥmad al-Bakrī (Amman: Bayt al-Afkār ad-Duwaliyya, 2007), 1008.

We can see the direct link of ethics to Islamic law *in toto*. For Ibn Rushd, there is a need for law for the society, although some individuals can act according to these virtues regardless of existing norms. However, as Ibn Rushd points out, not everyone has the ability to know what justice is. Thus, the law shows how justice can be reached and how everybody in the society must be an individual who regards his duties.[17]

If we look back on the discussions of the earlier authorities on Islamic law and ethics, we can see that they were aware of a link between ethics and law, but they did not equate them. This tendency, however, became prominent in the nineteenth and twentieth centuries, as we will see in the next chapter.

4 Contemporary Approaches for an Applied Islamic Law in Europe

4.1 Islamic Law as Islamic Ethics

This direct link of Islamic law to ethics, as we have seen it in Ibn Rushd's and al-Fārābī's approach, is missing in the writings of most Muslim jurists and scholars, although they do not think that there are no ethical implications of the norms in Islamic law. Be it as it may, in modern times, we have a shift in the development of Islamic law due to changing circumstances; Islamic law is, either partially or entirely, no more an applied nation's law. Thus, it became, and still is, largely only a part of the private religious lives of Muslim citizens.[18]

At the same time, scholars of Islamic Studies began to see Islamic law as ethics; these scholars included Kevin Reinhart, who stressed the results of the process of deriving norms from the relevant sources of *fiqh*.[19] For Reinhart, the categories of

17 Abū l-Walīd Ibn Rushd, *Talkhīṣ al-Khaṭāba*, ed. Muḥammad Salīm Sālim. Cairo: 1967, 68, 135, 145, 164 , 213–215, 229–238. For Ibn Rushd's understanding of law, see also Feriel Bouhafa, "Averroes' Corrective Philosophy of Law," in *Interpreting Averroes. Critical Essays*, ed. Peter Adamson (Cambridge: Cambridge University Press, 2019), 45–63; Serdar Kurnaz, "Ibn Rushd's Legal Hermeneutics and Moral Theory for a 'Living Sharia.'"

18 For the reduction of applied Islamic law mainly on the realm of the daily life of Muslims, see Brinkley Messick, "Fatwā, modern." *Encyclopaedia of Islam*, 3rd ed., accessed November 15, 2019, accessed November 15, 2019, dx.doi.org.proxy.ub.unifrankfurt.de/10.1163/15733912_ei3_COM_27049

19 Kevin Reinhart, "Islamic Law as Islamic Ethics," *The Journal of Religious Ethics*, 11/2 (1983): 186–203; for a more recent attempt, see Ahmad Badri Abdallah, "An Analysis of Islamic Jurisprudence (Fiqh) as Applied Islamic Ethics," *Islam and Civilisational Renewal* 5, no. 2 (2014): 183–203.

norms show us that an action is either obligatory, recommended, permissible, reprehensive, or forbidden. Since all actions are subject to these categories, Islamic law (*fiqh*) for Reinhart is more suitable to be Islamic ethics, since an action can be legal but its avoidance could be recommended, even forbidden. For example, if one signs a contract that contains an interest clause, which is forbidden according to Islamic law, then the contract can be valid, although this action is reprehensible.[20] Therefore, it is not wrong to state that Islamic law "stands as a significant example of a moral and legal theory of human behavior in which initial moral insights are systematically and self-consciously transformed into enforceable guidelines and attractive ideals for all of human life."[21]

However, we can discover a contrary development in faculties of Islamic theology in modern Turkey. Bedir points out that with the proclamation of the Turkish Republic, and with this the related reforms, Muslim scholars were forced to reflect on *fiqh* in terms of the Western law tradition. Textbooks, such as the one of Hayreddin Karaman (b. 1934), try to systematize *fiqh* in terms of law, like Law of Persons, Family Law, Inheritance Law, Law of Obligation, Property Law and International Law,[22] although *fiqh* does not have these rubrics. With this development, which according to Bedir begins with the codification of Ḥanafī law as *Majalla-i Aḥkām-i ʿAdliyye* during the later Ottoman period and the translation of Western law into Turkish, and further with the foundation of universities, which saw *fiqh* purely as law, *fiqh* lost its character of being ethics.[23] For Bedir, however, *fiqh* is a deontology and not merely law. Therefore, he rejects the systematization of Islamic law in terms of the structure of Western law. Bedir stresses that Islamic law contains both perspectives, legal and religious, and therefore is more than just law in the modern sense.[24] We see again here that the emphasis is on the ethical character of Islamic law, as was the case in Reinhart's observations.

Khaled Abou El Fadl (b. 1963), however, goes beyond Bedir and tries to see *fiqh* entirely as ethics; he specifically calls for a Quranic ethics. According to the Quran, if we follow Abou El Fadl, justice is one of the key concepts of Quranic ethics. Thus, Islamic law should always regard justice as the core point of argumentation and

20 Wael B. Hallaq, Sharīʿa. Theory, Practice, Transformations (Cambridge: Cambridge University Press, 2009), 246.

21 Reinhart, "Islamic Ethics," 199.

22 Hayreddin Haaman, *Mukayeseli İslam Hukuku.* 3 vols. (Istanbul: İz Yayıncılık, 2012).

23 The same is true for textbooks written in the Arab world. See Monique C. Cardinal, "Islamic Legal Curriculum: Are the Classics Taught Today?" Islamic Law and Society, 12, no. 2 (2005): 225, 242.

24 Murteza Bedir, "Fıkıh to Law: Secularization through Curriculum." *Islamic Law and Society* 11, no. 3 (2004): 378–401.

reflect on its traditional form to answer contemporary problems of Muslims all around the world. Abou El Fadl combines this idea with what he calls *dhikr* ('to have God in mind') in all of one's action. Thus, if we ask the Quran how a Muslim should act today, then we are not obliged to implement the Quranic verses word by word; rather, according to Abou El Fadl, we can discover ethical principles in the Quran, which we can extract from different rulings mentioned there.[25] These principles should guide a Muslim's life. Interesting is that Abou El Fadl does not only address Muslims living in countries where they are a minority, but he addresses all Muslims to rather regard the ethical character of the Quran and Islamic law in order to create a dynamic ethical system for solving daily life problems.

If we look closer at Abou El Fadl's approach, he seems to be influenced by Fazlur Rahman's (d. 1988) hermeneutics. Rahman, a Pakistani scholar who later taught and lived in the United States, tried to find a method to derive Islamic ethical principles from the Quran for a contemporary understanding of Quran and Islamic law. He not only addressed Muslims living in the diaspora but also in Muslim majoritarian countries. He suggests reading the Quran in its own historical circumstances, first in order to understand it as the Prophet and his Companions did, and thereafter to derive the ethical principles from Quranic utterances and only then to actualize it for contemporary times.[26]

In general, these above-mentioned approaches to Islamic law forced a shift in traditional Islamic law. Therefore, many scholars who were trained in Islamic law especially tried to find other hermeneutical tools to see Islamic law as ethics; on the other hand, the classical approach to Islamic law – to see it as a law system with ethical implications – continued to be pursued among these circles.

One of the tools is the use of the objectives of Sharia (*maqāṣid al-sharīʿa*). Others, however, saw that Muslims living as minorities, for example in Europe, needed a special *fiqh*, which was different from the *fiqh* in Muslim countries. They also largely made use of *al-maqāṣid*. Therefore, I want to highlight here the modern *maqāṣid* discourse and afterwards the discourse on minority law (*fiqh al-aqalliyyāt*), proposed by scholars like Ṭāhā Jābir al-ʿAlwānī (d. 2016) and Yūsuf al-Qaraḍāwī (d. 2022).

---

25 Khaled Abou El Fadl, "Qur'anic Ethics and Islamic Law." *Journal of Islamic Ethics* (2017), 7–28; Khaled Abou El Fadl, *Reasoning with God: Reclaiming Shariʿah in the Modern Age* (Lanham, MD: Rowman & Littlefield, 2014).

26 Fazlur Rahman, *Islam and Modernity: Transformation of an Intellectual Tradition* (Chicago: University of Chicago Press, 1982), 20–21.

4.2 The Objectives of Sharia [*maqāṣid ash-Sharīʿa*] in Modern Times

Contemporary scholars, despite their research field, concentrate very much on the classical term *maṣlaḥa* (roughly translated as 'public interest') and *maqāṣid*. In sum, this theory states that every ruling of Islamic law should secure an interest of humans or avoid anything harmful (so-called *mafsada*). The starting point for the evolution of the *maṣlaḥa* approach is that Quran and Sunna cannot answer and regulate everything. Scholars tried to find hermeneutical tools to solve problems according of Quran and Sunna, even if there was no direct link to them.

As it is impossible to describe the *maṣlaḥa* approach in its entirety, I will sum up the classification of *maṣlaḥa* and *maqāṣid* as an overview. There are first the accepted interests (*al-maṣāliḥ al-muʿtabara*). These are interests which are accepted either by Quran and/or Sunna, like the protection of wealth through the punishment of theft. On the second level, we find invalid interests (*al-maṣāliḥ al-mulġā*); although humans see some benefits in them, they are regarded as invalid. An example is the equal distribution of inheritance, although the Quran says that in some constellations, daughters inherit half of the amount that sons inherit. We find the unattested interests (*al-maṣāliḥ al-mursala*) on the third level; neither Quran nor Sunna provide direct information on the validity of regarding a certain *maṣlaḥa*. Scholars now have to elaborate which of those *maṣāliḥ* are acceptable interests and thus the theological bases for justifying an action. Thus, scholars saw a need for classifying the unattested interests in order not to contradict the religious sources. Accordingly, *maṣlaḥa* has three different categories: necessities (*ḍarūriyyāt*), needs (*ḥājiyyāt*), and improvements (*taḥsīniyyāt*). Needs and improvements are not defined by any scholar, but rather are only roughly described as interests to be regarded for society's sake (a disregard of these interests would harm, though not destroy, society); in contrast, necessities are strictly defined. Necessities are interests which should be protected, otherwise a society, not only *the Muslim* society, cannot exist. These necessities consist of the protection of the following five elements: life, reason, religion, descendant, and wealth. Scholars did not choose these categories arbitrarily. It is quite the reverse: They derived them from punishments (*ḥudūd*) mentioned in Quran and Sunna, like the punishment for murder (Q 4:92–93), for drunkenness (Q 5:90–91), for changing the religion (according to a Hadith),[27] for adultery (Q 24:2), and for theft (Q 5:38).[28]

---

27 Muḥammad b. Ismāʿīl al-Bukhārī, al-Jāmiʿ al-Musnad al-ṣaḥīḥ, Kitāb 88, Bāb Ḥukm al-Murtadd wa-l-Murtadda wa-Stitābatihim, Hadith No. 6922. This Hadith formulates punishment for apostasy, and scholars like al-Ghazālī derive from it the protection of religion.

Most of the classical scholars state that they have to regard the necessities to find solutions on daily life problems. In contemporary times, however, scholars decided to develop *maṣāliḥ* to be an independent source of law and called them more often *maqāṣid* ('objectives of the law') then *maṣāliḥ* ('[public] interest').[29] The outline of this approach is that every solution that is derived from the sources should regard the *maqāṣid,* or at least should not contradict them. Therefore, Muslim scholars understand even some Quranic verses differently than their wording, such as the punishment for theft. The Quran states that theft should be punished, according to Q 5:38, with the amputation of the hand. Since this punishment should protect wealth, and since today it is possible to protect wealth in different ways, the former punishment of amputation of the hand can be changed, e.g., with custody. Modern authors therefore criticize the classical *uṣūl al-fiqh* but try to use the concept on *maqāṣid* for modern times to tackle the question of the needs of modern-day problems in secular states. European scholars like Tariq Ramadan (b. 1962), for example, try to implement European values like freedom of speech, freedom of religion, etc. into the *maqāṣid*-system. The aim is the participation of Muslims in the society in which they live; *maqāṣid* as an ethical tool should guide them through their daily life.[30]

Thus, *maqāṣid* became a source for different disciplines like Islamic finance,[31] environmental ethics,[32] bioethics,[33] and political discussions on human rights.[34] Contemporary contributors to *maqāṣid,* like aṭ-Ṭāhir ibn ʿĀshūr (d. 1970), Aḥmad

28 Bassiouni, Menschenrechte, 146–61, 182–205; for a detailed analysis of different maqāṣid-approaches, see Felicitas Opwis, Maṣlaḥa and the Purpose of the Law. Islamic Discourse on Legal Change from the 4th/10th to 8th/14th Century (Leiden: Brill, 2010).

29 Opwis says: "What they all have in common despite their variety, and what distinguishes them from pre-modern authors, is their focus on the maqāṣid instead of maṣlaḥa. In the pre-modern period, most jurists focused on maṣlaḥa as a tool to derive legal rulings and as a criterion or standard by which to judge the correctness of rulings." Opwis, "New Trends in Islamic Legal Theory: Maqāṣid al-Sharīʿa as a New Source of Law?" *Die Welt des Islam* 57 (2017), 16.

30 Tariq Ramadan, *Radical Reform: Islamic Ethics and Liberation* (Oxford: Oxford University Press, 2008).

31 Ercument Aksak and Mehmet Asutay, "The Maqasid and the Empirics: Has Islamic Finance Fulfilled Its Promise?" In *Islamic Finance: Political Economy, Values and Innovation,* ed. Mehmet Asutay and Abdullah Turkistani (Berlin: Gerlach Press: 2015), 187–219.

32 Willis Jenkins, "Islamic Law and Environmental Ethics: How Jurisprudence (Usul al-Fiqh) Mobilizes Practical Reform," *Worldviews* 9, no. 3 (2005): 351.

33 Abdul Halim Ibrahim et. al., "Maqasid al-Shariah Based Islamic Bioethics: A Comprehensive Approach," *Journal of Bioethical Inquiry* 16 (2019): 333–45.

34 Bassiouni, Menschenrechte.

ar-Raysūnī (b. 1953), and Jasser Auda (b. 1966),[35] mainly criticize the limitation of essential necessities to five.[36] They say that there are more interests and necessities to be regarded than those mentioned in the classical sources. Consequently, we have different approaches to *maqāṣid*, like reinterpretation – this is the attempt to find, for example, freedom of religion in Quran – or the approach of extension, like the case of Rashīd Riḍā (d. 1935), who extended the *maqāṣid* in his study called *al-Waḥy al-Muḥammadī.*[37] Most scholars concentrate on extending the *maqāṣid* in such a fashion that also human rights are included. For example, Ibn ʿĀshūr is one of those scholars who stick to the classical *maqāṣid* but see them as a general category for humankind and divide *maṣlaḥa* into general and specific. Specific *maqāṣid* are those common to the classical approach to the *maqāṣid*, but in a more extended fashion by regarding not only the necessities as essential elements for the survival of the society, but rather all *maṣāliḥ* categories.[38] European authors also follow the trend of extension. Tariq Ramadan, for example, says that each *maqṣad* can be gained through reasoning and reading the two books of God: the Quran and the universe. The universe for him is like a book, which guides us to the truth – a modern trend, which can be seen in the writings of scholars of different Islamic disciplines. Ramadan tries to systematize the *maqāṣid* anew, in that he sets the protection of religion and the interest of humans on top. He divides the overall *maqāṣid* into three categories: protection of life, of nature, and of peace. According to him, these *maqāṣid* refer, again, to the protection or preservation of *maqāṣid*, such as dignity, knowledge, creativity, equality, freedom, and others.

The main problem of contemporary *maqāṣid* approaches, however, is that we do not know how most of the authors derive these *maqāṣid*; they do not describe how they gained these *maqāṣid* and why they propose particularly these in their writings. All these approaches must tackle the question of how to avoid arbitrariness in finding *maqāṣid.* Felicitas Opwis comments:

> Largely absent from contemporary discussions are questions about who determines the universals and the particulars derived from the sources. It comes as no surprise that, when comparing different interpretations of the purposes of the law, we find very diverse results. Duderija and Attia, for example, both identify "affection" (*mawadda*), "compassion" (*raḥma*), and "repose" (*sakīna*) as divine objectives in the realm of the family. But Duderija interprets

35 Jasser Awda, *Maqasid al-Sharia as Philosophy of Islamic Law* (London: International Institute of Islamic Thought, 2008).

36 For the overall criticism see Opwis, "New Trends."

37 For a detailed analysis see Yasir S. Ibrahim, "Rashīd Riḍā and Maqāṣid al-Sharīʿa," *Studia Islamica* 102/103 (2006): 157–98.

38 Muḥammad aṭ-Ṭāhir b. ʿĀshūr, *Maqāṣid aš-Šarīʿa al-Islāmiyya* (Beirut: Dār al-Kitāb al-Lubnānī, 2011).

these purposes as evidence for a gender-egalitarian Islamic family law, whereas Attia employs them to assert traditional gender hierarchies.[39]

From this point of view, many scholars tried to tackle the question of an "Islamic way of living" in the diaspora, presupposing that there is a diaspora, in which Muslim minorities live. Therefore, since the end of the 1990s, the discussion on Minority law (*fiqh al-aqalliyyāt*) started.

4.3 Islamic Minority Law [*Fiqh al-Aqalliyyāt*][40]

Although the discussions on jurisprudence or *fiqh* of minorities occurred as a technical term with al-ʿAlwānī's treatise on it, scholars already tried to solve the problems of Muslims in non-Muslim countries at the beginnings of the twentieth century. Rashīd Riḍā, for example, issued many fatwas concerning those questions, which were published also in the journal *al-Manār.* With the rise of the Muslim population in areas like Europe and USA, scholars, who later engaged in discussions on *fiqh al-aqalliyyāt*, issued isolated fatwas and then participated in founding academies for Islamic law. These academies focused on issuing fatwas and saw the *desideratum* for special issues for Muslim minorities in non-Muslim countries.[41] The *European Council for Fatwa and Research* played *inter alia* a decisive role in creating *fiqh al-aqalliyyāt:* many of the members later stood up for its development. At first, scholars like al-Qaraḍāwī tried to keep the link of this new type of ethical oriented juridical thinking with the traditional understanding of *fiqh* by looking for direct links within the school of the Mālikīs and Ḥanafīs. It was also prominent to refer to classical methods like *maṣlaḥa, maqāṣid* and legal precepts (*qawāʿid*).[42]

The starting point of their reflection on contemporary legal issues was the legal precept that every ruling is subject to changes due to changing times and circumstances.[43] Although scholars like al-Qaraḍāwī issued many fatwas in the 1990s

39 Opwis, "New Trends," 30.

40 The following chapter heavily relies on the analysis of Patrick Franke in his article "Fiqh al-Aqallīyāt," Bamberger Islam-Enzyklopädie, www.uni-bamberg.de/islamwissenschaft/bie.

41 For an overview of these academies and their specific approaches, see Ahmed Gad Makhlouf, *Das Konzept des kollektiven iǧtihād und seine Umsetzungsformen. Analyse der Organisation und Arbeitsweise islamischer Rechtsakademien* (Berlin: Peter Lang, 2018).

42 Franke, "Fiqh al-Aqallīyāt."

43 See for example Yūsuf al-Qaraḍāwī, *Fī Fiqh al-Aqalliyyāt al-Muslima. Ḥayāt al-Muslimīna Wasaṭ al-Mujtamiʿāt al-Ukhrā* (Cairo: Dār ash-Shurūq, 2001), 50–2.

and *fiqh al-aqalliyyāt* was popular in Arab countries, the first reflection on the concept of *fiqh al-aqalliyyāt* was made by the Iraqi scholar al-ʿAlwānī in his article on *fiqh al-aqalliyyāt.*

Al-ʿAlwānī stated that *fiqh al-aqalliyyāt* is different from the classical view on *fiqh*, which is close to a concept of law. For al-ʿAlwānī, *fiqh* should be a comprehensive understanding of religion: one should comprehend the religion anew in the new situation under which Muslims are living. For al-ʿAlwānī, this does not mean that one has to break the link to traditional *fiqh* entirely; rather, one can see it as important basis for the new type of *fiqh* that heavily gives credit for minorities living in secular states, respecting the law applied there. For al-ʿAlwānī, therefore, the classical distinction of the world in *Dār al-Islām* ('House of Islam') and *Dār al-Kufr* or *al-Ḥarb* ('House of Unbelief' or 'War') was untenable.[44] Not only al-ʿAlwānī, but almost the majority of scholars, even Salafī-oriented scholars, criticize this dichotomy. Therefore, instead of *Dār al-Kufr*, they often use other terms like House of Witness or House of Response/Acceptance, in order to imply that Muslims living in non-Muslim countries do not live in House of Unbelief. However, we can discover that these scholars, while they may assign these terms with positive connotations, still think within the dichotomy of Muslim and non-Muslim countries. This attitude was criticized by Tariq Ramadan, who insisted that Muslims in the so-called non-Muslim countries are not willing to see themselves as minorities but see themselves as part of the larger society. The interesting point is that most of these scholars are willing to accept non-religiously argued values like freedom of speech, equality, etc., and see the *fiqh al-aqalliyyāt* as a possibility for integration purposes, as assimilation of Muslims is for all of them a problem. For this sake, the majority accepts to respect all religious groups and have positive relationships; they issued many fatwas for that purpose, such as whether a Muslim can congratulate for Christmas, which for Muslims living in Germany, for example, and who were born there, is self-evident. Broadly accepted therefore are human rights under the scope of *maqāṣid al-sharīʿa.*

Because of the realignment of *fiqh*, there was a need for theoretical reflection, mainly shouldered by al-ʿAlwānī and al-Qaraḍāwī. They primarily concentrated on *ijtihād*, which is, since the efforts of Muḥammad ʿAbduh (d. 1905), a key concept for almost every renewal movement in modern times. Al-Qaraḍāwī, however, is the one who tries to use traditional rulings of *fiqh* more than al-ʿAlwānī. He only has a few restrictions on using rational argumentation, but his concepts lack epistemological reflections. A common point among the scholars is that *maqāṣid* is one of the core concepts for a new, legitimate *ijtihād.* Especially with the argument of

44 Ṭāhā Ǧābir al-ʿAlwānī, "Madḫal ilā Fiqh al-Aqalliyyāt." *Islāmiyyāt al-Maʿrifa* 19 (1999/2000), 9–29.

'necessity' (*ḍarūra*), i. e., a situation of emergency and urgent need, Muslims can refrain from classical views prohibiting something like buying a house with credit and interest (*ribā*). Since there is a necessity to buy a house, many scholars allow Muslims to buy houses with credit when there are no alternatives. This, again, led to critiques such as the polemic of Muḥammad Saʿīd Ramaḍān al-Būṭī (d. 2013), which states that Muslims everywhere in the world should regard the same rules.[45]

We can notice that with the *fiqh al-aqalliyyāt*, the scholars do not only try to give Muslims the opportunity to integrate in non-Muslim societies but also try to reestablish their authority, which they have lost during the changes in the nineteenth and twentieth centuries, in religious questions in all fields of human life, both in Muslim and non-Muslim societies. At the same time, *fiqh al-aqalliyyāt* is criticized for being far from a comprehensive set of guidelines, as it rather is a specific form of *fiqh* for Muslims as minorities.[46]

Ramadan criticizes the use of the term minority for Muslims in multi-cultural societies, but he again thinks in the dichotomy of Muslim and non-Muslim. However, he goes beyond the realm of *fiqh*, both in the suggested understandings of al-ʿAlwānī and al-Qaraḍāwī. Ramadan proposes a perception of Islam with European character (so-called European Islam, although Ramadan himself rejects this term).[47] He pleads for the term "ethical majority" in a pluralistic sense and rejects the term "minority" as a political term, because minority for him implies an unfamiliarity, which is not given for the majority of Muslims living in Europe. Nevertheless, he tries to find legitimizing arguments from the Muslim tradition to accept secular law and values such as human rights by focusing on Islamic ethics and on *maqāṣid*. His approach, however, is as arbitrary as the approach of those scholars, who focus on *fiqh al-aqalliyyāt* or, the latest version, *fiqh al-taʿāyush*, the concept of *fiqh* of living together.[48]

Scholars try to react to those critiques. Since Muslims in Europe do not want to see themselves as minorities (and with the critiques of the Tunisian thinker Mohamed Mestiri), scholars began to call *fiqh al-aqalliyyāt* "*fiqh* of citizenship," as *fiqh al-aqalliyyāt* is too close to thinking in terms of immigration. This would then enable scholars to design Islamic law for a pluralistic society. Thus, we can

---

45 Franke, "Fiqh al-Aqallīyāt."

46 Yohei Matsuyama, "Fiqh al-Aqalliyat: Development, Advocates and Social Meaning," Annals of Japan Association for Middle Eastern Studies 26, no. 2 (2010), 48.

47 For an overview and different conceptions on "European Islam," see Ertugrul Sahin, *Europäischer Islam. Diskurs im Spannungsfeld von Universalität, Historizität, Normativität und Empirizität*, Berlin: Springer, 2017.

48 Franke, "Fiqh al-Aqallīyāt."

discover, since the beginning of the twenty-first century, a movement from the term "minorities" to "citizenship" (*muwāṭana*).[49]

5 Conclusion

We have two different approaches today to give Muslims in multicultural societies the opportunity to respect their religious identity and still be a productive part of their multicultural society. One is the call for a European Islam, which tries to find philosophical and theological arguments for shared secular values by either respecting Quranic ethics or seeing the Islamic law tradition as ethics with highly dynamic nature for changes and adjustments. In contrast to this, scholars living in so-called Muslim countries suggest a concept that they call *fiqh al-aqalliyyāt* and try to find solutions for Muslims in what they call non-Muslim societies. They also try to make Islamic law as dynamic as possible, although there are trends which are restrictive on Muslims living in European societies. Andrew March found four different ethical attitudes in the realm of *fiqh al-aqalliyyāt:* The first one is a rigid understanding of Islamic law as a revelatory-deontological system. The second is a contractualist-constructivist understanding with emphasis on the principle of trusteeship (*amāna*) – here an integration of Muslims in non-Muslim societies is not possible, since they do not see themselves as part of this society but rather as people who come from the outside and have a contract to be there for a particular time. The third approach is what March calls a consequentialist-utilitarian approach regarding the objectives of the Sharīʿa. The last (fourth) comprehensive-qualitative approach, espoused by al-ʿAlwānī and al-Qaraḍāwī, emphasizes the principle of *daʿwa*, which is to invite people to convert to Islam. March points out that this invitation is not an offensive one; rather it is an invitation to convert to Islam by exemplifying a peaceful good life, by respecting the other, by being a citizen of a secular state, and by respecting the law. Due to this behaviour, according to this understanding, Islam will be widespread, and everyone can decide for himself to join in the religion or not.[50]

Especially this thinking in terms of *daʿwa* shows us that these scholars, although very progressive in their respectively traditional terms, think in the dichotomy of belief and unbelief. The attempts for an Islam with European character, on the other hand, try to overcome this dichotomy, yet do not have a principle that is

49 Alexandre Caeiro, "Fatwas for European Muslims: The Minority Fiqh Project and the Integration of Islam in Europe" (PhD diss, University of Utrecht, 2011), 71–72.
50 March, "Sources of Moral Obligation." Translation by Laura Radosh.

philosophically or theologically argued and justified: we do not really know what it means to demand a European Islam, since the term "European" is also vague. The European context itself is pluralistic. Their main point of argumentation is the historicity of the entire Muslim tradition and the fact that this tradition always incorporated laws, ideas, and philosophies of different cultures. Therefore, the Muslim tradition is subject to updates due to new circumstances. Thus, it will be exciting to follow the development of Islamic theology in Germany, which has been in the phase of establishment for more than ten years, and its contribution and reactions to these discussions.

References

Abdallah, Ahmad Badri. "An Analysis of Islamic Jurisprudence (Fiqh) as Applied Islamic Ethics." *Islam and Civilisational Renewal* 5, no. 2 (2014): 183–203.

Abou El Fadl, Khaled. "Qur'anic Ethics and Islamic Law." *Journal of Islamic Ethics* (2017): 7–28.

Abou El Fadl, Khaled. *Reasoning with God: Reclaiming Shari'ah in the Modern Age.* Lanham, MD: Rowman & Littlefield, 2014.

Aksak, Ercument and Mehmet Asutay. "The Maqasid and the Empirics: Has Islamic Finance Fulfilled Its Promise?" In *Islamic Finance: Political Economy, Values and Innovation*, edited by Mehmet Asutay and Abdullah Turkistani, 187–219. Berlin: Gerlach Press, 2015.

al-ʿAlwānī, Ṭāhā Ǧābir. "Madḫal ilā Fiqh al-Aqalliyyāt." *Islāmiyyāt al-Maʿrifa*, 19 (1999/2000), 9–29.

al-ʿAlwānī, Ṭāhā Ǧābir. *Towards a Fiqh for Minorities: Some Basic Reflections.* Translated by Ashur A. Shamis. London: International Institute of Islamic Thought, 2003.

al-Ghazālī, Abū Ḥāmid. *Iḥyāʾ ʿUlūm al-Dīn*, Beirut: Dār al-Maʿrifa, n.d.

al-Qaraḍāwī, Yūsuf. *Fī Fiqh al-Aqalliyyāt al-Muslima. Ḥayāt al-Muslimīna Wasaṭ al-Mujtamiʿāt al-Ukhrā.* Cairo: Dār ash-Shurūq, 2001.

al-Qaraḍāwī, Yūsuf. *Fiqh of Muslim Minorities: Contentions Issues & Recommended Solutions.* , Cairo: Al-Falah Foundation, 2003.

Awda, Jasser. *Maqasid al-Sharia as Philosophy of Islamic Law.* London: International Institute of Islamic Thought, 2008.

Bassiouni, Mahmoud. *Menschenrechte zwischen Universalität und islamischer Legitimität.* Frankfurt am Main: Suhrkamp, 2014.

Bedir, Murteza. "Fıkıh to Law: Secularization through Curriculum." *Islamic Law and Society* 11, no. 3 (2004): 378–401.

Bouhafa, Feriel. "Averroes' Corrective Philosophy of Law." In *Interpreting Averroes. Critical Essays*, edited by Peter Adamson, 45–63. Cambridge: Cambridge University Press, 2019.

Bouhafa, Feriel. "Ethics and *Fiqh* in al-Fārābī's Philosophy." In *Philosophy and Jurisprudence in the Islamic World*, edited by Peter Adamson, 11–27. Berlin: Walter de Gruyter, 2019.

Caeiro, Alexandre. "Fatwas for European Muslims: The Minority Fiqh Project and the Integration of Islam in Europe." PhD diss., University of Utrecht, 2011.

Cardinal, Monique C. "Islamic Legal Curriculum: Are the Classics Taught Today?" *Islamic Law and Society* 12, no. 2 (2005): 225–242.

Davison, Roderic H. “Tanẓīmāt.” *Encyclopaedia of Islam, Second Edition.* Edited by Peri Bearman, et al. Brill Reference Online, 2002-, accessed March 11, 2022, http://dx.doi.org/10.1163/1573-3912_islam_COM_1174.

Franke, Patrick. “Fiqh al-Aqallīyāt,” *Bamberger Islam-Enzyklopädie*; www.uni-bamberg.de/islam wissenschaft/bie.

Haaman, Hayreddin. *Mukayeseli İslam Hukuku.* Istanbul: İz Yayıncılık, 2012.

Hallaq, Wael B. *Sharīʿa. Theory, Practice, Transformations.* Cambridge: Cambridge University Press, 2009.

Ibn ʿĀshūr, Muḥammad al-Ṭāhir. *Maqāṣid aš-Šarīʿa al-Islāmiyya.* Beirut: Dār al-Kitāb al-Lubnānī, 2011.

Ibn Rushd, Abū l-Walīd. *Bidāyat al-Muǧtahid wa-Nihāyat al-Muqtaṣid.* Edited by Abū Aws, Yūsuf b. Aḥmad al-Bakrī. Amman: Bayt al-Afkār ad-Duwaliyya, 2007.

Ibn Rushd, Abū l-Walīd. *Talkhīṣ al-Khaṭāba.* Edited by Muḥammad Salīm Sālim. Cairo, 1967.

Ibrahim, Abdul Halim et. al. “Maqasid al-Shariah Based Islamic Bioethics: A Comprehensive Approach.” *Journal of Bioethical Inquiry* 16 (2019): 333–45.

Ibrahim, Yasir S. “Rashīd Riḍā and *Maqāṣid al-Sharīʿa.*” *Studia Islamica* 102, no. 103 (2006): 157–98.

Jenkins, Willis. “Islamic Law and Environmental Ethics: How Jurisprudence (*Usul al-Fiqh*) Mobilizes Practical Reform.” *Worldviews* 9, no. 3 (2005): 338–364.

Karaman, Hayreddin. *İslâm Hukuk Tarihi.* Istanbul: İz Yayıncılık, 1999.

Keller, Nuh Ha Mim. “Which of the Four Orthodox Madhhabs Has the Most Developed Fiqh for Muslims Living as Minorities.” *Q News, The Muslim Magazine*, accessed June 8, 2020, www.masud.co.uk/ISLAM/nuh/fiqh.htm

Kurnaz, Serdar. “Who is the Lawgiver? The Hermeneutical Grounds of the Methods of Interpreting Qur'an and Sunna (*istinbāṭ al-aḥkām*).” *Oxford Journal of Law and Religion* 6 (2017): 347–371.

Kurnaz, Serdar. “Ibn Rushd's Legal Hermeneutics and Moral Theory for a ‘Living Sharīʿa’ – an Alternative Approach to Islamic Law in Ibn Rushd's *Bidāyat al-Mujtahid.*” *Oxford Journal of Law and Religion* 8 (2019): 174–205.

Makhlouf, Ahmed Gad. *Das Konzept des kollektiven iǧtihād und seine Umsetzungsformen. Analyse der Organisation und Arbeitsweise islamischer Rechtsakademien.* Berlin: Peter Lang, 2018.

March, Andrew F. “Sources of Moral Obligation to non-Muslims in the ‘Jurisprudence of Muslim Minorities’ (*Fiqh al-aqalliyyāt*) Discourse.” *Islamic Law and Society* 16, no. 2 (2009): 34–94.

Matsuyama, Yohei. “Fiqh al-Aqalliyat: Development, Advocates and Social Meaning,” Annals of Japan Association for Middle Eastern Studies 26, no. 2 (2010): 33–55.

Messick, Brinkley. “Fatwā, modern.” *Encyclopaedia of Islam.* 3rd ed. Accessed November 15, 2019. dx.doi.org.proxy.ub.unifrankfurt.de/10.1163/15733912_ei3_COM_27049

Opwis, Felicitas. Maṣlaḥa *and the Purpose of the Law. Islamic Discourse on Legal Change from the 4th/10th to 8th/14th Century.* Leiden: Brill, 2010.

Opwis, Felicitas. “New Trends in Islamic Legal Theory: *Maqāṣid al-Sharīʿa* as a New Source of Law?” *Die Welt des Islams*, 57 (2017): 7–32.

Rahman, Fazlur. *Islam and Modernity. Transformation of an Intellectual Tradition.* Chicago: University of Chicago Press, 1982.

Ramadan, Tariq. *Radical Reform: Islamic Ethics and Liberation.* Oxford: Oxford University Press, 2008.

Reinhart, Kevin. “Islamic Law as Islamic Ethics.” *The Journal of Religious Ethics* 11, no. 2 (1983): 186–203.

Rudolph, Ulrich. “Al-Ghazālī on Philosophy and Jurisprudence.” In *Philosophy and Jurisprudence in the Islamic World*, ed. Peter Adamson (Berlin/Boston: Walter de Gruyter, 2019), 67–91.

Sahin, Ertugrul. *Europäischer Islam. Diskurs im Spannungsfeld von Universalität, Historizität, Normativität und Empirizität*, Berlin: Springer, 2017.

III. Law and Religion

Martin Heger

Der Wandel von einem personalen zu einem territorialen Rechtsverständnis in Mittelalter und früher Neuzeit

I Zum Thema

Durchmustert man heutzutage in Deutschland die Medien, wird immer wieder – gerade auch mit Blick auf Berlin – das Bild einer sich entwickelnden Paralleljustiz „an die Wand gemalt", wobei vor allem bestimmte Gruppen von Migranten bzw. deren Abkömmlinge die Durchsetzung ihrer tatsächlichen oder vermeintlichen Rechtspositionen nicht den staatlichen Institutionen anvertrauen, sondern lieber durch Angehörige der eigenen Gruppe gewahrt wissen wollen. Neben selbst ernannten „Richtern", die zwischen Streithähnen innerhalb einer Gruppe unter Umgehung staatlicher Instanzen, nicht notwendig freilich in illegaler Weise, einen Ausgleich zu vermitteln und mindestens moralisch auch durchzusetzen suchen, tritt dann auch schon mal eine auf ihren leuchtfarbigen Warnwesten als selbst ernannte „Scharia-Polizei" kenntlich gemachte Truppe junger Männer in Erscheinung, die zumindest den Anschein erweckt, als würde sie nach Art einer Privatpolizei in bestimmten, mehrheitlich von Muslimen bewohnten Stadtteilen nach Recht und Ordnung schauen, und zwar gemessen eben nicht an staatlichen Maßstäben, sondern an dem hierzulande formal nicht geltenden islamischen Recht der Scharia.[1] Soweit selbsternannte Tugendwächter bloß innerhalb der hier lebenden Gruppe der Muslime die Scharia als ethische Sollens-Ordnung[2] durchzusetzen suchen, mag man dies als moralische Anmaßung begreifen wollen; illegal ist es aber normalerweise nicht, solange einerseits die moralischen Vorgaben nur auf der Ebene der Moral – bzw. ausnahmsweise auch (staats-)rechtlich, aber nur soweit das Recht etwa an die Sittenwidrigkeit anknüpft, den Kirchen bestimmte Regelungen ihres Arbeitsrechts überlässt (so dass etwa ein katholischer Priester mit einer Heirat seinen Job verliert[3]) oder (wie beim in Art. 6 GG verfassungsrechtlich ver-

---

1 Zu diesem einführend *Matthias Rohe*, Das Islamische Recht, *Christine Schirrmacher*, Die Scharia.

2 Zum Wandel von einem rechtlichen zu einem vor allem ethischen Verständnis der Scharia vgl. Serdar Kurnaz ,+ (in diesem Band).

3 Dagegen verstößt die Kündigung eines katholischen Chefarztes durch ein katholisches Krankenhaus nach Scheidung und Wiederverheiratung gegen Europarecht (vgl. EuGH, Urt. v. 11.9.2018 – C 68/17).

https://doi.org/10.1515/9783111062631-007

bürgten elterlichen Erziehungsrecht) auch Moralvorstellungen seitens dazu berufener Akteure (z. B. der Eltern[4]) bestimmten Eingriffen in die Rechtssphäre anderer zugrunde gelegt werden dürfen (bestes Beispiel ist die seit 2012 explizit in § 1631d BGB zugelassene Beschneidung männlicher Kinder gerade aus religiösen Gründen), – sanktioniert werden und ihre Durchsetzung andererseits nicht mit staatlicherseits verbotenen Mitteln erfolgen soll (so befugt das Erziehungsrecht nach § 1631 Abs. 2 BGB die Eltern nicht dazu, mittels Gewalt ihre Kinder im Sinne bestimmter Moralvorstellungen zu erziehen, selbst wenn eine Erziehung in diesem Sinne mittels anderer Sanktionen zulässig wäre[5]). Aus staatlicher Sicht zum Problem wird es erst, wenn dessen seit dem Ausgang des Mittelalters (in Deutschland vor allem seit dem Wormser Reichstag von 1495[6]) etabliertes Gewaltmonopol durch den Auftritt als eine „Polizei“ erschüttert wird. Die staatliche Justiz hat dieses Auftreten demgemäß nach einem zwischenzeitlich vom Bundesgerichtshof (BGH) aufgehobenen Freispruch[7] „im zweiten Anlauf“ durch das Landgericht Wuppertal mit Geldstrafen sanktioniert;[8] Grundlage war allerdings der nach §§ 3, 28 Versammlungsgesetz strafbare Verstoß gegen das Uniformverbot bei Versammlungen, nicht dass sich eine Gruppe von Zivilisten als Privatpolizei zusammen getan hat.[9]

Weil das heutige deutsche Recht selbstverständlich von einer umfassenden Geltung im gesamten Territorium der Bundesrepublik Deutschland und einer Durchsetzung nur mittels den von der Rechtsordnung dafür vorgesehenen bzw. zumindest zugelassenen öffentlichen wie auch privaten Institutionen ausgeht, erscheint eine ethnisch oder religiös fundierte Paralleljustiz als Absage an dieses

4 So umfasst das elterliche Erziehungsrecht auch eine Erziehung zu bestimmten ethisch bzw. religiös geprägten Verhaltensweisen, so dass Eltern etwa mit Erziehungsmitteln sanktionieren können, wenn sich ihre noch nicht religionsmündigen Kinder nicht an die aus den religiösen Überzeugungen der Eltern folgenden Regelungen (z. B. Fasten, Unterlassen bestimmter Betätigungen, aber auch Kirchenbesuch) halten

5 Vgl. dazu die Strafverfolgung und Entziehung des Sorgerechts gegen Mitglieder der „Zwölf Stämme“, die aufgrund bestimmter Bibelstellen sich auch im Interesse ihrer Kinder zur Prügelstrafe verpflichtet sahen. Zur Strafbarkeit etwa AG Nördlingen, Urt. v. 23.11.2015, Az. 1 Ds 101 Js 108562/14 (https://www.lto.de/recht/nachrichten/n/ag-noerdlingen-urteil-1-ds-101-js-108562-14-zwoelf-staemme-schule-schlaege-rute/), zur Entziehung des Sorgerechts EGMR, Urt. v. 22.03.2018, Beschw.-Nr. 11308/16 u. a. (https://www.lto.de/recht/nachrichten/n/egmr-11308-16-sekte-zwoelf-staemme-koerperliche-zuechtigung-kinder-sorgerecht-entzogen/

6 Vgl. dazu nur *Adolf Laufs*, JuS 1995, S. 665 ff.; *Hans-Jürgen Becker*, NJW 1995, S. 2077 ff.

7 BGHSt 63, 66.

8 https://www.lto.de/recht/nachrichten/n/lg-wuppertal-26kls2018-scharia-polizei-uniform-verbot-salafisten-geldstrafen-verurteilt/.

9 Dieses Urteil ist nach einem Beschluss des BGH vom 29.4.2020 (Az. 3 StR 547/19) inzwischen rechtskräftig (vgl. https://www.lto.de/recht/nachrichten/n/bgh-3str547-19-urteile-shariah-police-wuppertal-rechtskraeftig/).

Grundprinzip sowie als Abkehr der betreffenden Gruppen von den Grundfesten unseres Staates. Und in der Tat ist es ein Problem für den Rechtsstaat, wenn bestimmte nicht allzu kleine Gruppen letztlich nicht (mehr) dem von der lokalen Rechtsordnung gebilligten Weg der Rechtsdurchsetzung vertrauen und deshalb auf innerstaatlich dafür nicht vorgesehene Institutionen zurückgreifen wollen. Das ist zu unterscheiden davon, dass bestimmte Komplexe in vielen Gesellschaften staatlicherseits bewusst privaten, vor allem religiösen Würdenträgern übertragen sind. In besonderem Maße gilt dies für das Ehe- und Familienrecht, aber auch im Bereich des internationalen Wirtschaftsrechts und des Sportrechts für die Schiedsgerichtsbarkeit.

Insgesamt ist die deutsche Rechtsordnung – auch im Vergleich zu anderen derzeitigen staatlichen Rechtsordnungen – freilich tendenziell wenig offen für außerstaatliche Refugien, wie etwa der Blick auf das Familienrecht lehrt. Während das deutsche Recht mit der obligatorischen Zivilehe für die Eheschließung seit Bismarcks Kulturkampf in den 1870er Jahren zwingend staatliche Akteure und die Beachtung staatlichen Rechts voraussetzt, finden sich in vielen anderen Ländern insoweit für außerhalb des vom Staat gesetzten Rechts offenere Regelungsmodelle. Möglich ist hier etwa oft auch alternativ eine Eheschließung nach religiösem Ritus. Allerdings ist es auch in diesen Ländern stets so, dass die etwa bei einer Eheschließung aktiven außerstaatlichen Akteure wie Priester etc. zu diesem Tun staatlicherseits zumindest befugt sind. Man kann daher wohl sagen, dass heute in der großen Mehrheit der Staaten diese territoriale Rechtsregimes aufbauen, die für alle Einwohner oder Anwesenden ihrerseits verbindlich sind und nur durch staatlicherseits dazu ermächtigte Personen umgesetzt werden können.

Rein religiös bindende Eheschließungen, die – wie die sog. Imam-Ehen in der Türkei[10] – bewusst außerhalb der staatlichen Familienrechtsordnung bleiben sollen, werden daher regelmäßig auch in den Staaten nicht anerkannt, welche grundsätzlich eine Eheschließung auch durch dazu ermächtigte religiöse Autoritäten für wirksam erachten. Da ihnen jede rechtliche Wirksamkeit abgesprochen wird, weshalb allenfalls eine religiös-sittliche Wirkung denkbar bleibt, hat sich der deutsche Gesetzgeber auch vor gut zehn Jahren dazu entschlossen, die seit Ende des 19. Jahrhunderts zur Durchsetzung der obligatorischen Zivilehe bestehende Strafbarkeit und schließlich auch das Verbot einer religiösen Eheschließung vor oder erst recht ohne Zivilehe zu streichen. In der Türkei gibt es dagegen bis heute ein strafbewehrtes Verbot religiöser Voraustrauungen; in der Schweiz sind solche zumindest weiterhin verboten (Art. 97 Abs. 3 SchwZGB).

---

10 Dazu *Gotthard Jäschke*, Die „Imam-Ehe“ in der Türkei, Die Welt des Islams, N. S., 4, (2–3), 1955, S. 164–201.

Eine Sonderform besteht in einigen, vor allem islamischen Staaten wie etwa Pakistan; hier steht das staatliche Recht vielfach unter dem Vorbehalt der Vereinbarkeit mit der Scharia oder einer Letztüberprüfung durch Scharia-Gerichte, so dass religiöse Wertungen unmittelbar auf den Inhalt etwa eines Strafurteils einfließen.[11] Ein relativ bekanntes Beispiel war die Konversion einer jungen Muslima zum Christentum und der sich daran anschließende Streit innerhalb der pakistanischen Justiz, ob es sich dabei um eine rechtlich zulässige Ausübung der Religionsfreiheit oder eine – aus islamisch-rechtlicher Sicht als „Abfall vom Islam" – todeswürdige Apostasie[12] handelt.[13]

Wenn man heute – wie wohl die Allermeisten nicht nur in den westlich-liberalen Staaten – in Fragen des anwendbaren Rechts (der Jurisdiktion) und auch von dessen Durchsetzung ein gleichsam natürliches Primat der modernen Territorial- bzw. Nationalstaaten sieht, muss man sich freilich immer vor Augen halten, dass über mehr als ein Jahrtausend in Europa das Recht neben dem heute herrschenden Territorialprinzip auch der Abstammung und damit dem sog. Personalitätsprinzip folgen konnte. Die Stellung in einer Rechtsordnung folgte jahrhundertelang der Zugehörigkeit zu einem Volksstamm wie etwa den Franken, Alemannen oder Sachsen. Vergleichbare Entwicklungen gab es im 19. und 20. Jahrhundert mit der Etablierung der Konsulargerichtsbarkeit, in vielen Kolonialgebieten und etwa in den USA, wo den Native Americans für ihre Reservatsgebiete bis heute eine eingeschränkte Jurisdiktionsgewalt zukommt.[14]

Vielfach ist die Rede insoweit auch von einem Stammesrecht; da sich die Gesellschaften allgemein – in den Worten Henry Maines – „from status to contract" entwickelt haben,[15] wäre dieses Stammesrecht der historische Vorläufer des modernen territorial gedachten Staatsrechts. Vor diesem Hintergrund soll nunmehr ein Blick auf das Personalitätsprinzip als Grundlage des anwendbaren (Stammes-) Rechts geworfen werden.

11 Dazu *Benedikt Naarmann*, Der Schutz von Religionen und Religionsgemeinschaften in Deutschland, England, Indien und Pakistan, 2015, S. 446 ff.

12 Zur Apostasie im islamischen Recht *Naarmann* (Fn. 11), S. 405 ff.

13 Vgl. NZZ v. 8.5.2019 (https://www.nzz.ch/international/christin-asia-bibi-nach-acht-jahren-haft-aus-pakistan-ausgereist-ld.1480237).

14 Vgl. die Entscheidung des US Supreme Courts vom 9.7.2020 im Fall „McGrint v. Oklahoma" (https://www.lto.de/recht/feuilleton/f/jimcy-mcgirt-halb-oklahoma-den-ureinwohnern-strafgewalt-us-supreme-court/).

15 *Uwe Wesel*, Geschichte des Rechts, 5. Aufl. 2022, Rn. 47 unter Hinweis auf *Henry Maine*, Ancient Law, 1861, Kap. 5 a.E.

II Stammesrechte

Friedrich Carl von Savigny, der berühmteste Jurist in der Gründungszeit der Berliner Universität, hat 1834 in seiner „Geschichte des Römischen Rechts im Mittelalter“ mit Blick auf den personalen Anwendungsbereich des Römischen Rechts in seinem Untersuchungszeitraum folgendes angemerkt: „... im Mittelalter, wo in demselben Lande, ja in derselben Stadt, der Lombarde nach lombardischen, der Römer nach römischem Recht lebte. Ja dieselbe Verschiedenheit des Rechts galt auch für die Germanen verschiedener Stämme, der Franke, der Burgunder, Gote lebten an demselben Orte jeder nach anderem Rechte“.[16]

Dass Franken nach fränkischem und Sachsen generell nach sächsischem (Stammes-)Recht lebten, folgte dabei der Entwicklung seit dem allmählichen Niedergang des (west-)römischen Reichs bis zu seinem Untergang im Jahr 476 unserer Zeit. In Folge der Völkerwanderung in der Spätantike und im frühen Mittelalter (datiert üblicherweise auf die Jahre 375 bis 568) kam es in ganz Europa häufig zu einem Nebeneinander verschiedener Volksstämme. Es entstanden teilweise unterschiedliche Rechtsordnungen für die zugezogenen Germanen und die verbliebenen Römer; so galt etwa im Westgotenreich ab 475 der Codex Euricianus zunächst für Goten wie Römer, bis dann unter Alarich II. speziell für die dort lebenden Römer die sog. Lex Romana Visigothorum erlassen worden ist, während parallel für die Goten der Codex Euricianus in Geltung blieb.[17] Andererseits wurde das lange so wirkmächtige Römische Recht im Jahr 532 unter dem oströmischen Kaiser Justinian zum Corpus Iuris zusammengefasst und bildete so eine weitgehend einheitliche Rechtsgrundlage im östlichen Teil des Römischen Reichs.[18] So galten im 6. Jahrhundert unserer Zeit im Westgotenreich aufgrund des Personalitätsprinzips unterschiedliche Rechte für die beiden großen Volksgruppen, während in Byzanz das Corpus Iuris als Territorialrecht Geltung beanspruchte.

In der im 8. Jahrhundert mit dem Machtantritt von Pippin, dem Vater Karls des Großen, beginnenden sog. fränkischen Zeit existierten auch auf dem Gebiet des heutigen Frankreichs und Deutschlands Volksstämme wie die Franken, Alemannen, Sachsen, Baiern etc., die zwar zumeist in bestimmten Gebieten siedelten, aber nicht als Territorial- oder gar Staatsvolk agierten, sondern durch persönliche Stammesstrukturen verfasst waren. Diese Volksstämme wiederum stützten sich –

16 *v. Savigny*, Geschichte des Römischen Rechts im Mittelalter, Bd. 1, 1834, S. 116.

17 *Heinrich Mitteis/Heinz Lieberich*, Deutsche Rechtsgeschichte, 19. Aufl. 1992, S. 94.

18 Vgl. nur *Jan Dirk Harke*, Römisches Recht, 2008, S. 20 ff.

wie Savigny gesagt hatte – auf ihre sog. Volksrechte. Die älteste solche Quelle ist die Lex Salica, das Stammesrecht der salischen Franken (Salier).[19]

Hierzu merken die bekannten Rechtshistoriker Ludwig Mitteis und Heinz Lieberich an: „Der stammesweisen Rechtsaufzeichnung entspricht, daß jeder nach seinem Stammesrecht, der lex originis beurteilt wurde; er stand ursprünglich nur mit seinem eigenen Stamm in Rechtsgemeinschaft; es galt das sog. Personalitätsprinzip. Jeder behielt sein Geburtsrecht, in welchem Stammesgebiet er sich auch aufhalten mochte, und mußte sich gegebenenfalls dazu bekennen (professio iuris). So konnte der in der germanischen Zeit noch undenkbare Fall eintreten, daß mehrere Rechte zusammentrafen".[20] Während etwa die Goten lediglich ihr – wenngleich für Goten und Römer unterschiedliches – Recht angewendet haben, „behandelten die Franken bei Verträgen und im Prozeß jeden Beteiligten nach seinem Geburtsrecht; die Gerichte kamen so in die Lage, stammesfremdes Recht anzuwenden; das Königsgericht urteilte jeweils nach dem Stammesrecht des Beklagten".[21]

Im hohen Mittelalter setzte sich dann zunächst in der Hochgerichtsbarkeit, zunehmend aber auch in der niederen Gerichtsbarkeit die Vorstellung durch, die Jurisdiktion bzw. die Rechtsprechungsgewalt an das Territorialitätsprinzip zu binden und nicht – wie noch nach dem Personalitätsprinzip – auch gegenüber verstreut siedelnden Untertanen außerhalb eines gerichtlichen Bannkreises zu gewähren.[22] Dahinter stand der Umstand, dass ursprünglich allein personell gedachte Herrschaftsbeziehungen zunehmend in einer dauerhaften, ja vererbbaren Herrschaft über ein Gebiet mündeten; die in diesem Gebiet lebenden Personen wurden nicht mehr primär über ihre Verwandtschaft als Gefolge eines Stammesfürsten, sondern aufgrund ihres Siedlungsorts als Untertanen des Territorialherren begriffen. Dieser und nicht mehr ihr Stammesoberhaupt wurde damit auch zum Gerichtsherren.

In den Städten des hohen und späten Mittelalters führte die Verleihung des Bürgerrechts an bestimmte Gruppen von Einwohnern letztlich dazu, dass diese nach dem Recht der Bürger leben konnten. Das bekannte Sprichwort „Stadtluft macht frei", das in dieser Fassung zwar erst im 19. Jahrhundert rückblickend geprägt worden ist, zeigte an, dass in eine Stadt gelangte Leibeigene nach Jahr und Tag ihre Freiheit erlangten und damit von ihrem Grundherrn nicht mehr herausver-

19 *Heinrich Mitteis/Heinz Lieberich,* (Fn. 17), S. 92.

20 *Heinrich Mitteis/Heinz Lieberich* (Fn. 17), S. 91.

21 *Heinrich Mitteis/Heinz Lieberich* (Fn. 17), S. 91.

22 *Heinrich Mitteis/Heinz Lieberich* (Fn. 17), S. 268 ff.

langt werden konnten.[23] Die Stadt als – durch ihre Mauern markiertes – Territorium bestimmte damit zwar nicht sofort, aber doch nach gewisser Zeit über die Rechtsverhältnisse in Bezug auf solche Neubürger.[24]

Eine Sonderstellung nahmen in vielen Städten traditionell die Juden ein, die nicht nur zumeist in eigenen Stadtteilen und abgegrenzt von der übrigen Bevölkerung, sondern eben auch weitgehend nach eigenem Recht lebten.[25] Dies führte zwar zu der bekannten Ghettoisierung, verhinderte andererseits aber auch eine Amalgamierung mit der Bevölkerungsmehrheit und erlaubte den Juden, ihren Glauben zugleich als ihre Rechtsordnung beizubehalten und mit Leben zu erfüllen. So war es möglich, dass in den christlich dominierten Städten bis in frühe Neuzeit die Jüdische Gemeinde gegenüber ihren Angehörigen Verstöße gegen Vorschriften des Jüdischen Rechts nach demselben sanktionierte.[26] Zugleich erleichterte der Fortbestand des Jüdischen Rechts in den Ghettos den Erhalt eines Netzwerks zu den gleichartigen Rechtsordnungen in anderen jüdischen Vierteln in ganz Europa; unterstützt wurde dies noch durch Responsen, als gutachterliche Auskünfte besonders rechtskundiger Rabbiner, welche von einzelnen Gemeinden angefordert und versandt worden sind.

Außerhalb der Städte richteten sich die Rechtsbeziehungen auf der obersten Ebene nach dem Lehnsrecht.[27] Es entstanden die typischen Lehnspyramiden mit dem König an der Spitze und mehreren Gruppen bzw. Schilden von Lehnsmännern. Wenngleich das Lehnsgut von Anfang an zumeist das Nutzungsrecht an einem abgegrenzten Territorium beinhaltete, begründete das Lehnsrecht doch zunächst eine primär persönliche Berechtigung für einen Gefolgsmann des Lehnsherrn. Zunächst sollte das Lehen den Lehnsmann wirtschaftlich in die Lage versetzen, seinem Lehnsherrn treue Dienste zu erbringen, so dass der Lehnsherr Lehen nur an seine Dienstmannen vergab. Im Vordergrund stand hier noch ein personal gedachter Dienst- und Treueverbund von Lehnsherr und Vasall, wobei ersterer letzteren durch die Beleihung mit einem Lehnsgut und die damit verbundene Berechtigung zur Ziehung der Früchte und Nutzungen daraus dazu in den Stand

23 *Karl S. Bader/Gerhard Dilcher*, Deutsche Rechtsgeschichte: Land und Stadt – Bürger und Bauer im Alten Europa, Bd. II, 1999, S. 353 ff.

24 Zur Rechtsstellung von Bürgern und Fremden in der mittelalterlichen Stadt näher *Karl S. Bader/Gerhard Dilcher* (Fn. 23), S. 445 ff.

25 Zum Judenrecht einführend *Hans Peter Benöhr*, JuS 1989, S. 8 ff.; *Karl S. Bader/Gerhard Dilcher* (Fn. 23), S. 464 ff. m. w. N. – Ausf. *Guido Kisch*, Forschungen zur Rechts- und Sozialgeschichte der Juden in Deutschland während des Mittelalters, 1955.

26 Dazu näher Hendrik Pekarek, Verbrechen und Strafe in der Jüdischen Rechtstradition, 2021.

27 Näher zur Lehnsverfassung im Mittelalter *Heinrich Mitteis/Heinz Lieberich* (Fn. 17), S. 178 ff.

setzte, seinen Verpflichtungen gegenüber dem Lehnsherrn etwa zur Heerfolge und zur Begleitung bzw. Beratung (in Latein: auxilium et consilium) nachzukommen.

Im Laufe des Mittelalters veränderte sich der Blickwinkel; in den Vordergrund trat die Berechtigung des Lehnsmannes am Lehnsgut, im Regelfall einem nutzbaren Stück Land, welches nunmehr auf den Erben des Lehnsmannes übergehen konnte oder sogar sollte. Der Lehnsherr konnte daher nicht mehr seine Gefolgsleute aussuchen und diese durch die Nutzungen aus dem Lehen alimentieren, sondern musste nunmehr zumeist den Sohn des Lehnsmannes mit dessen vormaligen Lehen beleihen; erst dadurch wurde letzterer wiederum dem Lehnsherrn gegenüber zu den genannten persönlichen Diensten verpflichtet. Diese Dienste wurden zusehends durch Zahlungspflichten abgelöst; es entwickelte sich eine Art Steuer, die wiederum dem Lehnsherrn ermöglichte, die zuvor persönlich vom Lehnsmann zu erbringende Beratung und Heerfolge durch professionelle Beamte und Söldner „einzukaufen". Diese sog. „Verdinglichung" des Lehnsrechts führte im Spätmittelalter und in der frühen Neuzeit dazu, dass vor allem die großen Vasallen gegenüber dem Lehnsherrn nur noch durch ein loses Treueband verbunden blieben und faktisch mehr und mehr zu Herrschern innerhalb der zum Lehen erhaltenen Territorien aufstiegen.[28]

Die aus dem mittelalterlichen Lehnsrecht folgende doppelte Rechtsbeziehung an einem Territorium zwischen Lehnsherr und Vasall (jenem stand das formale Obereigentum, diesem dagegen das vererbliche Nutzeigentum am Lehnsgut zu[29]) wurde noch dadurch herausgefordert, dass sich im ausgehenden 16. Jahrhundert zurückgehend auf die Staatslehre von Jean Bodin[30] in Europa zusehends der Gedanke an eine einheitliche und unteilbare Souveränität des Territorialherrn durchgesetzt hatte, die in einem Widerspruch zu einer mehrfach gestuften Herrschaftsbeziehung stand; dies und die in der ersten Hälfte des 16. Jahrhunderts in Westeuropa einsetzende und mit dem Augsburger Religionsfrieden von 1555 manifestierte Glaubensspaltung, womit es in der Hand des jeweiligen Territorialherrn lag, welcher Glaube und damit auch welche daraus folgende Glaubensordnung in seinem Gebiet vorherrschen sollte (cuius regio eius religio), führte zugleich zur Auflösung der für Westeuropa im Mittelalter noch prägenden universalen katholischen Kirche und eines seit der Kaiserkrönung Karls des Großen im Jahr 800 in Anknüpfung an das frühere Römische Reich universell gedachten Hl. Römischen Reichs, welches sich freilich im ausgehenden Mittelalter zunehmend auf seine

---

28 Zum Übergang zur Landesherrschaft *Heinrich Mitteis/Heinz Lieberich* (Fn. 17), S. 261ff.

29 Näher *Martin Heger*, Der Nießbrauch in usus modernus und Naturrecht, 2004, S. 101ff.

30 Dazu *Elisa Hoven*, JuS 2007, S. 10ff.

deutschen Kernbestandteile (unter Einschluss von Burgund und Oberitalien) fokussiert hatte.

Innerhalb des Hl. Römischen Reichs Deutscher Nation[31] war den Territorialherrn mit dem Westfälischen Frieden ab 1648[32], wiewohl formal immer noch Vasallen des Königs bzw. Kaisers, dann sogar der Abschluss von Bündnissen mit auswärtigen Mächten gestattet, sofern sich dieser nur nicht gegen den Kaiser als den obersten Lehnsherrn und das Reich richtete. Das ursprünglich primär personell gedachte Lehnsband war damit vollends zu einer territorialen Herrschaftsmacht geworden; deshalb wird das formal weitgehend unverändert fortbestehende Lehnsrecht spätestens mit Beginn der Neuzeit nur noch als „leere Form“[33] betrachtet, die dann 1806 mit dem Ende des Reichs auch formal aufgegeben wurde,[34] indem die Großvasallen zu unabhängigen Landesherren wurden und die mit kleineren Gütern beliehenen „Reichsstände“ mediatisiert, d. h. der neuen Territorialherrschaft untergeordnet wurden.

Insgesamt hat sich im hohen Mittelalter das zuvor für die individuelle Rechtsposition maßgebliche Personalprinzip in vieler Hinsicht in ein Territorialprinzip verwandelt; maßgeblich für das für eine Person an einem bestimmten Ort zu einer bestimmten Zeit geltende Recht war nicht mehr deren Abstammung, sondern – so wieder Ludwig Mitteis und Heinz Lieberich – „die Zugehörigkeit zu einem Lande; und auf die in einem Lande vorfallenden Tatbestände wurde jetzt nur noch das Landrecht angewandt (in Latein: „quod est in territorio, etiam est de territorio“). Das war eine notwendige Entwicklung, da in den Marken und im Osten [des Reiches] Angehörige verschiedener Stämme lebten und die geistlichen, bald auch die weltlichen Fürstentümer mit den alten Stämmen nichts mehr zu tun hatten. Trotzdem ist die Erinnerung an die Stammesrechte nicht ganz verblaßt. Noch die Goldene Bulle (1356) unterscheidet terra juris Franconici und Saxoninici [also Gebiete des Fränkischen und des Sächsischen Rechts]. Das fränkische Recht war durch Siedler und Kaufleute weit verbreitet worden und fand nur an dem durch den Sachsenspiegel bestimmten Gebiete des „gemeinen Sachsenrechts“ seine Grenze.“[35]

---

31 Zu dessen Verfassung *Mückl*, Jura 2006, S. 602 ff.; zur Geschichte *Klaus-Peter Schroeder*, JuS 2006, S. 577 ff.

32 Zu den damals erfolgten Änderungen der Reichsstruktur vgl. *Klaus-Peter Schroder*, JuS 1995, S. 959, 960 f.; zu den Folgen *Martin Heckel*, JuS 1988, S. 366 ff. und *Christoph Link*, JZ 1998, S. 1 ff.

33 *Heinrich Mitteis*, Der Staat des hohen Mittelalters, 7. Aufl. 1962, S. 424. – Dazu krit. *Hans K. Schulze*, Grundstrukturen der Verfassung im Mittelalter, Bd. I, 3. Aufl. 1995, S. 72 f.

34 Dazu *Klaus-Peter Schroeder*, JuS 2006, S. 577 ff.

35 *Heinrich Mitteis/Heinz Lieberich* (Fn. 17), S. 227.

III Frühneuzeitliche Entwicklungen

Nach der zunehmenden Territorialisierung im ausgehenden Mittelalter und zu Beginn der Neuzeit, insbesondere aber nach der Durchsetzung von Bodins Gedanken einer unteilbaren Souveränität des jeweiligen Souveräns im ausgehenden 16. Jahrhundert, welche zumeist auf den Territorialherrn oder den Herrscher eines Staates projiziert wurde, trat die Idee einer Jurisdiktion kraft Personalitätsprinzip auch über verstreut in verschiedenen Territorien lebende Angehörige eines Volksstammes noch weiter zurück. Der bretonische Jurist Bertrand d'Argentré (1519–1590) – ein Landsmann und Zeitgenosse Bodins – hat es so formuliert: „et finitae potestatis finita jurisdictio et cognitio; ideo et statuta extra territoria sua sine usu sunt".[36] Wo die staatliche Macht endet, ende auch die Rechtssetzungs- und Rechtsdurchsetzungsgewalt des Territorialherren.[37] Außerhalb des beherrschten Territoriums seien seine Gesetze dagegen „sine usu", mithin außer Gebrauch; das galt dann natürlich auch für außerhalb dieser Grenzen lebende Angehörige der gleichen Volksgruppe, die konsequent nunmehr primär der Jurisdiktionsgewalt des dortigen Territorialherren unterstanden.

Diese Formulierung knüpft an an die gängige Änderung des Verständnisses vom Römischen Recht als dem gemeinen Recht (ius commune), welches im hohen und späten Mittelalter noch als universal geltende, gleichsam sakrale Rechtsordnung bzw. „ratio scripta" begriffen wurde, hin zu der zu Beginn der Neuzeit aufkommenden Vorstellung, das Römische Recht sei als Gemeines Recht nur insoweit anwendbar als es in einem Gebiet zu der fraglichen Zeit tatsächlich auch in Gebrauch sei; nicht die Universalität des Rechts begründe seine Anwendung mehr, sondern die Rezeption dieses Rechts durch tatsächlichen Gebrauch, in den Worten von Hermann Coring galt mithin das Erfordernis eines „usu receptum".[38] Nicht (mehr) in Gebrauch befindlichem Römischem Recht wurde daher seit dem 17. Jahrhundert zunehmend die Fortgeltung als gemeines Recht verweigert; lokale Rechtsstatuten konnten damit als Ausdruck des örtlichen Rechtsgebrauchs das römisch-gemeine Recht verdrängen, zeigte doch ihre Existenz, dass dieses nicht mehr per se in Geltung war, sondern allenfalls aufgrund neuerer Rechtssetzung.[39] Dadurch und durch die parallel einsetzende Kodifikation einiger (zumeist freilich

36 Zitiert nach *Frederick Alexander Mann*, Studies in International Law, 1973, S. 18.

37 *Florian Jeßberger*, Der transnationale Geltungsbereich des deutschen Strafrechts, 2011, S. 42 Fn. 5.

38 *Ulrich Eisenhardt*, Deutsche Rechtsgeschichte, Rn. 254.

39 *Martin Heger*, ZJS 2010, S. 29, 30f.

nicht aller) Rechtsmaterien in den Territorien[40] sowie – subsidiär – auch auf Reichsebene (hierfür ist insbesondere die 1532 erlassene Peinliche Halsgerichtsordnung Kaiser Karl V., zumeist bezeichnet als „Constitutio Criminalis Carolina“, zu nennen[41]) wurde der Gedanke, dass in einem Territorium ein für dieses gesetztes Recht allgemein – d. h. für alle Rechtsunterworfenen – gelten sollte zunehmend durchgesetzt. Das galt freilich nicht für alle Rechtsgebiete gleichermaßen.

So bildete noch bis ins 18. Jahrhundert hinein, wie etwa der Völkerstrafrechtler Florian Jeßberger konstatiert, – trotz mancher Anfechtung – „die lex patriae die allgemein anerkannte Grundlage der Bestrafung. Strafrecht war Stammesrecht.“[42] In ähnlicher Weise wurde auch das Ehe- und Familienrecht bis ins späte 19. Jahrhundert fast überall durch religiöse Regeln geprägt. Solange – sieht man von der Ausnahme der jüdischen Gemeinden ab, die allerdings seit dem späteren Mittelalter vielfach nach Osten abgedrängt worden waren – die Territorien in Europa jeweils für sich religiös weitgehend homogen waren, führte die Anknüpfung familienrechtlicher Regelungen an die religiöse Ordnung zwar formal zu einer Anknüpfung an die Person bzw. deren Konfession; der Sache nach galt damit aber gleichwohl in einem Territorium nur eine – wenngleich konfessionell determinierte – Familienrechtsordnung. Der frühneuzeitliche Territorialstaat übernahm im „konfessionellen Zeitalter“ faktisch das aufgrund der religiösen Prägung des Territoriums geltende Ehe- und Familienrecht und legte dessen Vollzug in die Hände religiöser Beamter. So war etwa in protestantischen Gebieten die Verheiratung eines Geistlichen der Regelfall und eine Ehescheidung im Prinzip möglich (wenn auch faktisch selten), während in katholischen Gebieten das Zölibat einer Eheschließung des Priesters entgegenstand und allenfalls in den im kanonischen Recht vorgesehenen extremen Ausnahmefällen eine Eheauflösung denkbar sein konnte.

Erst das Nebeneinander verschiedener Religionszugehörigkeit in einem Territorium, wie es im 18. Jahrhundert zunehmend möglich wurde, führte dazu, dass aus der personalen Anknüpfung des religiösen Eherechts innerhalb einzelner Territorien verschiedene Rechtsregimes resultierten, die letztlich dem Personalitätsprinzip folgten.

Während mithin bereits seit dem hohen Mittelalter boden- und vermögensbezogene Rechtsverhältnisse zunehmend nach dem Territorialitätsprinzip anhand des maßgeblichen Ortes nach dem dort geltenden Landrecht gelöst wurden und das

40 Als Prototyp für eine Stadtrechtsreformation in Deutschland wird regelmäßig das Nürnberger Stadtrecht von 1469 genannt.

41 Textausgabe von *Friedrich-Christian Schroeder*, Die Peinliche Gerichtsordnung Kaiser Karls V. von 1532 (Carolina), 2000; dazu *Klaus Geppert*, Jura 2015, S. 143 ff.; *Alexander Bechtel*, ZJS 2017, S. 641 ff. und 2018, S. 20 ff.

42 *Florian Jeßberger* (Fn. 38), S. 43.

Lehnsrecht die rechtlichen Beziehungen zwischen Lehnsherr und Vasall ebenfalls danach regelte, wo sich das Lehnsgut befand, folgten die Regelungen des Strafrechts noch bis zum Ende der frühen Neuzeit zu einem erheblichen Teil, das Familienrecht sogar noch weit in die Moderne hinein vorrangig dem Personalitätsprinzip. Für das Eherecht war die enge Verbindung vor allem der Eheschließung mit den dafür von den Religionsgemeinschaften gemachten Vorgaben der wesentliche Grund, so dass religiöse Heterogenität erst das Personalitätsprinzip in seinen Wirkungen sichtbar werden ließ.

Dagegen war das Strafrecht seit Beginn der Neuzeit aus seiner zuvor noch engeren Verknüpfung mit kirchenrechtlichen Sanktionsregelungen gelöst worden. Auf den Kirchenbann folgte seit 1519 nicht mehr automatisch die Reichsacht. Gleichwohl blieb das in der frühen Neuzeit in vielen europäischen Staaten geschaffene bzw. umgebildete Strafrecht aus der Sicht der meisten zeitgenössischen Juristen „Stammesrecht". Der Grund war wohl, dass man bereits damals zögerte, einen Fremden für ein Verhalten haftbar machen zu wollen, welches nach der Rechtsordnung des Territoriums, aus dem er gekommen ist, nicht als strafbar eingeschätzt wurde. Dieser Gedanke sollte im Zuge der Eroberung der Kolonien weitergetragen werden. Schon zur Zeit der Kolonisierung Amerikas durch Spanien (und Portugal) im 16. Jahrhundert lebten die Spanier nach ihrem Recht; die indigenen Völker wurden zwar in einer recht bekannten grundsätzlichen Diskussion – immerhin – als Menschen angesehen, doch wurde ihnen natürlich nicht die gleiche Rechtsstellung gewährt. Augenfällig ist das beim Institut der Sklaverei vor allem von aus Afrika stammenden Menschen; deren mindere Rechtsstellung folgte letztlich auch dem Personalitätsprinzip. Noch kurz vor Abschaffung der Sklaverei in den USA wurde in einem berüchtigten Grundsatzurteil des Supreme Courts 1857 die Rechtstellung von Sklaven bzw. Schwarzen generell weitestgehend negiert (Dred Scott v. John F. A. Sandford).[43]

Während in den europäischen Mutterländern spätestens im 19. Jahrhundert das Territorialitätsprinzip durchgesetzt wurde, nahmen die Kolonisten regelmäßig ihr Recht in die Kolonien mit, wo es dann in verfahrensmäßig vereinfachter Weise für europäische bzw. weiße Siedler gelten sollte, während für die indigene bzw. einheimische Bevölkerung ein deutlich anderes, z.T. weiter an den vorgefundenen Stammestraditionen orientiertes Recht etabliert wurde.[44]

Und auch außerhalb der Kolonien – wie etwa in China, Japan und der Türkei – galt ab Mitte des 19. Jahrhunderts vielfach das Konsularrecht, aufgrund dessen

43 60 U.S. 393 (1856)

44 Zum Strafrecht in den deutschen Kolonien ausf. *Ralf Schlottau*, Deutsche Kolonialrechtspflege, 2007; *Heger*, Koloniales Strafrecht, S. 161 ff.

Rechtsstreitigkeiten unter Europäern regelmäßig nicht nach dem territorial geltenden Recht und nicht vor der örtlich zuständigen Gerichtsbarkeit, sondern vor Konsulargerichten nach im Regelfall vereinfachtem Heimatrecht entschieden wurden; für die deutsche Konsulargerichtsbarkeit etwa in Shanghai.[45]

IV Aktuelle Fragen

Migrationsströme, die bereits in nachrömischer Zeit im Zuge der Völkerwanderung das Personalitätsprinzip zum Durchbruch brachten, stellen bis heute eine Herausforderung für das Recht dar. Das gilt in besonderem Maße für das Familien- und Strafrecht, weil beide Rechtsmaterien in starkem Maße in den Nationalstaaten kulturell überwölbt sind.[46]

Und weil das Strafrecht nach heutiger Auffassung angesichts des Schuldprinzips nur bei nachgewiesener Schuld des Angeklagten im Sinne eines diesem persönlich vorwerfbaren Fehlverhaltens eingreifen kann, stellt das Mitbringen von Rechtsvorstellungen aus fremden Rechtskreisen bzw. Rechtskulturen gerade heute eine Herausforderung für die das Territorialrecht durchsetzende staatliche Justizordnung dar. Ein Beispiel ist der sog. Ehrenmord;[47] hier wird von den im Inland aktiven Tätern immer wieder angeführt, in ihrer Heimat sei ein solches Verhalten zur Verteidigung der Familienehre faktisch geboten. Die deutsche Justiz hat bei der strafrechtlichen Bewertung denn auch immer wieder geschwankt – klar war zwar die Strafbarkeit wegen Totschlags, doch wurde im Rahmen einer hier durchaus nahe liegenden und schärferen Strafbarkeit wegen Mordes immer wieder erwogen, ob ein niedriger Beweggrund in der Tötung zum Erhalt der (vermeintlichen) Familienehre gesehen werden kann, weil dem Täter aufgrund der Prägung aus seiner vormaligen Heimat gerade nicht bewusst war, dass aus deutscher Sicht sein Verhalten sittlich auf niederster Stufe steht, dachte er doch gerade an etwas irgendwie Ehrerhaltendes.

Das gilt freilich auch umgekehrt, wenn nämlich das deutsche Strafrecht versucht, auch Verhaltensweisen im Ausland zu erfassen, wenn und soweit die Person eigentlich in Deutschland lebt. Beispiele sind die Abtreibung durch deutsche

45 Zu diesem Nebeneinander mit Blick auf die deutsche Kolonie Kiautschou näher *Martin Heger*, Das Strafrecht der „Musterkolonie“ Kiautschou, in: Michael Jäger/Benjamin Langer/Mingchao Mao (Hrsg.), Ost-westliche Erfahrungen der Modernität: der chinesisch-deutsche Ideenaustausch und die Bewegung des 4. Mai 1919, 2020, S. 57 ff.

46 Dazu *Martin Heger*, Flucht und Migration als Herausforderung für das staatliche Strafrecht, in: Berliner Wissenschaftliche Gesellschaft (BWG), Jahrbuch 2015/2016, 2018, S. 95 ff.

47 Näher *Erol Pohlreich*, „Ehrenmorde“ im Wandel des Strafrechts, 2009.

Staatsangehörige etwa in den Niederlanden oder – seit neuerem – Zwangsverheiratung (§ 237 StGB) und weibliche Genitalverstümmelung (§ 226a StGB) bei hierzulande lebenden Ausländern auf „Heimaturlaub". Hier gilt inzwischen das Personalitätsprinzip, so dass auch Auslandstaten gegenüber Deutschen oder gewöhnlich hierzulande lebenden Ausländern nach deutschem Strafrecht vor deutschen Strafgerichten verfolgt werden können (§ 5 Nr. 6 c und 9a StGB).

Im Familienrecht hat man dagegen vor wenigen Jahren das Eheschließungsalter territorialisiert; wurde zuvor eine ausländische Ehe hierzulande auch anerkannt, wenn ein Partner minderjährig war, soll dies nach dem Willen des Gesetzgebers heute ausscheiden. Da damit einer Reihe von bislang anerkannten ausländischen Ehen hierzulande per se die Wirksamkeit abgesprochen würde, hat das BVerfG dieser Tage vom Gesetzgeber eine gewisse Einschränkung der absoluten Nichtigkeit von Minderjährigenehen verlangt.[48] Weil Art. 6 GG grundsätzlich auch im Ausland geschlossene Ehen innerstaatlichem Schutz unterstellt, bleibt eine weitestgehende Annullierung derselben allein aufgrund des Territorialitätsprinzips zumindest fragwürdig; mit Recht hat es daher das OLG Frankfurt auch nach der erwähnten Gesetzesänderung abgelehnt, die Ehe einer zur Zeit der Trauung erst 17jährigen Bulgarin, die inzwischen volljährig mit Mann und Kind nach Deutschland gekommen ist, aufzuheben.[49] Soweit freilich die Ehe erzwungen wurde oder die Minderjährigkeit ausgenutzt worden ist, sprechen die Grundrechte des Betroffenen für eine Einschränkung des Schutzes der Ehe.

Bibilographie

Bader, Karl S. und Gerhard Dilcher. *Deutsche Rechtsgeschichte: Land und Stadt – Bürger und Bauer im Alten Europa*, Bd. II.Heidelberg/Berlin/New York: Springer, 1999.

Bechtel, Alexander. *Die Constitutio Criminalis Carolina von 1532 – Wegbereiter einer eigenständigen deutschen Strafrechtsdogmatik* – Teil 1/2. Zeitschrift für das juristische Studium (ZJS) 2017, S. 641–646 und 2018, S. 20–28.

Becker, Hans-Jürgen: *Das Gewaltmonopol des Staates und die Sicherheit des Bürgers: Der Ewige Landfriede – vor 500 Jahren.* In: Neue Juristische Wochenschrift (NJW) 1995, S. 2077–2081.

Eisenhardt, Ulrich. *Deutsche Rechtsgeschichte*, 7. Aufl., München: C.H. Beck, 2019.

Geppert, Klaus. Die Peinliche Halsgerichtsordnung Karls. V. (die „Carolina"). In: Juristische Ausbildung (Jura) 2015, S. 143–153.

Harke, Jan Dirk. *Römisches Recht.* München: C.H. Beck, 2008.

Heckel, Martin. *Der Westfälische Friede als Instrument internationaler Friedenssicherung und religiös-weltanschaulicher Koexistenzordnung.* In: Juristische Schulung (JuS) 1988, S. 336–341.

48 BVerfG, Beschl. v. 1.2.2023 – BvL 7/18.

49 OLG Frankfurt, FamRZ 2019, 1853.

Heger, Martin. „Das Strafrecht der „Musterkolonie“ Kiautschou.“ In: *Ost-westliche Erfahrungen der Modernität: der chinesisch-deutsche Ideenaustausch und die Bewegung des 4. Mai 1919*, herausgegeben von Michael Jäger, Benjamin Langer und Mingchao Mao. Berlin, de Gruyter, 2020, S. 57–67.

Heger, Martin. *Der Nießbrauch in usus modernus und Naturrecht.* Berlin: Duncker & Humblot, 2004.

Heger, Martin. *Flucht und Migration als Herausforderung für das staatliche Strafrecht.* In: Berliner Wissenschaftliche Gesellschaft (BWG), Jahrbuch 2015/2016, Peter Lang, Frankfurt a. M. 2018, S. 95 ff.

Heger, Martin. „Koloniales Strafrecht.“ In: *(Post)Koloniale Rechtswissenschaft – Geschichte und Gegenwart des Kolonialismus in der deutschen Rechtswissenschaft*, herausgegeben von Philipp Dann, Isabel Feichtner und Jochen von Bernstorff, Tübingen: Mohr Siebeck, 2022, S. 161–188.

Heger, Martin. *Recht im „Alten Reich“ – Der Usus modernus*, Zeitschrift für das juristische Studium (ZJS) 2010, S. 29–39.

Hoven, Elisa. *Jean Bodin (1530 bis 1596) – Wegbereiter des modernen Staates.* In: Juristische Schulung (JuS) 2007, S. 10–14.

Jäschke, Gotthard. *Die „Imam-Ehe“ in der Türkei.* In: Die Welt des Islams, N. S., 4, (2–3), 1955, S. 164–201.

Jeßberger, Florian. *Der transnationale Geltungsbereich des deutschen Strafrechts.* Tübingen: Mohr Siebeck, 2011.

Kisch, Guido. *Forschungen zur Rechts- und Sozialgeschichte der Juden in Deutschland während des Mittelalters.* Zürich: Europa-Verlag, 1955.

Kurnaz, Serdar. → Im Band

Laufs, Adolf. *Frieden durch Recht – der Wormser Reichstag.* In: Juristische Schulung (JuS) 1995, S. 665–671.

Link, Christoph. *Die Bedeutung des Westfälischen Friedens in der deutschen Verfassungsentwicklung – Zum 350jährigen Jubiläum eines Reichsgrundgesetzes.* In: Juristenzeitung (JZ) 1998, S. 1–9.

Maine, Henry Sumner. *Ancient Law.* London: John Murray, 1861,

Mann, Frederick Alexander. *Studies in International Law.* Oxford, Clarendon Press, 1973.

Mitteis, Heinrich. Der Staat des hohen Mittelalters. 7. Aufl., Weimar: Hermann Böhlaus Nachfolger, 1962.

Mitteis, Heinrich und Heinz Lieberich. *Deutsche Rechtsgeschichte*, 19. Aufl., München: C.H. Beck, 1992.

Mückl, Stefan. *Das Heilige Römische Reich deutscher Nation: Idee, Verfassung, Untergang.* In: Juristische Ausbildung (Jura), 2006, S. 602–610.

Naarmann, Benedikt. *Der Schutz von Religionen und Religionsgemeinschaften in Deutschland, England, Indien und Pakistan.* Tübingen, Mohr Siebeck, 2015.

Pekarek, Hendrik. *Verbrechen und Strafe in der Jüdischen Rechtstradition.* Berlin: Duncker & Humblot, 2021.

Pohlreich, Erol. *„Ehrenmorde“ im Wandel des Strafrechts.* Berlin: Duncker & Humblot, 2009.

Rohe, Matthias. *Das Islamische Recht.* München: C.H. Beck, 2009.

v. Savigny, Friedrich Carl. *Geschichte des Römischen Rechts im Mittelalter*, Bd. 1. Heidelberg: J. C. B. Mohr, 1834.

Schirrmacher, Christine. *Die Scharia: Recht und Gesetz im Islam.* Holzgerlingen: SCM Hänssler, 4. Aufl. 2015.

Schlottau, Ralf. *Deutsche Kolonialrechtspflege.* Frankfurt et al.: Peter Lang, 2007.

Schroeder, Friedrich-Christian. *Die Peinliche Gerichtsordnung Kaiser Karls V. und des Heiligen Römischen Reichs von 1532 (Carolina).* Leipzig: Reclam, 2000.

Schroder, Klaus-Peter. *Der Dreißigjährige Krieg, das Alte Reich und Samuel von Pufendorf (1632–1694).* In: Juristische Schulung (JuS) 1995, S. 959–965.

Schroeder, Klaus-Peter. *Mythos, Wirklichkeit und Visionen: Die Geschichte vom langen Leben und Sterben des Heiligen Römischen Reiches Deutscher Nation.* In: Juristische Schulung (JuS) 2006, S. 577–582.

Schulze, Hans K.: *Grundstrukturen der Verfassung im Mittelalter,* Bd. I. 3. Aufl., Stuttgart: Kohlhammer, 1995.

Wesel, Uwe. *Geschichte des Rechts.* 5. Aufl. München: C.H. Beck, 2022.

Elisa Klapheck

Towards a Jewish Theology of Secular Law

> The Sages taught: One who sees the Sages of Israel recites: Blessed is, who has shared of his wisdom with those who revere him. One who sees Sages of the nations of the world recites: Blessed is, who has given of his wisdom to humans of flesh and blood. One who sees kings of Israel recites: Blessed is, who has shared of his glory with those who revere him. One who sees kings of the other nations of the world recites: Blessed is, who has given of his glory to humans of flesh and blood. (B. Berakhot 58a)

The First Commandment: A Legal System

From a rabbinical or Talmudical viewpoint, the commandment to form a legal system has the highest priority. It is placed even before the commandment to recognize God as the one God of Israel. Accordingly, the first of the Seven Noahide Commandments concerns the judiciary:

> The descendants of Noah, [i.e., all of humanity], were obligated to observe seven commandments: The commandment of establishing a legal system; and the prohibition against blessing [i.e., cursing] the name of God; and the prohibition of idol worship; and the prohibition against forbidden sexual relations; and the prohibition of bloodshed; and the prohibition of robbery; and the prohibition against eating a limb from a living animal. (B. Sanhedrin 56a)

Here the understanding of *b'nei Noah*, children of Noah, means that all of humanity stems from the biblical story of the flood. As Noah and his family were the only human beings to survive, he became the father of all humankind after him.[1] The story marks an end and a new beginning. In the end, God makes a covenant and promises that he will never annihilate the world again. But in the rabbinical understanding, the Noahide covenant also contains a legal codex – a primordial rule of law for human beings.[2] This legal code is further elaborated in the Talmud as the Seven Noahide Commandments.

Although usually translated as the Seven Noahide Laws, I am purposefully calling them "commandments" to underline their equal rank to the Ten Commandments. Yet the word commandment is itself a difficult translation for the many dif-

Translation: The contribution was translated in English by Laura Radosh.

Note: All citations of Torah and commentary are based on sefaria.org, last accessed 30 Nov. 2021.

1 Gen. 6:9 to 9:17.
2 Gen. 9:1–17.

https://doi.org/10.1515/9783111062631-008

ferent Hebrew expressions for the laws found in the Torah and rabbinic literature – *dinim, mishpatim, chukim, mishnayot, mitzvot, takkanot, etc.* The Ten Commandments are in Hebrew, for example, *asseret ha-dibrot*, which is perhaps best translated as "the ten statements." In Jewish jargon today, all injunctions, whether positive or negative, are subsumed under the term *mitzvot*, which is again difficult to translate. I understand it primarily as "obligation," but in the end, the literal translation is irrelevant.

Of greater importance for an attempt to arrive at a Jewish theology of secular law is the *order* of the Noahide commandments. A statement all of its own is made with the very first commandment: the injunction to create a legal system. The order can be read as prioritizing, or as a set of preconditions: the first commandment as the requirement for the second, and so on. However, key here is not only the order of the commandments but also and equally the order of biblical events. The flood in the book of Genesis takes place around fifty chapters before the Israelite nation is founded at Mount Sinai in the book of Exodus. Thus, in the rabbinical understanding, the Noahide Commandments were revealed long before the Ten Commandments. This means that the first Noahide commandment to form a legal system already applied to those who later received the Torah with the Ten Commandments. The Talmudic rabbis emphasized that the Noahide Commandments apply to the Jews as to all peoples. That at least is their interpretation of the events in Marah.

In the Torah, Marah is the site on the Sinai Peninsula where the Israelites arrived after crossing the Sea of Reeds and after the drowning of Pharaoh with his horses and riders.[3] According to the narrative in Exodus 15, the rejoicing of the Israelites was short-lived. In Marah, where they arrived afterwards, they had nothing to drink for three days, for the water there was bitter, giving Marah its name (*mar* means 'bitter'). The crisis became the first conflict between God and his people. Dramatic as the situation seemed, its immediate solution appeared simple. Moses, at God's behest, threw a piece of wood into the water, making it potable. The more long-term solution to resolving future crises between God and his people is stated in the next, easy to overlook sentence: "There [in Marah] he [God] gave them laws and statutes (*chok u-mishpat)*, and there he tried them" (Ex. 15:25).

As a result of this first crisis, God gave the Israelites *chok* and *mishpat*, "laws and statutes." But what was meant by these terms, as they are both expressions for rulings, the rabbis explain as follows in the Talmud:

> The Jewish people were commanded to observe ten laws when they were in Marah: Seven that the descendants of Noah already accepted upon themselves, and God added to them

3 Exod. 15:22.

> the following commandments: ritual laws (*chukim*), and Shabbat, and honoring one's father and mother. (B. Sanhedrin 56b)

This interpretation makes it clear that as far as the Talmudic scholars were concerned, the children of Israel were already bound to the Noahide Commandments. Hence, from the beginning, they were within the same *human* context as all other peoples, and this remained so after the giving of the Torah at Mount Sinai. In Marah, however, still at quite a distance from Mount Sinai, three further laws were added to the original Seven Noahide Commandments: the first addition is called *chukim*, which I translate as "ritual laws." Elsewhere, the rabbis define *chukim* as those ritual laws whose reasoning cannot be grasped with logic. The prime example of *chukim* in the Torah is the almost magical ritual with the red heifer.[4] Unlike the Seven Noahide Commandments, which must be seen as universal laws, the three additions shape an Israelite identity. This holds true for ritual laws, which define the specific Israelite cult, as well as for the introduction of Shabbat as a ritual and social custom, and for honoring one's father and mother, which can be read as honoring one's heritage or ancestors.

The Secular Traditions of All Peoples

The rabbinical value placed on the secular traditions of other peoples is encompassing. It is said, for example, that before the Torah was revealed, there were already as many as twenty-six generations who found secular paths to the Torah:

> And there is a path, I will show him the salvation of God" [Ps. 50:23] ... "And there is a path [*derech*]" – meaning not one, but two paths take you to salvation – since Rabbi Ishmael son of Rav Nachman said: *Derech eretz* [literally: the way of the world] precedes Torah by 26 generations, since it is written "and to guard the way [*derech*] to the Tree of Life" [Genesis 3:24]. "Way" is the *derech eretz*, and only after that comes Tree of Life [*etz chayim*] which is Torah. (Vayikra Rabah 9:4)

This rabbinical statement can be understood to mean that the secular path taken by the twenty-six generations can be measured against the Torah, and even that their ways are equally promising. Because they are linked here to the benchmark of the Torah, they act as a kind of prehistory to the revelation of the Torah. And

4 Num. 19; The Torah section that delineates the requirements for this ritual is called "Chukat" (the epitome of ritual decrees). This *parashah* is the basis for the rabbinical definition of *chukim* as laws whose meanings cannot be grasped by understanding alone.

because they are within the context of the revelation, they uphold similar standards in a continuum that continues to be valued even *after* the Torah is given.

By interpreting the secular paths of earlier generations as leading to Torah, the Midrash not only relates the traditions of other peoples to the Torah, but also vice versa. The religious legal tradition of the Torah can, from the very beginning, be thought of as being in a possible relation to the secular legal traditions of other civilizations. But I would go even further to state that in this passage the rabbinical writings admit that a secular legal system is a necessary precondition for divine revelation, and for a monotheistic relationship to God.

And in fact, this order comes up repeatedly in the Torah: *first* there is a secular legal framework and *then* divine revelation. The best example is in the portion of the book of Exodus in which the revealing of the Ten Commandments is described. This section is called "Yitro," the name of Moses's father-in-law. According to the Torah, Yitro was not an Israelite, but a Midianite priest. Moses comes to him after fleeing Pharaoh, and marries Yitro's daughter Zipporah. It is Yitro who, in chapter 18 of Exodus, recommends that Moses create a secular legal system:

> You shall also seek out from among all the people capable men who fear God, trustworthy men who spurn ill-gotten gain. Set these over them as chiefs of thousands, hundreds, fifties, and tens, and let them judge the people at all times. Have them bring every major dispute to you, but let them decide every minor dispute themselves. Make it easier for yourself by letting them share the burden with you. (Exod. 18: 21–22)

These verses describe the fulfillment of the first Noahide commandment. Although there is not yet a Torah, responsibility is delegated to people who must make judgements on their own, while carrying collective responsibility for their decisions with Moses. Just as the Talmud stresses that the first Noahide commandment to establish courts of justice cannot be overestimated in its exceptional importance for humanity, it should not be underestimated that it is here a non-Israelite, even a Midianite priest, whom the Israelites have to thank for the establishment of a secular judicial system in the desert. It is not until after chapter 18 that the people become prepared for the revelation of God, which appears in chapter 20 as the Ten Commandments on the two Tablets of the Law.

Religio-secular tension

I would like to make a case for taking the order of events suggested by Torah and Talmud seriously, and reading the secular framework as a rabbinically recognized precondition for revelation. First, however, we must delineate the term "secular." Naturally, in the rabbinical discourse on law, it has nothing do to with the modern concept of secularism, in which society is increasingly secularized and religion becomes less and less important. Neither does "secular" in the rabbinical sense have anything in common with the Latin meaning of the word, which referred to the "secularization" of church property or its transfer to the state. The rabbinical tradition offers its own understanding of "secular," one which permeates the sensibilities of most conscious Jews to this day, including most Orthodox Jews.[5]

The story that best illustrates the rabbinical understanding of how the Jewish religion had become secular is the Talmudic legend of the Oven of Akhnai. David Biale cites this story in his book *Not in the Heavens: The Tradition of Jewish Secular Thought* as proof of the rabbinic accomplishment of creating a rabbinical/secular legal tradition with roots in the Torah.[6] In the story of the Oven of Akhnai, Rabbi Eliezer is outvoted by the other rabbis despite the "revelatory" proof that he brings in the form of divine miracles. The others answer laconically to these demonstrations that they do not follow miracles but decide by majority. To underline their position they quote the Torah, where it is written regarding legal disputes: "according to the majority you shall incline." It is not clear whether God is happy with the outcome of this story. At the end God laughs, "my children have defeated me, my children have defeated me." They have turned the divine arsenal, the law and majority rule, against their maker. And while we do not know what God thinks of this, what is clear, and emphasized by God in the Torah itself, is the fact that the Torah is not in the heavens, but in the world – *Lo ba-shamayim hi.* Human beings carry the responsibility for the law.

The simple act of being "in the world" necessitates taking worldly paths in order to do justice to the divine; *secular* instruments such as majority rule are employed to fulfill divine commandments. This indicates the rabbis' secular understanding of their religious responsibility. Secular is by no means the opposite of religious. Rather, the opposite of secular is theocratic, meaning that God rules alone and his laws are set in stone, infallible and unquestionable. And it is the job of God's representatives (for example, priests) to make sure that his laws are fulfilled as "God's will." "Secular" means instead that God's laws are "in the world," where they are further developed by people. That makes them fallible and necessitates corrections (*takkanot/tikkun*) and an unending process of negotiation. The Talmud, in which the rabbis interpret and enlarge upon the laws in unending debates, is itself a "secular" work. And the story of the Oven of Akhnai shows the extent to which the rabbis were aware of this fact.

---

5 In the nineteenth century, the founder of modern Orthodoxy, Samson Raphael Hirsch, propagated the concept of Torah *im derech eretz*, or Torah together with worldly education/occupations.

6 David Biale, *Not in the Heavens. The Tradition of Jewish Secular Thought* (Princeton: Princeton University Press, 2011).

This understanding of "secular" means that, from the outset, the Torah, and more so the Talmud, contains something that I have elsewhere called a "religio-secular tension" (*religiös-säkulares Spannungsfeld*).[7] It is caught between two understandings of law. On one side is God as lawgiver. On the other side are people as the lawgivers of secular order. Yet this tension is already established in the Torah itself, and even wanted by the Torah.

Two "first" commandments

Let us return to the Noahide commandments. I am less interested in the oft-repeated Jewish interpretation, according to which the Noahide commandments are proof of the rabbis' religious tolerance and mean that peoples without knowledge of the God of Israel should also be valued by the Jews. I am instead, or perhaps in contrast, interested in what the recognition of the secular legal traditions of other peoples might mean theologically for the development of the Jewish legal tradition. Does the first Noahide commandment, as a universal commandment for humanity to give the community a legal system – one which, according to the rabbis, is also grounded in Torah – lay the cornerstone for a specifically Jewish theology of secular law?

It is only at first glance that the Noahide commandments are a "light" version of the Ten Commandments, lacking the Jewish elements such as monotheism as a starting point or the commandment of Shabbat. In a comparison with the first Noahide commandment to establish courts of justice, the completely different tone of the Ten Commandments is worth investigating. In particular the first of the Ten Commandments is a direct expression of God's theocratic aspirations:[8] "I (*anochi*) the Eternal am your God ..." Here, a divine "I" speaks in a theocratic style directly to a "you," the Israelite people: "I the Eternal am your God who brought you out of the land of Egypt, the house of bondage ... you shall ... you shall not ..." (Exod. 20:1–14; Deut. 5:6–18). In contrast, the first Noahide commandment requests in a secular tone to establish a system of law with regulations, courts, and judgments independent of any relation to God.[9]

7 Elisa Klapheck, "Das religiös-säkulare Spannungsfeld des Judentums," in *Machloket/ Streitschriften, vol. 1 Säkulares Judentum aus religiöser Quelle*, contributions by Ruth Calderon and Elisa Klapheck (Berlin: Hentrich & Hentrich, 2015), 9–47.

8 Ibid., 12 and 28.

9 The rabbinical debate on the transparent nature of the legal system can be found in the Babylonian Talmud, Sanhedrin 56b.

A Jewish theology of secular law can of course only be founded on the interaction of *both* first commandments – the first of the Noahide commandments and the first of the Ten commandments. It must be based on the secular traditions of all peoples *and* on the Torah. Even in the Toseftah, the rabbinical code of law edited parallel to the Mishnah, the Jews' legal system is deemed equal to the secular legal systems of other peoples. The Toseftah also lists the seven Noahide commandments: "The descendants of Noah were obligated to observe seven commandments: the commandment of establishing a legal system [*dinim*]," etc.[10] Then the text asks what is meant by *dinim:* "Just as Israelites [the Jewish people] are commanded to establish law courts in their neighborhoods, so too, Noahides are commanded to establish law courts in their cities" (Toseftah Avodah Zarah 9:4).

Here the order is reversed. Just as the Jewish people are given the task of creating a secular justice system, so too were the Noahides given the task. But there is a hint hidden in this reversal. It makes clear that the secular judicial yardstick of the first Noahide commandment is from the beginning contained within the Torah. It is exactly this part of the Israelite legal canon that non-Jewish peoples too – humanity as a whole – can be expected to follow.

Nahum Rakover, in his comprehensive study *Law and the Noahides*, pinpoints an overlap, recognized by the sages, of the first Noahide commandment and the laws of Israel.[11] In this context, Rakover highlights those rabbinical commentaries that aim, through their evaluation of the Noahide commandments, to find a general standard that is also acceptable for the Jewish tradition. For the sages, the decisive attribute is "just" and "righteous." If a people gives itself just laws, thus also ensuring justice for Jews, then, from a Jewish viewpoint, these laws must be accepted.[12] The question that poses itself next is whether the "just" laws of the others can be seen as part of the Jewish legal tradition. On this point, the rabbinical commentaries analyzed by Rakover disagree. Some scholars see a fundamental difference between the laws laid down by God for the Jewish people and the generally applicable secular laws. Others see an intersection by means of the criterion "just."

10 The entire passage reads: "Noah's Children [Noahites] were commanded concerning seven commandments: concerning a legal system [*dinim*], concerning blasphemy, concerning idolatry, concerning sexual immorality, concerning murder, concerning theft, and concerning [eating] a limb torn from a living animal" (Tosefta Avodah Zarah 9:4).

11 Nahum Rakover, *Law and the Noahide Laws. Law as a Universal Value* (Jerusalem: Library of Jewish Law, 1998).

12 Maimonides, the authoritative eleventh-century Jewish philosopher and halachist so central to Orthodox Judaism, stated in his codex, the Mishneh Torah: "Anyone who accepts upon himself and carefully observes the Seven Commandments is of the Righteous of the Nations of the World and has a portion in the World to Come" (Kings and Wars 8:11).

In any case, the Noahide commandments lead to the theologically surprising insight that God seems to want a multi-religious world, into which he dispersed his beloved Israelites.

In the changing social realities in which the Jewish people has lived over the centuries, this reality of the law has necessarily been constantly renegotiated. That is the context in which we should read Samuel's Talmudic principle from the third century: *dina de-malkhuta dina* ('the law of the country is the law'). Usually it is understood as meaning that the laws of a non-Jewish state can be recognized as long as they are not in contradiction to the laws of the Torah. Independent of the history of the dictum, its impacts, and the varying positions taken throughout the centuries on the extent to which the laws of non-Jewish states should be recognized, particularly when they are in conflict with the Torah, the rabbinical tradition has emphasized the applicability of the secular laws of non-Jewish states for Jews as well. But usually this is understood only for Jews in the diaspora who are adapting to the conditions "in exile."

Yet from the preceding analysis, we can see that *dina de-malkhuta dina* has theological potential; namely, as an expression of the first Noahide commandment *together with* the Israelite legal canon. *Dina de-malkhuta dina* is, in each case, the secular framework within which the rabbinical discourse on the law took place in the Babylonian Talmud. And indeed, the influence of Babylonian law on the history of Jewish law can hardly be overemphasized.

Reversibility of Law into Commandment (Franz Rosenzweig)

My efforts to formulate a Jewish theology of secular law that acknowledges the tension between religious and secular law – a tension already laid down in the Torah – between the laws of God as revealed on Mount Sinai and the laws as negotiated by human beings, led me to a noteworthy debate from around a century ago between Franz Rosenzweig and Martin Buber. Over the course of the years 1923–1924, in private correspondence and in publications, the two held a dispute on whether it is possible for revelation to come in the form of "laws."[13] The contro-

13 See Martin Buber, "Heruth on Youth and Religion" (1919, reprinted in 1923), trans. Eva Jospe, in Asher Biemann (ed.), *The Martin Buber Reader Essential Writings* (New York: Palgrave, 2002), 125–38; Franz Rosenzweig, "The Builders: Concerning the Law" (1924) in Rosenzweig, *On Jewish Learning*, ed. and trans. Nahum Glatzer (Madison: University of Wisconsin Press, 1955). See also Buber's letters from 1924–5 in Nahum N. Glatzer and Paul Mendes-Flohr (eds.), *The Letters of Martin Buber:*

versy took place within the context of a discussion on the existential ability to experience God – or whether "divine freedom" (*Gottesfreiheit*) is something that people can know and, through their acts, bring into being.

Buber, in his lecture "Cherut on Youth and Religion," defended the opinion that there was no such thing as a revelation of laws. "The image of man to which we aspire," he wrote, "is incompatible with the acceptance of traditional law ... in a one-time revelation, transmitted in its entirety and binding for all time."[14] In the lecture's title, the Hebrew word *cherut* ('freedom') can also be spoken as *charut* or 'engraved,' associating it with the tablets. The rabbis were aware of these two possible readings. "Read not charut ['graven'] but cherut ['freedom']," as is stated in Pirkei Avot (Chapters of the Fathers).[15] The Jewish laws should not be understood as fixed in stone, but recognized for their liberatory potential. Buber offered a similar interpretation of the changing meanings:

> God's writing on the tablets constitutes freedom; the religious forces persistently strive to rediscover those symbols of divine freedom again. God's original tablets are broken. The religious forces of eternal renewal persistently strive to restore the blurred outlines of divine freedom on the second tablets, the tablets of the teaching and the law.[16]

But for Buber, the renewal of divine freedom could not mean "an acceptance of Jewish teaching . . . as something finished and unequivocal; nor can we commit ourselves to Jewish law if this law is taken to mean something closed and immutable."[17]

The controversy between Buber and Rosenzweig must be placed within the project of the Jewish Renaissance – a renewal of Jewish tradition by bringing religious experience into modern life. Rosenzweig answered Buber's play on the words *charut/cherut* with another Talmudic wordplay. He chose a citation that referenced the word "building" in its double sense of a fixed architecture and a creative process, to be renewed: "And all your children [*banayikh*] shall be taught of the Eternal, and great shall be the peace of your children" (Isaiah 54:13). Do not read your children [*banayikh*], but your builders [*bonayikh*]" (B. Berakhot 64a).[18]

Rosenzweig's interpretation of *banayikh* and *bonayikh* reveals his typical restorative and renewing approach. For him, Torah scholars were those who re-

---

A Life of Dialogue, trans. Richard and Clara Winston and Harry Zohn (Syracuse: Syracuse University Press, 1996).

14 Martin Buber, "Heruth on Youth and Religion," 133–4.

15 Pirkei Avot 6:2, Mishnah.

16 Martin Buber, "Heruth on Youth and Religion," 135.

17 Ibid.

18 See Franz Rosenzweig, "The Builders."

stored the tradition, not in the old way, but rather in a new way of building and thinking – a *neues Denken.*

This is the framework within which Rosenzweig's affirmation of "the law" should be understood. Rosenzweig, however, makes a distinction between "law" and "commandment." The commandment is experienced as an intrinsic part of the human being; the law, in contrast, is the external way in which the commandment is elaborated.

> The imperative of the commandment makes no provision for the future; it can only conceive the immediacy of obedience. If it were to think of a future or an Ever, it would be, not commandment nor order, but law. Law reckons with times, with a future, with duration. The commandment knows only the moment ... Thus the commandment is purely the present. ... All of revelation is subsumed under the great today. God commands "today," and "today" it is incumbent to obey his voice. It is in the today that the love of the lover lives, in this imperative today of the commandment.[19]

Buber retorted:

> I do not believe that revelation is ever a formulation of Law. It is only through man in his self-contradiction that revelation becomes legislation. This is the fact of man. I cannot admit the Law transformed by man into my will, if I am to hold myself ready as well for the unmediated Word of God directed to a specific hour of life.[20]

Rosenzweig countered that for him, too, revelation was not equivalent to legislation:

> Even for him who observes the law, revelation is not what you call law-giving. On this Day [*bajom hase; Exodus* 19:1] – that is his theory of experience as well as yours. He as well as you deems it unfortunate that the commandment issued "on that day" should give rise to the old law. We do not consciously accept the fact that every commandment can become law, but that *the law can always be changed back into a commandment*, a fact you know so well.[21]

For Rosenzweig, the legal validity of the law was connected to its reversibility back into a commandment. The immediate power of the commandment, with its existential meaning for all things, must reside behind each law.

---

19 Franz Rosenzweig, *The Star of Redemption*, trans. William W. Hallo (New York: Holt, Rinehart and Winston, 1970 [1921]), 177.

20 Buber to Rosenzweig, 24 June 1924 in Glatzer and Mendes-Flohr, *The Letters of Martin Buber*, 315.

21 Rosenzweig to Buber, 29 June 1924, in ibid., 316 (emphasis is my own).

This idea, which can be conceived of as a theory of a "relative law" – the relation of the law to the commandment – was drawn from Rosenzweig's theological interpretation of a "first commandment." He, too, in *The Star of Redemption*, elevated one commandment above all others, one to which every other commandment and law within the Torah could be traced: "You shall love the Eternal your God with all your heart and with all your soul and with all your might."[22]

The commandment to love was, for Rosenzweig, the commandment of all commandments. But love as a commandment can only be formulated as a positive directive, and can only be experienced by people as pure presence. God's imperative of "love me" is, as Rosenzweig says, "simply incapable of being law; it can only be commandment."[23] Only in the concretization of loving one's neighbor does the Torah express the commandment to love in the negative, in the form of "you shall not," hence as a "law" that sets limits.

> They cannot assume the garb of laws except as prohibitions, as the delineation of the boundaries of that which can on no account be reconciled with love of neighbor. Their positive aspect, their "you shall," can only be expressed in the form of the one-and-all commandment of love. The commandments in the garb of positive laws are for the most part ritual laws; they are the sign language of the love for God, amplifications, that is, of the "first tablet."[24]

The Law of Liberation

The idea of summarizing all laws in one commandment was not new. In rabbinical Judaism, until Christianity achieved religious hegemony, there had been multiple attempts to reduce all Jewish laws to one single principle. Hillel consolidated it in the famous statement: "That which is hateful to you do not do to another; that is the entire Torah, and the rest is its interpretation. Go study" (B. Shabbat 31a). In the talmudic tractate Makkot, the sages attempted to consolidate the 613 laws of the Torah into one moral principle that ends with the word *tzedek*, justice and righteousness.[25] In this context, it is revealing to look also at the Talmudic debate on the recitation of the Ten Commandments. Originally, they were recited in services before the *Shema* (the affirmation of monotheism). But because members of proto-Christian sects became ever more insistent that the true revelation

22 Franz Rosenzweig, *The Star of Redemption*, 176. "Thou" in the translation has been changed to you to reflect Rosenzweig's use of the informal "du" in German.

23 Ibid., 177.

24 Ibid., 216.

25 B. Makkot 23b-24a.

was the Ten Commandments and that the ritual laws were only secondary, the rabbis took the Ten Commandments out of the daily liturgy.[26] With this, a creative rabbinical tradition of interpreting the laws could develop, one which consciously embraced the diversity of sometimes contradictory laws, while at the same time creating a taboo around determining a first or primary principle. For any such principle would by necessity imply a weighting, and mean that some laws would be overruled. This taboo made it possible for all of the laws to continue to apply equally – at least theoretically – even when they were diametrically opposed, no longer practiced, or in contradiction to newer laws.

Yet in *The Star of Redemption*, Rosenzweig establishes a "first" commandment – the commandment to love. At the same time, he distinguishes between the two tablets. The commandments to love God are phrased predominantly in a positive manner on the first tablet. The second tablet, on the other hand, is made up of mostly negative phrases, stating that which is incompatible with loving one's neighbor. These negative commandments, as prohibitions spoken by God, implicitly also contain the commandment to love God. But in their "you shall not," they at the same time hold a secular potential, specified by human beings in other laws. In the end, it is on the second tablet that the first Noahide commandment is mirrored. The five commandments on the second tablet, which forbid murder, adultery, theft, false witness, and coveting one's neighbors' possessions, are found in similar wording in the seven Noahide commandments, as prohibitions against "forbidden sexual relations; and bloodshed; and robbery." And as prohibitions, they necessitate a judicial system to penalize transgressions.[27]

Rosenzweig's disinterest in the second First Commandment – the Noahide commandment to establish secular courts of justice – can be seen in the fact that it plays no role in his discussion of the reality of the commandments/laws. Most likely this is also due to his ambivalent attitude toward the role of the state in personal religious renewal. For the man who wrote his dissertation, "Hegel and the State," on Hegel's political theology of the state in conflict with the Christian subject (Jesus), this tension was not an issue for his Jewish understanding of the commandments/laws. In fact, in *The Star of Redemption*, Rosenzweig conceives of the Jewish people as outside political history. The Jewish holidays instead celebrate a redeemed eternity beyond the necessity of a legal secular system. Christianity in contrast, as Rosenzweig saw it, shapes the state of the world through both state and church. For Rosenzweig, a Jewish theology of secular law, perhaps combined with a renewal of the Jewish legal tradition as not only the rit-

26 B. Berakhot 12a; Y. Berakhot 1:5; see also Sifre Devarim 6:34

27 Exodus 20: 13–14; B. Sanhedrin 56b.

ual enactment of the commandment to love but also as a dynamic of religion and secularity in the present political world, was an impossibility.

But that need not mean that Rosenzweig's theory of relational law is not useful to the present analysis. Distinguishing between the mostly positively formulated commandments on the first tablet and the negative laws on the second creates a tension between the two tablets. It also points toward the second First Commandment because the creation of a legal system is implicit in the prohibitions of the second tablet.

In order to articulate a theology of secular law, it is imperative to think both tablets *together* – to recognize their internal connection, as was the custom in rabbinical Judaism, *without* prioritizing one side over the other. It is precisely within the tension between the first and the second tablet or, put another way, between the theocratic claim that God expresses toward his people and the secular striving of human beings, that we can first recognize a Jewish theology of secular law. The two tablets are eternally connected and the tension between them is fundamental to this connection. The two sides interpenetrate one another.

God's theocratic claim is however not fixed. Let us look again at the start of the first of the Ten Commandments: "I the Eternal am your God who brought you out of the land of Egypt, the house of bondage." Here, God presents himself as a commandment, or as a legal structure, namely the first of the Ten Commandments. But his presentation of himself as an eternal law includes an active gesture: "... who brought you out of the land of Egypt, the house of bondage." The kind of law that emerges from this first commandment need not be fixed and repressive; it can also be emancipatory. There have always been two understandings of the function of law. One sees it as cementing a preexisting, hierarchical order, while the other understands law as a means to enable liberation and emancipation.[28]

God's theocratic "I" as the start of an emancipatory movement can become a liberating inspiration in a secular system of law. The inner, legal connection between God and the liberation from slavery, oppression, and disenfranchisement can constitute a dynamic understanding of the law. Taking God as the starting point of this legal conception would lead to writing laws that would change society. This conception of law understands itself as against repressive legal orders that uphold static, hierarchical structures in which human beings have a fixed status (royalty, slave, worker, etc.). It is the beginning of a Jewish theology of secular law. It presupposes a secular legal order (that is, a state under the rule of law), while link-

28 Hauke Brunkhorst, "Internalisierung der Transzendenz. Die wiederholte Aufhebung der alteuropäischen Tradition in den Rechtsrevolutionen Europas," *Babylon. Beiträge zur jüdischen Gegenwart* 23 (March 2010), 63 and 65.

ing it to a theocratic legal dynamic that leads out of "Egypt, the house of bondage." Not a secular legal system alone, but a secular legal system in connection with a theocratic claim can bring an emancipatory legal logic into society and act as a corrective to current laws. In a Jewish theology of secular law, those laws hold true that aid the emancipation from injustice, oppression, and benightedness. These are also paths that lead to and reflect the Torah and how its religio-secular approach unfolds within secular legal systems. The Torah is truly no longer in the heavens.

References

Biale, David. *Not in the Heavens. The Tradition of Jewish Secular Thought.* Princeton: Princeton University Press, 2011.

Klapheck, Elisa. "Das religiös-säkulare Spannungsfeld des Judentums." in *Machloket/ Streitschriften, vol. 1 Säkulares Judentum aus religiöser Quelle*, contributions by Ruth Calderon and Elisa Klapheck, 9–47. Berlin: Hentrich & Hentrich, 2015.

Rakover, Nahum. *Law and the Noahide Laws. Law as a Universal Value.* Jerusalem: Library of Jewish Law, 1998.

Buber, Martin. "Heruth on Youth and Religion" (1919, reprinted in 1923). Translated by Eva Jospe. In *The Martin Buber Reader Essential Writings*, edited by Asher Biemann, 125–138. New York: Palgrave, 2002.

Rosenzweig, Franz. "The Builders: Concerning the Law" (1924). In Rosenzweig, *On Jewish Learning*, edited and translated by Nahum Glatzer. Madison: University of Wisconsin Press, 1955.

Glatzer, Nahum N. and Paul Mendes-Flohr, eds. *The Letters of Martin Buber: A Life of Dialogue.* Translated by Richard and Clara Winston and Harry Zohn. Syracuse: Syracuse University Press, 1996.

Rosenzweig, Franz. *The Star of Redemption.* Translated by William W. Hallo. New York: Holt, Rinehart and Winston, 1970 [1921].

Brunkhorst, Hauke. "Internalisierung der Transzendenz. Die wiederholte Aufhebung der alteuropäischen Tradition in den Rechtsrevolutionen Europas." *Babylon. Beiträge zur jüdischen Gegenwart* 23 (March 2010): 61–73.

IV. Legal Pluralism in Concrete Action

Stephan M. Probst

Halacha and Medical Law at the End of Life

Introduction

Medicine is able to extend life more effectively than ever before and thus fulfill the halachic command of *pikuach nefesh.* Many diseases that would have proven deadly in the past can now be either healed by modern medicine or at least treated as chronic conditions. Thus, our life expectancy is much longer than that of previous generations. However, we must take into consideration that over time, the last chapters of our lives may be riddled with chronic diseases, pain, and other restrictions. The risk of suffering from dementia and requiring a high level of care is also a valid cause of concern. Ethical and legal foundations for medical interventions at the end of life have necessarily become the focus of controversial scientific and societal debate.

If we take a critical look at the day-to-day operations of our care facilities, doctors offices, and medical clinics, we must admit to sometimes believing in the omnipotence of our high-tech medicine far beyond what is healthy. We also have to ask ourselves if the additional time bought by modern medicine is actually always worth living. Our post-modern society measures the value of a person not so much by their humanity as by their independence, achievements, and status. The value a person attributes to their own life is influenced significantly by the value others attribute to it. That is one reason why no one wants to become dependent upon others for care due to chronic illness and debilitation. Some either wish or are compelled by societal expectation to exercise their right to self-determination by maintaining control over the end of their lives, or in some cases, by even prematurely ending life itself.

Studies have shown during the last few years that a majority of people consider being able to determine the time and the circumstances of their own death to be the epitome of autonomy and self-determination. In a 2003 study of 700 German physicians published in 2015, 20 % of physicians polled admitted to having been asked to partake in physician-assisted suicide. Altogether, 40 % could imagine participating under certain circumstances, while 40 % could not at all, with the remaining 20 % undecided. The study also showed that in 10 % of all deaths accompanied by doctors, pain medications were prescribed in doses intended to shorten life. In about 50 % of those cases, treatment was either shortened or ceased in

Note: Summary of the Workshop "Medical Law" at the 2019 Annual Conference

https://doi.org/10.1515/9783111062631-009

order to decrease life expectancy. Euthanasia by request was listed in 1% of cases as the result of accompaniment by the physician at end of life. The study showed that doctors partake in the complete spectrum of possible end-of-life interventions, from the limitation (via withholding or withdrawing) of treatment, to physician-assisted suicide, to euthanasia upon request (Schildmann et al. 2015).

As part of the necessary debate about the multitude of questions surrounding the end of life, we encounter within society diverse concepts of dignity, what constitutes both good living and good dying, as well as the rights and responsibilities of citizens, doctors, and other health-care professionals. Awareness and knowledge of the halachic or Jewish-medical approach to such questions may be helpful when practical solutions are sought for issues residing in the legal grey zone and/or in response to moral conflicts.

The Nearly Absolute Value of Life and the Principle of Autonomy

Judaism is known for its notably high estimation of earthly life. This is not surprising given the history of the Jewish people of being faced since olden days through the present with persecution and pending threats of annihilation. What rabbi and philosopher Leo Baeck deemed "endlose Lebenspflicht" is a normative core principle of Judaism (*pikuach nefesh* or 'the unending duty to live').[1] Its theological foundation stems from the halachic concept that life has been given to humanity from God and is, so to speak, "on loan." Thus, humanity is obligated to take care of that which has been borrowed from the Creator by maintaining health. Considered "God given," life itself takes priority over all else. The value and dignity of an individual life cannot be altered or reduced by suffering, lack of productivity, debility, or physical or psychological constraints, regardless of how much longer a person has to live. Judaism teaches that the frail and suffering are in particular need of help, and that the presence of God is immanent in our elders.

> One who enters to visit the sick person should sit neither on the bed nor on a chair; rather he should wrap himself in his prayer shawl with trepidation and awe, and sit before the sick person below him, as the Divine Presence is above the head of the sick person, as it is stated: "God will support him on the bed of illness," and he must treat the Divine Presence with deference. (B. Talmud, Shabbat, 12b)

1 Leo Baeck, *Das Wesen des Judentums*, in *Leo Baeck Werke*, ed. Albert Friedlander et. al. (Gütersloh, Germany: Gütersloher Verlagshaus, 2019, 199.

No consensus exists in our diverse, postmodern society dictating that a person must choose life. Furthermore, no such consensus exists as to what constitutes a good life or a good death. Individuals are on their own when it comes to sorting through and making sense of a plethora of value systems and lifestyle choices. Thus, the principle of autonomy has become the accepted ethical framework by default for everyone. According to Article 1 of the German constitution, "human dignity shall be inviolable. To respect and protect it shall be the duty of all state authority."[2]

Autonomy, as seen within the medical world, is an expression of individual freedom and as a right of refusal. Free people are permitted to decline interference from others in both how they live and how they die. Since an obligation to choose life does not exist, all medical interventions – including those that extend and save lives – require the consent of the patient.

The Wish to Die at the End of Life

People who experience the final phase of their lives as unbearable and hopeless due to their suffering often express the wish to die. This concerns not only their family members, but also their medical providers and caregivers – especially when they are Jewish. They most commonly fear that a conversation about death may destroy hope too soon or become too emotional. Another fear is that talking about end-of-life preferences might result in wishes being expressed that the caregiver may not want or be allowed to fulfill. The Halacha forbids any measures that hasten death even by a moment. According to German law, euthanasia is a punishable offense. In Germany, businesslike assistance with suicide was banned in November of 2015. Even though suicide itself is not punishable, assisting suicide in certain cases was.

> One may not close the eyes of a dying person (gosses); one who touches him to move him is a murderer. R. Meir would say: "It is compared to a sputtering candle which is extinguished as soon as a person touches it – so, too, whoever closes the eyes of a dying person is considered to have taken his soul." (Beraita, Semachot 1:4)

German Criminal Code Section 216[3]

> Killing upon request

2 Artikel 1, GG, Grundgesetz für die Bundesrepublik Deutschland.
3 § 216 StGB, Strafgesetzbuch für die Bundesrepublik Deutschland.

1. Whoever is induced to kill at the expressed and earnest request of the person killed incurs a penalty of imprisonment for a term of between six months and five years.
2. The attempt is punishable.

German Criminal Code Section 217[4]

Facilitating suicide as recurring pursuit

1. Whoever, with the intention of assisting another person to commit suicide, provides, procures or arranges the opportunity for that person to do so and whose actions are intended as a recurring pursuit incurs a penalty of imprisonment for a term not exceeding three years or a fine.
2. A participant whose actions are not intended as a recurring pursuit and who is either a relative of or is close to the person referred to in subsection (1) is exempt from punishment.

The wish to die is usually much more complex than assumed. It can be brought about by a person having exhausted their will to live, as well as from acceptance of impending death and the wish to not fight against it anymore. The wish to die can express itself acutely via suicide or as a sincere and serious wish to hasten death as part of the right of self-determination. At the bedside of a terminally ill person, a conversation about the wish to die can be such a relief as to mitigate the death wish itself. Discussing the wish to die can open the door to palliative care – care which can successfully ease the patient's suffering such as to counteract their wish to die sooner. Thus the remaining time to live is sometimes reinvigorated with purpose and content. It often comes to the fore in conversation with the dying that the wish to die and the will to live often coexist, as well as just how much they change over time in their respective intensity. Proper understanding of the wish to die and its causes is a prerequisite for competent accompaniment of people who wish to die (Probst 2017; Kremeike et al. 2019).

Avoiding discussions about the wish to die – whether because the fulfillment of the wish to die or even a discussion thereof might be considered punishable – does not protect the terminally ill in any way, but rather strengthens their suffering and vulnerability. Thus, open discussion of these questions is of great importance from legal, ethical, halachic, psychological, and medical perspectives.

4 § 217 StGB, Strafgesetzbuch für die Bundesrepublik Deutschland.

The Distinction between Sustaining Life and Prolonging Dying

The Jewish understanding of life as on loan from God limits the right to self-determination of the ill. In contrast to secular laws, the Halacha insists upon the sustenance of life, prohibiting not only the killing of another human being, but also suicide. The Halacha implicitly states that even a life drawing to a close is of infinite and indivisible value. It is forbidden to do anything that would change the condition of the dying person once the dying process has begun. The life in the process of ending must be honored and the natural dying process left to unfold, undisturbed and without being hastened. "A dying person (*gosses*) is considered to be alive in every respect ... whoever touches him is a murderer – one should wait a short while, as perhaps he is in a swoon" (Maimonides, Mishne Torah, Hilchot Avel, 4:5).

When seen in light of the above reference, modern medicine blurs the boundary between life and death such that it becomes difficult to determine when the dying process has commenced and when the ill person has become a *gosses*. The religious obligation to sustain and save life often leads to an over-estimation of the power of medicine. Thus, therapies are often continued that prolong suffering, and in the worst-case scenario, actually lead to people either wanting to die or increasing an already existing wish to do so. This demonstrates the importance of doctors having candid conversations with the ill and their families about the wish to die and to flush out the causes for such wishes together. Patients who wish to die (because they are being kept alive by medical interventions that are extending the irreversible death process) do not need to take matters into their own hands in order to die. They are not going against the Halacha by exercising their autonomy as a patient and choosing to refuse a therapy in order to die instead. On the contrary, it would be questionable for a physician in this case to give an ill person and their family false hope and to respond to the wish to die with a reminder of the obligation to save life and encourage the patient to continue to participate in a futile therapy.

During the twelfth century, Rabbi Judah ben Samuel of Regensburg (1150–1217) detailed the difference between two diametrically opposed interventions at the end of life: namely, actively inducing death (which is also forbidden to do to a *gosses*) via assisted suicide and suicide on the one hand, and the removal of impediments to dying on the other. In the case of a gosses, allowing death to occur is a mitzvah and in no way murder or suicide. In some cases, it can even be the fulfillment of a wish to die:

> If person is suffering terrible pain, and he tells someone: "You can see that I am not going to live; kill me, as I cannot suffer any more," one may not touch him ... whereas Saul was permitted [to shorten his life] to prevent a desecration of the divine name before Israel.
>
> If a person suffers great pain, and he knows he cannot live, he may not commit suicide. This we learn from Rabbi Chanina ben Teradyon, who did not want to open his mouth. But if there are factors preventing a speedy demise – such as a man chopping wood in the vicinity of a dying man's home, and the noise of the chopping prevents the soul from escaping – we remove the chopper from there. Likewise we do not place salt on his tongue to prevent his death. But if he is dying and says, "I cannot die until you put me in a different place," they may not move him from there. (Sefer Chassidim, chapter 723, followed by chapter 234)

Palliative Care

Palliative care at its best affirms life and regards dying as a normal process. This kind of care neither hastens nor postpones death. It aims to preserve the best possible quality of life until death (EAPC 2009). Unfortunately, the German term for allowing the death process to occur, namely, *passive Sterbehilfe*('passive euthanasia'), is highly confusing and in Germany historically problematic. In order to make clear that no active hastening of death is occurring, in German one now only uses the term *Sterbenlassen* ('allowing death to occur'). Allowing death to occur may entail abstaining from a therapy prolonging death or interrupting a recently commenced therapy. The goal is to allow the terminally ill and dying person to die of their illness. Respect for life and the dying patient form the ethical foundation. When the therapeutic interventions used by the physicians to control or fight the disease no longer have positive effects upon the patient and only prolong suffering, those interventions are no longer indicated. At that point, the patient should be able to expect the doctor to halt the unnecessary treatments. This does not mean that the physician is killing the patient via negligence, but rather that the illness is allowed to take its natural course. It also does not mean that a patient is being given up on or that something useful is being kept from them. On the contrary, it means that they are being protected from false or contraindicated measures. Under no circumstances may a dying person be given a deadly amount of medication. The Halacha gives these exact instructions, as well as the injunction to halt any interventions which have commenced but prove to be contraindicated once in progress. We have to know how to turn the words in to practice and be able to recognize in individual, specific cases what is getting in the way of the person being able to die. We must clearly define and delineate which modern means constitute illegal physician-assisted death and what constitutes contemporary impediments to dying.

> It is forbidden to cause the dying to die quickly, such as one who is moribund over a long time and cannot die, it is forbidden to remove the pillow from under him on the assumption that certain bird feathers prevent his death. So, too, one cannot remove the key of the synagogue from beneath his head, or remove him so that he may die. But if there is something that delays his death, such as a nearby woodchopper making a noise, or there is salt on his tongue, and these prevent his speedy death, one can remove them, for this does not involve any action at all, but rather the removal of the preventative agent. (Rema (R. Moshe Isserles) on Shulchan Aruch, Yoreh Deah, 339:1)

Furthermore, Rabbi Solomon Eger (1786–1852), in his commentary on Yoreh Deah 339:1, quotes another rabbinic authority (Beit Yaakov, 59), who states: "It is forbidden to hinder the departure of the soul by the use of medicines." In the Talmud we find a very early and prominent precedent for allowing death to occur by removing any procedure that artificially extends the dying process. First there are the prayers of the students that must be interrupted by the servant so that the rabbi's soul is able to leave his body, thereby ending his torturous and dignity-robbing dying process:

> It is related that on the day that Rabbi Yehuda HaNasi died, the Sages decreed a fast, and begged for divine mercy so that he would not die. And they said: Anyone who says that Rabbi Yehuda HaNasi has died will be stabbed with a sword. The maidservant of Rabbi Yehuda HaNasi ascended to the roof and said: "The upper realms are requesting the presence of Rabbi Yehuda HaNasi. May it be the will of God that the lower worlds should impose their will upon the upper worlds." However, when she saw how many times he would enter the bathroom and remove his phylacteries, and then exit and put them back on, and how he was suffering from his intestinal disease, she said: "May it be the will of God that the upper worlds should impose their will upon the lower worlds." And the Sages, meanwhile, would be be silent, i. e., they would not refrain from begging for mercy so that Rabbi Yehuda HaNasi would not die. So she took a jug (kuza) and threw it from the roof to the ground. Due to the sudden noise, the Sages were momentarily silent and refrained from begging for mercy, and Rabbi Yehuda HaNasi died. (B. Talmud, Ketubot 104a)

When Continuing to Live Means Only Torture and Pain

Sometimes the remaining life span of a dying person is taken up by the most horrible torture and pain, or the inability to breathe destroys every remaining bit of quality of life. As we have already determined, this can lead to a person wishing to be freed by death. From both a legal (and a halachic) perspective, a life that is filled with suffering need not be tolerated at any cost. The alleviation of suffering takes priority overextending life. In order to attain an acceptable level of symptom alleviation, the law allows that the risk be taken that in the process of treating symptoms, the medication used may unintentionally accelerate the dying process. In Germany, the description used during the last few years has referred to *Therapien am Lebensende* ('therapies at the end of life') to describe this situation. This term has replaced the previous *indirekte Sterbehilfe* ('indirect euthanasia'), not least of all in order to gain distance from an otherwise illegitimate, purposeful overdose of pain medication. Any such attempt to purposely shorten life would be an act of euthanasia in disguise. From a legal and moral perspective, the intention behind the action to improve quality of life at the end of life is what counts, as long as it is by no means an attempt to hasten death (Kučera 2016, CCAR 1992, Jacob 1995).

Both liberal rabbis and orthodox decisors of Jewish law follow this argumentation, and consider the alleviation of suffering the fulfillment of such a significant mitzvah, that they are willing to take the risk that death might be hastened in the process involuntarily (Steinberg 2003). Yet the fear that a consequent pain management regiment or treatment of symptoms using opioids and benzodiazepines in the case of asphyxiation attacks may lead to hastened death has been shown by science to be mostly a hypothetical consideration. New studies show that the early inclusion of palliative medical expertise leads to less aggressive treatment and that patients live longer rather than shorter, with better quality of life. Even palliative sedation – as a last resort in the case of unmanageable pain – does not hasten death, but rather enables a peaceful transition into death. Palliative medicine does not espouse giving up or a fatalistic view, nor does it come into conflict with the mitzvah of *pikuach nefesh.* It can in many but not all cases provide ill patients who wish to die with positive and life-affirming options. (Sykes and Thorns 2003; Temel et al. 2010; Probst 2019)

Patient Autonomy at the End of Life

No one can truly place themselves in the situation of a suffering, terminally ill person. Proverbs 14:10 tells us: *The heart knows its own bitterness.* When a patient cannot even consider palliative sedation as an acceptable alternative to the suffering they see coming, some wish to use their freedom of choice to ultimately use the right, by their own choice, to end their own lives ahead of schedule. If these patients are practicing Jews, the following questions arise: Do extreme situations exist in which a person may return the gift of life to the Creator? Are an individual's dignity and autonomy valued more highly than the injunction to sustain life? The ban against suicide and assisted suicide —even under the pressure of unbearable pain – is supported with reference to the ancient narrative about the death as a martyr by Rabbi Chanina ben Teradyon. As we read earlier, Rabbi Judah ben Samuel of Regensburg referred to this narrative. The extensive description of the exact conditions found in the Talmud are worthy of careful consideration:

> They took Rabbi Chanina ben Teradyon and wrapped a Torah scroll around him, and encompassed him with faggots of vine branches, to which they set fire. They brought woolen tufts, soaked them with water, and laid them to his heart, so that his soul should not depart quickly. (...) His disciples said to him: "Open your mouth that the fire may penetrate." He replied, "Better is it that He who gave the soul should take it, and that a man should do himself no injury." Then the executioner said to him: "Master, if I increase the flame and remove the woolen tufts from off thy heart, will you bring me a taste of the of the life of the world-to-come?" "Yes," said Chanina. "Swear it," demanded the executioner. Chanina took the oath. Forthwith the officer increased the flame and removed the woolen tufts from over Chanina's heart, and his soul departed quickly. (B. Talmud, Avodah Zarah, 18a)

At the beginning of his martyrdom, Rabbi Chanina ben Teradyon clearly disagrees with the advice of his students to breathe in smoke and flame, because to do so would constitute actively shortening his life. As his torturous execution continues, he agrees not only to the removal of the wool, but also in the face of increasing pain and torture, he also explicitly allows the intensification of the very flames which will bring him the salvation of death. In the halachic discussion during the past few decades, some scholars have seen this in extreme cases as support for active assistance in dying. They have considered whether loss of dignity in the face of increasing mental or physical incapacitation, or if unmanageable or intolerable pain which exhaust the will of the elderly to live are justifications for both suicide and assisted suicide alike. In the wake of the brutal crusades during the Middle Ages, the Ashkenazic tradition changed its judgment of suicide. Fear of impending torture and torturous execution became valid justifications for killing oneself and thus, suicide was no longer deemed murder of the self: "In a time of persecutions, it is allowed to kill oneself if one is afraid of suffering" (Piskei ha-Tosafot, Cod. Parma 2421 [De Rossi 107], fol. 49a).

Today it is valid to ask if impending dementia and painful end-of-life conditions resulting from terminal illness can be seen in a similar light (Kravitz 1995, Klein and Teutsch 2018). If this comparison is deemed legitimate, the same would apply to assisted suicide. Otherwise, instigating a person to commit suicide or assisting suicide is considered even worse than the suicide itself. The helper minimally violates Leviticus 19:14, which states "do not put a stumbling block before the blind." The aide is guilty of misleading the sick to think that a forbidden act may be permissible. Worse, he enables the patient to commit the forbidden act, thereby encouraging the patient to commit a sin (Dorff 2003, p. 183).

You Shall Love Your Neighbor As Yourself

In order to allow for a milder position in regard to passive euthanasia, suicide, and physician-aided dying, scholars also work with the following analogy: At the time that the death penalty still formally existed in antique Jewry, those slated to die must be granted an execution as free from pain and fear as possible. The talmudic expression for securing a humane death during execution is *mitah yafah.* The obligation to do so is is found in Leviticus 19:18: "You shall love your neighbor as yourself." In the same fashion as an ill person approaching a painful or undignified dying process, a person awaiting execution faces an inescapable, foreseeable, and likely painful and undignified death. Byron L. Sherwin asks why a convicted criminal is guaranteed a gentle and speedy death when the same is withheld from an innocent ill person (Sherwin 1990, 93–101).

Gosses, Treifah, Chayyeh Sha'ah

The talmudic concepts of treifah and chayyeh sha'ah are both plausible and helpful – albeit not completely uncontroversial – in making a halachic assessment of the unclearly defined situation modern medicine has created in which the ill hover for long periods of time in the grey zone between life and death. When the Halacha mentions a dying person, it is most often referring to a gosses. This is a person who, regardless of cause, has entered the dying process and can be expected to die within seventy-two hours. Rabbi Moshe Feinstein described a gosses as "comparable to a clock that is running down." He goes on:

> Hakadosh Baruch Hu declared that death shall be the experience of man. Thus, there is a finite time that man can live. The gosses is an individual whose time has come. Lacking any specific pathology, he is not classified as a treifah but as a normal member of society. Shortening his life is tantamount to taking the life of a healthy person. This is why the sages warn that a gosses should not be touched. But this prohibition does not apply to the treifah. (Feinstein 1996)

Several scholars suggest that modern dying often fits more into the category of the treifah, one who is clearly and severely terminally ill and will die within twelve months. The diagnostic capabilities available to modern medicine today make it more possible than ever to offer reliable prognoses and to recognize illnesses which, despite maximum use of all possible therapeutic uses, will inevitably end in death within twelve months. According to Maimonides, a treifah person is alive yet dying (Mishneh Torah, Issurei Bi'ah 1:12).

In talmudic criminal law, the distinction between treifah and gosses played a significant role. To state it simply, whoever killed a gosses was punished as a murderer. However, someone who killed a treifah was not seen according to talmudic criminal law as a murderer subject to earthly punishment. That person's guilt and punishment was left solely to the Creator. According to some rabbis and scholars, the consideration of a special category treifah allows for a more lenient assessment of allowing death to occur, suicide, and in some cases, assistance with suicide for some ill who are classified as treifah. A person must not agree with a treifah's wish to die or recommend assistance with dying; however, it is acceptable to approach their wish to die with empathy and respect. The suicide of treifot should not be considered murder of self, but rather accepted (Segal 2002).

As demonstrated by a passage from the Babylonian Talmud, which introduces the important term chayyeh sha'ah, the diagnosis of the status of a treifah for medical therapy decisions is relevant in terms of the Halacha. The fact that a treifah may still have a significant life expectancy and yet be faced with inevitable death and poor quality of life may have led to a unique situation requiring special consideration. This may account for what initially appears to be quite a strange diction in the Babylonian Talmud:

> Rava says that Rabbi Yohanan says, and some say that it was Rav Chisda who says that Rabbi Yochanan says: If there is uncertainty as to whether a patient will live through his ailment or die from it, the patient may not be treated by gentile doctors, due to the concern that a gentile doctor may kill him [or let him die]. But if it is certain that he will die from his affliction if he does not receive medical attention, the patient is treated by them, as it is possible that a gentile physician will save him. (B. Talmud Avoda Zarah 27b)

Rabbi Elliot N. Dorff comments:

> It is clear, then, that the Talmud defines 'the life of the hour' (*chayyeh sha'ah*)[5] as the time a person lives after being diagnosed as having a terminal illness. After that time, we need not try to cure a person who, as far as we know, cannot be cured, and therefore we may employ the services of a nearby gentile doctor rather than going to the trouble of hunting for a Jewish one. This is probably not because the rabbis assumed that Jewish doctors are more skilled than gentile ones; it is rather because they were worried that gentile doctors might not do their best in healing Jews and might even do things that would hasten a Jewish patient's death. In our setting, this means that if the patient is dying of a terminal disease, we may relinquish aggressive medical treatments, even if it is effective in prolonging vital organs. We then may, and probably should, concentrate instead on relieving pain. (Dorff 2003, 204)

5 Translation is my own.

The talmudic ruling may thus be construed that we may interpret the Halacha while making end-of-life decisions with a gentle flexibility, which also acknowledges the death wishes of a terminally ill patient and accepts them in extreme individual cases. Keeping in mind that the tosafot to Avodah Zarah 27b articulate the general principle that the proper objective of medical care of a patient is to act in the patient's benefit. It is not always to the patient's benefit to continue living, and in most cases the patient knows best what is best for them and what constitutes quality of life. Nonetheless, the general position in Judaism is as follows, noting that Rabbi Dorff speaks not only for conservative Jews:

> A Jew may not commit suicide, ask others to help in committing suicide, or assist in the suicide of someone else. Withholding or withdrawing machines or medications from a terminally ill patients, however, does not constitute suicide and is permitted. In my view, one may withhold or withdraw artificial nutrition or hydration from a such a patient, for that, too, falls outside the prohibitions of suicide and assisted suicide. (Dorff 2000)

Legal Uncertainty Despite or Due to Section 217 of the German Criminal Code

Much more controversial and less clear than the halachic discussion regarding the permissibility of physician-assisted suicide or the complex considerations around usage of the categories gosses, treifah and chayyeh sha'ah are the discussion and jurisprudence in Germany since the enactment of German Criminal Code Section 217 in November 2015. The legal implications have yet to be clarified in depth. Professionals who accompany the dying are unsettled as they must fear that a conversation around the wish to die could be interpreted as providing suicide assistance – especially in cases in which the professionals can relate to a patient's wish to die, deem certain suicides acceptable, and then accompany patients who intend to end their own lives.

Shortly following the enactment of this law, 151 legal scholars published a resolution against Section 217 in *medstra*, the German medical criminal law journal. Since April 2019, the German Federal Constitutional Court (Bundesverfassungsgericht) has heard numerous petitions from deathly ill patients, palliative care physicians, and professional suicide assistants against the ban of assisted suicide on a professional basis. In the meantime, the decision of the Federal Constitutional Court's judges remains awaited in response to a judgment passed by the Federal

Administrative Court in 2017.[6] At that time, the Federal Administrative Court (Bundesverwaltungsgericht) decided that in extreme individual cases, the state could not bar a terminally ill person's access to sedatives intended for suicide. This was precipitated by the Federal Institute for Pharmaceuticals and Medicinal Products' (Bundesinstitut für Arzneimittel und Medizinprodukte [BfArM]) decision to deny a petition of such a patient. Does the state's responsibility to protect life take a back seat to the right of the individual to choose suicide? Representatives of the German Foundation for Patient Protection made their positions clear in the media, stating their opinion that "a federal agency may not assume the prohibited work of suicide assistance." In contrast, the Federal Court of Justice (Bundesgerichtshof) pardoned two physicians in July 2019 who accepted the death wishes of their patients, did not try to prevent them, and accompanied them while they committed suicide.

Voluntary Stopping of Eating and Drinking (VSED)

Since 2017, the question of whether or not voluntary stopping of eating and drinking (VSED) presents a legal opportunity for a person to choose their own death by initiating the process leading to death (Jox et al. 2017). The German Federal Medical Association (Bundesärztekammer) stated its position to Section 217 not to consider accompaniment of VSED as suicide assistance. The German Association of Palliative Medicine (DGP) stated in February 2019 that the voluntary refusal to eat and drink should neither be considered suicide nor a discontinuation of therapy. VSED should be considered a unique category of action (DGP 2019). In the meantime, physicians are increasingly recommending VSED to patients who express the continuous and justified wish to die. A medieval midrash touches upon refusal to eat and drink as a "natural" means of causing death:

> It happened that a woman who had aged considerably appeared before Rabbi Yose ben Chalafta. She said, "Rabbi, I am much too old. Life has become a burden for me. I can no longer taste food or drink, and I wish to die." Rabbi Yose answered her: "To what do you ascribe your

6 On 26 February 2020, three months after the conference took place that this text was written for, the German Federal Court announced its decision that Section 217 is in violation of the Basic Law (*Grundgesetz*) and declared it nullified. While the removal of suicide assistance from the criminal code is seen as generally positive, many questions remain as new questions arise. The Federal Court acknowledged the reasoning and motivation for Section 217 while defining the right to suicide as an expression of self-determination (as well as that of a self-determined death) as so fundamental, that all necessary rules and regulations need be subordinate to this right without impediment.

longevity?" She answered that it was her habit to pray in the synagogue every morning, and despite occasional more pressing needs, she had never missed a service. Rabbi Yose advised her to refrain from attending services for three consecutive days. She heeded his advice and on the third day she took ill and died. (Yalkut Shimoni, Ekev 871)

Is refusal to partake in life-sustaining daily prayer in the synagogue or refusal to imbibe life-sustaining nourishment and drink suicide? And how shall VSED accompaniment by physicians be assessed? Is it suicide assistance and thus a violation of the law set forth in German Criminal Code Section 217? How is this seen in terms of the Halacha? May a Jew voluntarily refuse food and drink in order to hasten death? May a Jewish physician suggest VSED as a course of action and may that physician accompany the patient who chooses this path?

The Difference between VSED and the Natural Process of Dying

In order not to conflate this controversial discussion with cases which pose no halachic, ethical or legal conflicts, the difference between VSED and the loss of appetite and thirst which accompanies end-stage illnesses must be delineated. The absence of the need to eat and drink and a catabolic metabolic status as a result of a serious illness or symptom of old age do not constitute VSED. In these cases, the cessation of the need to eat and drink are not voluntary. Extended periods of abstention from food and drink often proceed natural death. Furthermore, the refusal of a conscious patient who refuses artificial nutrition due to an obstructive and growing tumor or a patient whose swallow reflex is disturbed by a stroke does not constitute VSED, but rather refusal of a medical treatment. Cicely Saunders, the founder of the modern hospice movement, is credited with the statement that a terminally ill person does not die because they do not eat, but rather does not eat because they are dying. If the cases in which conscious, mentally stable patients who are able to swallow and do feel hunger and still refuse food and drink in order to end their lives are considered, then VSED is not such a frequent phenomenon. In daily practice, VSED presents a spectrum of different choices of action rather than a separate and distinct entity in itself.

Is Voluntary Cessation of Eating and Drinking Tantamount to Suicide?

Regardless of presence of or delineation from additional and sometimes difficult to separate symptoms of terminal illnesses, the uncertainty remains as to whether "real" VSED is truly to be considered suicide. From the perspective of medical ethics and philosophy, VSED is most often seen as a form of passive suicide – in the sense of "letting oneself die as a negative form of killing of self," or as "killing of self via intentional abstention" (Simon and Hoekstra 2015, Birnbacher 2015). This definition is in harmony with the established definition of suicide – namely, that of one of the venerated experts in the field of suicidology, the rabbi's son, Émile Durkheim: "On appelle suicide toute mort qui résulte médiatement ou immédiatement d'un acte positif ou négativ, accompli par le victime elle-même."[7] The current World Health Organization (WHO) definition is as follows: "Suicide is an act with a fatal outcome which the deceased, knowing or expecting a fatal outcome, had initiated and carried out with the purpose of provoking the changes he desired" (De Leo et al. 2006, p. 8). Considering the resulting potential destructive effects upon (palliative) care and accompaniment of seriously ill people, this classification is rejected in particular by palliative medicine practitioners (Alt-Epping 2018), and it has been requested for some time now that VSED be defined as its very own course of action. VSED should neither be equated with a cessation of treatment nor with suicide, given the vast differences. For one thing, there is no harm committed by one's own hand, and in contrast to the situation upon imbibing a lethal cocktail (after which there is no going back), VSED involves a more extended process during which there are days remaining during which the person's mind may change. VSED can be interrupted or ended until a certain point, and because there are no effects from the outside, death occurs naturally. It is stressed that VSED is not a distinct course of action and at the end of life is part of a fluid continuum from existing to completely absent feelings of thirst and hunger. The more these feeling subside, the clearer it becomes that VSED is not suicide but rather, at a certain point, the normal abstention from eating and drinking that occurs during the dying process. An early decision to voluntarily abstain from eating and drinking, as we have already determined, is more of a seldom exception. Then, however, it is more of a unique form of ending life and not a form of suicide (Birkhardt and Hanke 2014).

7 Émile Durkheim, *Le suicide: étude de sociologie* (Paris: Alcan, 1897), 3.

The story about Rabbi Yose ben Chalafta and the elderly woman could be an indication that, from the perspective of the Halacha, VSED should be seen as its own category of action – meaning the ending of one's life but not the murder of one's self. Judaism differentiates between ending one's life and committing suicide (Probst 2017a). As previously mentioned, suicides during a time of persecution are considered a separate category (Piskei ha-Tosafot, loc. cit.). The death of the elderly woman in the story from the midrash is brought about by her abstention from attending prayer; however, she was seemingly not ill enough to die, but rather weary of life itself. However, she is permitted to bring about her own death without committing the sin of suicide. She is also not ending her life in opposition to God, but rather acts out of her own free will. She is aware of what her abstention from synagogal prayer will lead to and wishes to reach this goal. The fear of unbearable suffering as a result of sickness or old age, and/or the fear of torture during a time of persecutions are justifications for why VSED does not count as murder of self and why a person may hasten their own death.

VSED from a Legal Perspective

The points in the argumentation against considering VSED as suicide differ completely from the attributions listed by the lawgiver for the criminal offense of assistance according to Section 217 of German Criminal Law. These attributions do not apply to the ending of one's life in itself, but rather primarily in regard to suicide influenced by third parties. Due to the necessary degree of commitment required to carry out VSED, a high degree of autonomy is a prerequisite. Outside influences from third parties are not typical for VSED, which is solely accompanied in a palliative fashion – one which does not differ from the kind of support that other people suffering from terminal illness receive. Even if VSED were considered suicide according to Section 217, accompaniment (according to Tolmein 2018) would not be a punishable offense, as such accompaniment is void of the intent to encourage suicide, but rather marked by the desire to support and care for the patient who desires to die and requires care during the process of VSED. As the decision of the ill must be respected, the physician cannot prevent VSED. The obligation to guarantee care and support does not apply here because VSED is not an accident. The only possible rescue would be to force feed or hydrate, against the will of the patient. No legal basis for this course of action exists in Germany, except in the German penal code.[8] In comparison, VSED does not count as an accident ac-

8 Section 101 of the Federal Penal Code; See Tolmein 2018.

cording to the Halacha, and the Jewish counterpart to the obligation to provide care, the principle of *lo ta'amod al dam re'echa,* does not apply here: "How do we know that if one sees his fellow drowning in a river, or a wild animal mauling him, or robbers attaching him, one must save him? Therefore it is said: 'Neither shalt thou stand idly by the blood of the neighbor (Lev. 19:16).'"[9]

There is, however, concern that with the ban against businesslike provision of suicide assistance, organizations focused upon such suicide assistance could offer "VSED programs" as an alternative. Businesslike conditions and potentially resulting group pressure would lead to the question if the patient would truly remain decisional and responsible for their actions, and if there then might be a violation of Section 217. Such an approach would contradict the life-affirming foundation of the Halacha. A patient's wish to die and harm to self via VSED are not condemned by the Halacha. However, convincing others to hurt themselves and end their lives, especially when carried out in a businesslike fashion, is prohibited:

> It once happened that a man uncovered a woman's head in public. She came before Rabbi Akiva, and he required the man to give her four hundred zuz as a fine. Said the man to him, "Rabbi, allow me some time," and R'Akiva concurred. The man observed the woman standing at the door of her house, then she broke a jug containing about an issar of oil before her. She uncovered her head, and bent down so as to put oil on her head with her hand. The man brought witnesses of this to R'Akiva, saying, "To one such as this I should give four hundred zuz?" Said R'Akiva to him, "What you say is nothing, for even though one is not permitted to do damage to onesself, if one does so there is no penalty, whereas if another does damage to him, that other is culpable" (Mishna, Baba Kamma, 90b).

Conclusion

Responses to terminally ill patients' wish to die are not always clear from a legal perspective. They require special consideration from ethical perspectives that reflect on the values and concepts – both those held by the patients and their professional helpers – of what constitutes a good death. The Halacha requires Jews, when in doubt, to "choose life" (Deut. 30:19); however, Jewish tradition also teaches that humans must accept death and recognize that "there is a time to die" (Eccles. 3:2). From experience, it is difficult for Jews to accept impending death, yet this may not lead to exaggerated care. Accompaniment of terminally ill patients requires a high degree of respect for the dying. Care means that in each case in which the ill patient trusts a physician with the wish to die, they evaluate the specific situation together to determine which biblical verse applies to the situation at

9 B. Talmud, Sanhedrin, 73a.

hand, and how they might best fulfill it. Care means not only considering the well-being of a person, but rather also respecting their will for themselves at the end of life – both legally and in terms of the Halacha. In conversation between the patient (and/or their legal decision-maker), their family, the doctors, and the rabbi, the patient emerges with authentic decisional capability. Dialogue assures that a patient is able to make a personal, reflective, authentic, voluntary, legal and Halacha-congruent decision. A one-size-fits-all approach will not work, especially when it comes to the possibilities involved in a personal decision to influence the dying process by abstaining from food and drink. Even though it remains controversial, consensus exists that no one has the right to force a person to eat if that person has decided voluntarily to commence with VSED. Furthermore, no medical providers would wish to abandon a terminally ill patient who turns to VSED, just because they themselves cannot accept VSED. On the contrary, the obligation always remains to alleviate suffering. People who have decided to undergo VSED have the same right to humane, medical, and caregiving accompaniment. We must not forget: "Treatment of a patient is not directed towards an abstract concept, but rather towards the actual sick (or dying / S.P.) person. Every ill person is different from every other ill person – even though they have the same illness. And, thus, the doctor must cure the sick person and not the disease" (Leibowitz 1982).

References

Alt-Epping, Bernhard. "Con: Der freiwillige Verzicht auf Nahrung und Flüssigkeit ist keine Form des Suizids." *Zeitschrift für Palliativmedizin* 19, no. 1 (2018): 12–15.

Birnbacher, Dieter. "Ist Sterbefasten eine Form von Suizid?" *Ethik in der Medizin* 27, no. 4 (2015): 315–324, doi: 10.1007/s00481-015-0337-9.

Birkhardt, Jürgen and Hanke, Roland Martin. "Freiwilliger Verzicht auf Nahrung und Flüssigkeit. Eine ganz eigene Handlungsweise." *Deutsches Ärzteblatt* 111, no. 14 (2014): A590–A592.

Bundesärztekammer. "Verbot der geschäftsmäßigen Förderung der Selbsttötung (§217 StGB): Hinweise und Erläuterungen für die ärztliche Praxis." *Deutsches Ärzteblatt* 114, no. 7 (2017): A334–A336.

Central Conference of American Rabbis. Questions and Reform Jewish Answers: New American Reform Responsa. New York: Central Conference of American Rabbis, 1992.

De Leo, Diego, et al. "Definitions of suicidal behavior. Lessons learned from the WHO/EURO Multicentre Study." *Crisis* 27 (2006): 4–15.

Deutsche Gesellschaft für Palliativmedizin. "Positionspapier der Deutschen Gesellschaft für Palliativmedizin zum freiwilligen Verzicht auf Essen und Trinken, Deutsche Gesellschaft für Palliativmedizin, Oktober 2019." Accessed 1 June 2020. https://www.dgpalliativmedizin.de/dgp-aktuell/deutsche-gesellschaft-fuer-palliativmedizin-positioniert-sich-erstmals-zum-sterbefasten-achtung-des-patientenwillen-hoert-nicht-beim-freiwilligen-verzicht-auf-essen-und-trinken-auf.html

Dorff, Elliot N. "Physician-Assisted Suicide and Euthanasia (Approved by the Rabbinical Assembly Committee on Jewish Law Standards Mar. 1997)." In *Life and Death Responsibilities in Jewish*

Biomedical Ethics, edited by Aaron L. Mackler, 407–434. New York: The Jewish Theological Seminary of America, 2000.

Dorff, Elliot N. *Matters of Life and Death. A Jewish Approach to Modern Medical Ethics.* Philadelphia: The Jewish Publication Society, 2003.

Durkheim, Émile. *Le suicide. Étude de sociologie.* Paris: Presses Universitaires de France, 1897. Reprint Alcan 1973.

European Association for Palliative Care. "White Paper on standards and norms for hospice and palliative care in Europe: part 1." *European Journal of Palliative Care* 16, no. 6 (2009): 278–289.

Fehn, Sabrina and Andé Fringer,. "Facetten des freiwilligen Verzichts auf Nahrung und Flüssigkeit – Notwendigkeit, Sterbefasten differenzierter zu betrachten." *Schweizerische Ärztezeitung* 98 (2017): 1161–1163.

Feinstein, Moshe. *Responsa of Rav Moshe Feinstein. Volume 1: Care of the Critically Ill.* Translated and Annotated by Moshe Dovid Tendler. Hoboken: Ktav Publishing House, 1996.

Hoekstra, Nina Luisa, Micha Strack, and Alfred Simon. "Bewertung des freiwilligen Verzichts auf Nahrung und Flüssigkeit durch palliativmedizinisch und hausärztlich tätige Ärztinnen und Ärzte. Ergebnisse einer empirischen Umfrage (n = 255). *Zeitschrift für Palliativmedizin* 16 (2015): 68–73.

Jacob, Walter and Moshe Zemer, eds. *Death and Euthanasia in Jewish Law, Essays and Responsa.* Pittsburgh, Tel Aviv: Rodef Shalom Press, 1995.

Jacob, Walter. "Drugs to Relieve Pain." In Jacob, et.al., *Death and Euthanasia in Jewish Law*, 167–168.

Jox, Ralf J., Isra Black, Gian Domenico Borasion, and Johanna Anneser. "Voluntary stopping of eating and drinking: is medical support ethically justified?" *BMC Medicine 15* (2017): 186–190, doi: 10.1186/s12916-017-0950-1.

Klein, Birgit E. and David A. Teutsch. "Quality of Life at End of Life: The Evolution of Key Concepts." *Journal of Jewish Ethics* 4, no. 2 (2018): 163–197.

Kravitz, Leonard. "Euthanasia." In Jacob, et.al., *Death and Euthanasia in Jewish Law*, 11–25.

Kremeike, Kerstin, Klaus Maria Perrar, Reinhard Lindner, Kathleen Bostroem, Thomas Montag, and Raymond Voltz. "Todeswünsche bei Palliativpatienten – Hintergründe und Handlungsempfehlungen." *Zeitschrift für Palliativmedizin* 20 (2019): 323–335.

Kučera Tom. "Halacha, Aggada und Sterbehilfe." In *Jüdische Positionen zur Sterbehilfe*, edited by Elisa Klapheck, 61–87. Berlin: Hentrich & Hentrich Verlag, 2016.

Leibowitz, Yeshayahu. "The General and the Particular in the Theory of Medical Practice" (Hebrew). In *Emunah, Historiah, ve-Arakhim*, 240–241. Jerusalem: Academon, 1982.

Probst, Stephan. "Wie gehen wir damit um und was sollen wir antworten, wenn uns unheilbar Kranke um Beihilfe zum Suizid bitten?" *Suizidprophylaxe. Theorie und Praxis* 44, no. 1 (2017): 12–17.

Probst, Stephan. "Suizid und Suizidprävention im Judentum." *Suizidprophylaxe. Theorie und Praxis* 44, no. 4 (2017): 124–128.

Probst, Stephan. "Die palliativmedizinische Begleitung jüdischer Patienten und Palliative Care aus jüdischer Sicht." *Zeitschrift für Palliativmedizin* 20, no. 1 (2019): 31–38.

Schildmann, Jan, Birte Dahmen, and Jochen Vollmann. "Ärztliche Handlungspraxis am Lebensende, Ergebnisse einer Querschnittsumfrage unter Ärzten in Deutschland." *Deutsche Medizinische Wochenschrift* 140, no. 1 (2014): 1–6. doi:10.1055/s-0034-1387410.

Segal, Sheila. "Pain and Suffering." In *Behoref Hayamim. In the Winter of Life. A Values-Based Jewish Guide for Decision Making at the End of Life*, edited by David Teutsch and Debora Waxman, 78–99. Wyncote: Reconstructionist Rabbinical College Center für Jewish Ethics, 2002.

Sherwin Byron L. *In Partnership with God, Contemporary Jewish Law and Ethics*. Syracuse: Syracuse University Press, 1990.

Simon, Alfred and Nina Hoekstra. "Sterbefasten – Hilfe im oder Hilfe zum Sterben?" *Deutsche Medizinische Wochenschrift* 140 (2015): 1100–1102.

Steinberg, Avraham. "Terminally Ill." In *Encyclopedia of Jewish Medical Ethics*, compiled and written by Avraham Steinberg. Translated by Fred Rosner, 1046–1088. Jerusalem, New York: Feldheim Publishers, 2003.

Sykes, Nigel and Andrew Thorns. "The use of opioids and sedatives at the end of life." *The Lancet Oncology* 4 (2003): 312–318.

Temel, Jennifer, Joseph A. Greer, Alona Muzikansky, et. al. "Early Palliative Care for Patients with Metastatic Non-Small-Cell Lung Cancer." *Journal of Clinical Oncology*. 30, no. 4 (2010): 394–400, doi: 10.1056/NEJMoa1000678.

Tolmein, Oliver. "Der freiwillige Verzicht auf Nahrung und Flüssigkeit und rechtliche Fragestellungen in der deutschen Debatte." *Zeitschrift für Palliativmedizin* 19, no. 3 (2018): 141–148.

Liliana Ruth Feierstein

"He was lain to rest in the Darkening of the Tides …": Death and Burial in the Field of Tension between Competing Laws in Latin America

In memoriam Alberto Dines z'l

> We have two pictures before us: one shows the serene face of an old man dressed in rabbinical garb … The text next to the portrait makes it clear that it is Isaac Aboab, 1605–1693, the first rabbi of the Americas. Pernambuco, Brazil 1642–1648. In the second image we see a funeral procession of countless men and women. Visibly moved, they accompany the two coffins. The caption says: "More than four thousand people accompany on foot the coffins of the couple Stefan Zweig." The two images highlight the history of the Jews in Brazil.
>
> Heinrich Lemle, *O drama judaico*[1]

Two depictions, two descriptions, two rabbis. Between them, 300 years. Towards the end of World War II, Heinrich (Henrique) Lemle (1909–1978) published a small book in Latin American exile in 1944 entitled *O drama judaico* (The Jewish Drama). In the epilogue, the author explains that he chose this setting, in which a Dutch-Sephardic rabbi and an Austrian-Jewish writer enter into conversation, as a symbol of Jewish history in Brazil.

As the first rabbi on American soil, Isaac Aboab da Fonseca (1605–1693) came from Amsterdam to then Dutch Recife in 1642[2] and served in the first synagogue on

Note: English translation by Ian Leveson. This article was first published under the title "Ruht er im Dunkeln der Gezeiten …": Tod und Begräbnis im Spannungsfeld konkurrierender Gesetze in Lateinamerika, in: Jahrbuch des Dubnow-Instituts/Dubnow Institute Yearbook 18 (2019), Göttingen: Vandenhoeck & Ruprecht/Brill Deutschland GmbH 2022, 341–360, doi.org/10.13109/9783666370991.341.

1 Heinrich Lemle, *O drama judaico* [The Jewish drama], Rio de Janeiro: Dois Mundos, 1944 p. 144 (translation here and below, unless otherwise noted, by the author); on Heinrich Lemle, see *Em Memoria do grão-rabino Dr. Henrique Lemle z. l.* [In memory of Grand Rabbi Dr. Henrique Lemle of Blessed Memory] (Rio de Janeiro: Associação Religiosa Israelita do Rio de Janeiro, 1978); the quotation in the title ("Ruht er …") is taken from Stefan Zweig, *Der begrabene Leuchter* (Frankfurt a. M.: Fischer, 1992), 62.

2 Mauritsstad (today part of Recife) was the capital of New Holland (*Dutch Brazil*) between 1630–1654.

https://doi.org/10.1515/9783111062631-010

the entire continent, *kahal zur yisrael.*[3] Religious freedom may not have existed for long, but with Aboab, Judaism nevertheless crossed the Atlantic.

Three centuries later, Heinrich Lemle went to Brazil and he too founded a synagogue, the *Associação Religiosa Israelita* in Rio de Janeiro, and shortly thereafter buried Latin America's most famous exile, Stefan Zweig (1881–1942), as well as his wife, Lotte (1908–1942). He concludes his booklet with a picture of the Brazilians' farewell to Zweig.

Using the example of death and burial cultures, this essay aims to focus on the tension between Jewish and state law in Brazil and Argentina. Embodied by a rabbi, Jewish law reaches America with Aboab de Fonseca and finally established itself there with the founding of a cemetery. Three hundred years later, the relationship between the "competing laws" is marked by emigration, the experience of exile, secularization, democracy and dictatorship – and it is no coincidence that the cemeteries will be one of the main arenas of dispute.

Who do the dead belong to?

"Greetings to all my friends! May they yet see the dawn after the long night! I, all the more impatient, go before them!" These are probably the last sentences Stefan Zweig wrote down. In any case, they are the last lines of the farewell letter, the *Declaração,* which he wrote in February 1942 at his home in Petrópolis and left to posterity. The beginning of the letter was addressed to the host country:

> Before I retire from life of my own free will and with clear senses, I must fulfil one last duty: to thank this wonderful country of Brazil, which has given me and my work such good and hospitable tranquillity. With every day I have learned to love this country more, and nowhere would I rather have rebuilt my life from the bottom up, after the world of my own language, for me, has perished and my spiritual home Europe has *destroyed itself.*[4]

The suicide of Stefan Zweig and his wife Lotte Altmann is well known, as are the photos of the funeral that circulated at the time. Rabbi Lemle and Cantor Israel Fleischmann, who conducted the ceremony, are to be seen in them. According to tradition, Lemle read a passage from Zweig's play *Jeremiah,* while the Eastern Eu-

---

3 Aboab da Fonseca was later one of the scholars who pronounced the ban against Baruch Spinoza.

4 Stefan Zweig, *Declaração* (Declaration), 22 February 1942, quoted in Alberto Dines, *Tod im Paradies. Die Tragödie des Stefan Zweig* (Death in Paradise. The Tragedy of Stefan Zweig) (Frankfurt: Edition Büchergilde, 2006), 618.

ropean Jewish friends felt a slight uneasiness. An ironic remark whispered in Yiddish made the rounds: *"Di galokhim senen schojn gekumn!"*[5]

What is less known, however, is what this incident triggered on various levels. Brazilians were shocked, and mourned the loss of one of their favorite writers, to whom they had granted asylum.[6] Zweig's suicide, however, also provoked a tremendous conflict with and within the Jewish community. It was a problem in which two structures of law – more than that, two sources of authority and legitimacy – clashed.[7] At the center of contention was the burial of the dead: should this be according to religious precepts or in accordance with the laws of the land?

Death is the most radical moment of life. It is therefore not surprising that in particular religions, including Judaism, strongly ritualize this event. A secular state cannot escape these ceremonies, but connotes them differently.[8] The *haskalah* was confronted with this difficulty from the beginning. The correspondence of 1772 between Moses Mendelssohn (1729–1786) and Rabbi Jacob Emden (1697–1776) from Hamburg, for example, testifies to this, concerning the three days that had to elapse before a funeral according to state law, in order to be able to safely exclude an apparent death.[9] Since, according to Jewish law, burial must take place within one day, a conflict arose between *halachah*, new scientific findings, and state law.

---

5 *galochim* (Yiddish, 'Christian clergymen'). The irony is based on the fact that the Reform rabbis and cantors took to wearing robes like those used by Protestant pastors. The quotation is from the journalist Aron Neumann (ibid., 616).

6 Legend has it that the news of Zweig's death so deeply moved Brazil's then President Getúlio Vargas and his supporters that they finally revised their hitherto rather positive view of European fascism. Although Brazil had already declared war on the Axis powers before, reluctantly and under pressure from the United States, after Zweig's death the country even sent a unit of more than 25,000 soldiers, the *Força Expedicionária Brasileira*, to Italy. Mexico, too, not only granted asylum to tens of thousands of supporters of the Spanish Republic, but in 1944 sent the *Escuadrón 201*, an air force unit, to fight alongside the Allies in the Philippines.

7 For Jewish perspectives on the tensions between state and religious law, see Gil Graff, *Separation of Church and State. Dina de-Malkhuta Dina in Jewish Law, 1750–1848*, (Tuscaloosa: University of Alabama Press, 2003; Mark Washofsky, "Halakhah and Political Theory: A Study in Jewish Legal Response to Modernity," *Modern Judaism* 9, no. 3 (1989): 289–310; Elisa Klapheck, "Das religiös-säkulare Spannungsfeld des Judentums," in *Machloket/ Streitschriften*, ed. Ruth Calderon and Elisa Klapheck (Berlin: Hentrich & Hentrich, 2015), 1: 9–47.

8 See the classic works of Émile Durkheim, *Les formes élémentaires de la vie religieuse. Le système totémique en Australie* [Basic Forms of Religious Life. The Totem System in Australia] (Paris, 1912) and Arnold van Gennep, *Les rites des passage* [Rites of Passage] (Paris, 1909).

9 See Moses Mendelssohn, *Briefwechsel (1761–1785)*, ed. Reuven Michael et al, in *Gesammelte Schriften. Jubiläumsausgabe* (Collected Writings, Anniversary edition), ed. Alexander Altmann et al. (Stuttgart: Frommann-Holzboog, 1994), 20/2: on the confrontation, see also Graff, *Separation of Church and State*, 36.

Brazil is particularly suitable for the concretization of this hitherto rather generally presented confrontation, because here different categories of Jewish reality can be observed: that of the Western Jews and the *Wissenschaft des Judentums* that they brought to Latin America, and that of the majority Eastern European Jews who had already lived in the communities for a longer time. This confrontation has been very impressively reconstructed by the journalist Alberto Dines (1932–2018), whose father attended Zweig's funeral as a representative of the Jewish community of Rio de Janeiro.[10] Among the many people who made their way to Zweig's house after hearing the sad news was a small group of men from the *ḥevra kaddischa'* (burial society), led by Rio de Janeiro's Chief Rabbi Mordechai Tzekinovsky, who came from Eastern Europe. In the run-up to the event, there were extensive debates about how to deal with Zweig's suicide from a Jewish perspective.[11] Dines describes them as follows:

> Despite the strictness of Jewish law regarding the burial of suicides . . . Rabbi Tzekinovsky is in favor of transferring the bodies ... so that both remain with their fellow believers. As their equals, without distinction.
>
> *Adonai natan, adonai lakach*, the Lord gives, the Lord takes away – the law is clear, ... the burial society is very rigorous. ... But the rabbi ... favours a different interpretation ...: "My attitude was probably influenced by admiration for the writer. His words, his works, especially his *Menorah* [by which he referred to the novella *The Buried Candelabrum: A Jewish Legend*] made a deep impression on me. I could not reconcile myself to the idea that this man would be utterly rejected and his soul forever banished from his people."[12]

Thus, in order to obtain the transfer of the Zweigs' bodies, a delegation of the Jewish community went to Petrópolis with the appropriate mandate. The mayor, however, argued that Stefan Zweig had left a detailed will, "and yet he said nothing about wishing to be buried in a Jewish cemetery."[13] Rabbi Tzekinovsky replied:

> *We* answered: "Was there any mention in the will regarding his wish to be buried in a non-Jewish cemetery?" ... *We are of* the opinion that a person does not have to mention what is indisputable: he knew ... that he would be buried in the midst of his people, in a Jewish cemetery, and consequently he did not need to raise this subject in his will. ... It is a human duty to allow the dead man his rest in the bosom of his own, of the people into which he was born."[14]

10 See Dines, *Tod im Paradies* [Death in Paradise].

11 Taking one's own life is forbidden by Jewish law. Although suicides are also buried in the Jewish cemetery, there is a separate area for them, usually at the edge of the cemetery.

12 Dines, *Tod im Paradies* [Death in Paradise], 612 (emphasis in original).

13 Ibid., 613.

14 Ibid. (author's emphasis). Dines quotes Rabbi Tzekinovsky's statements from a letter to him in 1980.

In what name does the rabbi use the personal pronoun "we" here? Who is answering? Does he mean "We Jews?" Or rather "We, the Jewish community," as a cultural collective with a distinct religious and cultural self-understanding, a minority within the Brazilian majority society? Its position had to be negotiated with the authorities, especially with regards to funeral rituals. Therefore, Tzekinovsky also put halachic arguments to the mayor: "[We] ask ... you to take into account the fact that his people's cemetery and his religion must have priority."[15]

As a representative of the city, the mayor reacted with irritation: if the Jewish community insisted on taking both bodies, he could not prevent it. However, he feared that the residents of Petrópolis would be "very disappointed" and would respond with "great indignation and great anger."[16] For the *ḥevra kaddisha,* this was "[n]o more, no less: an open threat against the Jews."[17] At first, the Jewish community did not give way. Its chairman, the Polish tailor Henrique Nussenbaum, even managed to obtain a personal audience with President Getúlio Vargas (1882–1954) at his vacation residence. Dines recounts the conversation as follows: "'Mr. President, he is *ours* ....' Vargas replied simply: "It is the people of Petrópolis who want him here.'"[18] There was nothing more to be done. "Deeply saddened and despairing, we withdrew. Later we learned that someone had gone to Petrópolis to hold a [Jewish] 'service' in the municipal cemetery of Petrópolis. *We* disapproved of this," Tzekinovsky recounts.[19]

Several thousand people followed the funeral procession; it was a sea of flowers. Earlier, the Brazilians had brought the coffins to the *Academia de Letras* for the wake. Nussenbaum made minimal demands so that the Jewish rite would be preserved there as well: "Flowers and wreaths should be placed in another room and the coffins should remain closed."[20]

Finally, there was a Jewish funeral after all. Rabbi Lemle and Cantor Fleischmann performed the Kaddish at the state cemetery. In a foreign country. In a foreign cemetery. At the neighbors.

---

15 Ibid., 614.

16 Ibid.

17 Ibid.

18 Ibid., 616.

19 Ibid., 614 (author's emphasis). It was later noted that Zweig himself had wished "'to be buried in the cemetery of Rio de Janeiro in the most modest and discreet manner'" (according to an instruction to his publisher Abraham Koogan, 18 February 1942, quoted in Dines, *Tod im Paradies* [Death in Paradise], 615).

20 Ibid.; In Judaism, coffins are traditionally kept closed.

On foreign soil

Di galokhim senen schoyn gekumn. Heinrich Lemle thus accepted a compromise that no Orthodox rabbi had been willing to make: a Jewish burial ritual on foreign soil. Foreign not only because the burial took place in a non-Jewish cemetery,[21] without the *tahara*, the ritual cleansing of the dead,[22] but also because Lemle had only arrived in Brazil in 1940.

Born in Augsburg in 1909, he had studied at the Jewish Theological Seminary in Breslau as well as at the *Hochschule für die Wissenschaft des Judentums* in Berlin and then – like many rabbinical students at the time – earned his doctorate at the University of Würzburg (with the dissertation *Mendelssohn und die Toleranz auf dem Grunde des Naturrechts und der Naturreligion*; 1932). He worked as a youth rabbi in Mannheim and Frankfurt am Main and was incarcerated in Buchenwald during the course of the November pogroms of 1938, but was nonetheless released three weeks later through the intervention of Lily Montagu.[23] He fled via England to Brazil in 1940, after having endured an interim internment on the Isle of Man. In 1951, he founded the first Center for Jewish Studies in Latin America at the University of Rio de Janeiro.

The linking of different languages as well as biblical and literary texts forms a constant in the tradition of Jewish scholarship, especially among rabbis in Latin American exile, who interwove religious with secular sources in their weekly sermons and articles. In this case, however, the focus was not solely on Zweig's suicide and its political implications – on a global scale and for Brazil in particular – but on the Austrian-Jewish author himself, and more specifically on his own interpretation of Jewish sources.

21 On the problem of the secularization of cemeteries and the cultural treatment of death, see Philippe Aries, *Essais sur l'histoire de la mort en Occident du Moyen Age à nos jours* [Essays on the History of Death in the West from the Middle Ages to the Present], Paris 1975; also Thomas W. Laqueur, *The Work of the Dead. A Cultural History of Mortal Remains*, Princeton, N. J., 2015. On the importance of the cemetery in Judaism, see Ariel Bar-Levav, *We Are Where We Are Not. The Cemetery in Jewish Culture*, in Jewish Studies 41 (2002), 15–46.

22 On Jewish traditions regarding death and mourning, see Maurice Lamm, *The Jewish Way in Death and Mourning*, New York 2000 and Leonor Slavsky, *La espada encendida. Un estudio sobre la muerte y la identidad étnica en el judaísmo* [The Burning Sword. A Study of Death and Ethnic Identity in Judaism], Buenos Aires 1993.

23 Lily Montagu (1873–1963), British social worker. Born and raised in a Jewish Orthodox family, she chose, influenced by Claude Montefiore, the path of liberal Judaism, for which she engaged herself resolutely in Europe. After 1938, she worked from London to free rabbis interned in camps and to enable them to emigrate. On Montagu's biography, see Ellen M. Umansky, *Lily Montagu and the Advancement of Liberal Judaism. From Vision to Vocation* (New York: Mellen, 1983).

In his essay *A vida e a morte de S. Zweig à luz da história judaica* ('The life and death of S. Zweig in the light of Jewish history'), Lemle again addressed Zweig's drama *Jeremias* and affirmed: "God is always with the defeated."[24] In doing so, he was concerned – entirely in the Jewish tradition – with an interpretation on various levels: about *Jeremias*, Zweig's exile, and his suicide in the wake of the self-destruction of his intellectual homeland. At the same time, it was important to Lemle and other rabbis in South America – despite the great recognition and admiration shown for the writer Zweig – to reaffirm the commandment to (continue) living and thus to make it clear that suicide was not an admissible Jewish way. This is also to be seen against the background that Fritz Pinkuss (1905–1994), from 1936 rabbi of the Jewish community in São Paulo, reported in his memoirs: that there were numerous Jewish exiles who wanted to follow Zweig's lead.[25]

In 1949, a few years after the publication of *O drama judaico*, a *machsor* ('prayer book for the High Holidays') appeared for the first time in its entirety in Portuguese. It was based on the joint translation work of Lemle and Pinkuss. The *machsor* was followed by a *siddur* ('daily prayer book') whose composition was strongly based on the *Unity Prayer Book of Liberal Judaism* (*tefillot le-kol ha-schana*), which had been published in Breslau in 1929 under the leadership of Rabbi Caesar Seligmann (1860–1950) from Frankfurt.[26] With the support of Seligmann, who lived in exile in Britain, this central manifestation of liberal Judaism was thus also linguistically transferred to the South. This was followed by other, more didactic works on the history and basic concepts of Judaism, which were intended to serve internally for the cultural education of youth and externally for the dismantling of anti-Semitic stereotypes in Brazilian society.

These publications not only proved to be milestones in the history of liberal Judaism in Latin America, but also illustrate the cultural transfer activity of German-speaking Jews and – although they formed a minority in the Latin American communities – their influence on Judaism there.

With the founding of the umbrella organization CENTRA (*Arbeitsgemeinschaft der jüdischen Gemeinden und Organisationen zentraleuropäischen Ursprungs in Lateinamerika*) in Montevideo in 1956, they succeeded in bringing together more than twenty congregations from nine different countries which followed the Breslau

24 Zweig published *Jeremias in* 1917 as a reaction to the First World War. The first performance in Zurich was a great success.

25 Fritz Pinkuss, *Lernen, Lehren, Helfen. Sechs Jahrzehnte als Rabbiner auf zwei Kontinenten* [Learning, Teaching, Helping. Six Decades as Rabbi on Two Continents] (Heidelberg: Universitätsverlag Winter, 1990), 65.

26 On the *tefillot le-kol ha-schana*, see Annette Böckler, *The "Einheitsgebetbuch." History, Theology, and Post-War Reception of the Last Pre-War German Jewish Prayer Book* (manuscript).

Central European tradition, thus ensuring its continuation. CENTRA's work finally culminated in 1962 with the constitution of the *Seminario Rabínico Latinoamericano* in Buenos Aires – the first and only rabbinical seminary on the entire subcontinent. A bridge between the three different groups of German-speaking, Eastern European, and Sephardic Jews was first built by Rabbi Marshall Meyer (1930–1993). As a North American scholar "neutral" to the three groups, he had come to Buenos Aires as a student of Abraham Joshua Heschel in 1959 and later became a protagonist of the resistance to the Argentine dictatorship of the 1970s and early 1980s. He was particularly known for his extraordinary commitment to humane prison conditions for political prisoners and in the search for Jewish *desaparecidos.*[27] Many years later, some Jewish families in Argentina adopted a custom common to victims of the Shoah and placed plaques with the names of murdered persons on the graves of their relatives in order to create – as an asylum, as it were – a place of remembrance for those who could not be buried.[28]

(Un)holy ground

On the threshold between life and death, cemeteries also represent the tensions between the different laws – those of Judaism and those of the state. This concerns, for example, the exclusion of those classified by *halachah* as unclean *(tmeym)*, the relative location within the burial ground of graves for suicides, or the time span between death and burial. The conflicts between these laws and their interpretation is by no means mere practice but has (had) significant effects on the political life of Latin America. The simultaneous existence of both traditions of law and

27 *Desaparecidos:* "disappeared," kidnapped and murdered by the military, whose bodies were never found. On Marshall Meyer, see Diego Rosenberg, *Marshall Meyer. El rabino que le vio la cara al diablo* [Marshall Meyer. The rabbi who looked the devil in the face] (Buenos Aires: Capital Intelectual, 2010); Mariela Volcovich, *Marshall T. Meyer. El hombre, un rabino* [Marshall T. Meyer. The man, a rabbi] (Buenos Aires: Generico, 2009); Sebastián Carassai, "Violencia política, dictadura militar y memoria. La Argentina de los años setenta y ochenta a partir del Archivo Marshall T. Meyer" [Political Violence, Military Dictatorship and Memory. Argentina in the 1970s and 1980s, starting from the Marshall T. Meyer Archive], Estudios Ibero-Americanos 43, no. 2 (2017): 380–396.
28 On this, see the film *Kadish,* dir. Bernardo Kononovich (2009) as well as Liliana R. Feierstein, "Trauer und/oder Melancholie. Religiös-kulturelle Spuren in der Trauerarbeit über polititsche Gewalt in Argentinien" [Grief and/or Melancholy. Religious-Cultural Traces in Mourning Political Violence in Argentina], *Jahrbuch Zentrum Jüdische Studien Berlin-Brandenburg* 2 (2015): 85–101, and Feierstein, "A Quilt of Memory. The Shoah as a Prism in the Testimonies of Survivors of the Dictatorship in Argentina," *European Review* 22, no. 4 (2014): 585–593.

thought, as already suggested by the Jewish scholar Samuel of Nehardea (3rd century) in the Talmud, allows for enrichment through mutual questioning.[29]

"'It matters not. Wherever a Jew lies buried, the site becomes holy ground.' ... Where he lies, his message will be."[30] With this allusion to Zweig's legend *The Buried Candelabrum*, Rabbi Tzekinovsky tried to offer comfort to the publisher Abraham Koogan,[31] Stefan Zweig's young friend. Koogan considered the official state funeral service in Petrópolis an exaggerated stage show and was therefore horrified.[32]

The burial of the dead, especially there being a (permanently undisturbed) burial-ground, is so significant in Jewish culture that the founding of the majority of communities in the "New World" has its origins in a group of *ḥevra kaddisha.* In Buenos Aires, the metropolitan region with the largest Jewish population in the subcontinent, the Jewish community in 1894 still consisted of a small group, but the first article of the statutes already stated: "[T]he funerals [are] to be strictly according to Mosaic law and custom" and Article 2 stipulates "for this, as far as means are available, to support needy co-religionists within the bounds of possibility."[33]

In the second major center of São Paulo, efforts to acquire a cemetery site began in 1915, and permission was not granted until 1919.[34] Tensions with the city administration were enormous, since the halachic requirement that only Jews be buried there contradicted the laws of the Republic of Brazil, which did not tolerate differential treatment between Brazilian citizens. In particular, it was contrary to the right of all citizens, regardless of denomination, to be buried in a cemetery of their choice – a democratization of the previously common practice of burying non-Catholics in an area for apostates. The dispute centered on

29 See the article by Elisa Klapheck in this book.

30 Dines, *Tod in Paradies* [Death in Paradise], 615.

31 Abrahão (Abraham) Koogan, born in Bessarabia in 1912 and died in Rio de Janeiro in 2000, was a bookseller, one of Zweig's closest friends in Brazil and the publisher of his books. Koogan was an original in the Latin American publishing world: from umbrella salesman to a man of books, he specialized mainly in medical and psychological subjects and was the first publisher of Freud's works in Brazil. See Alberto Dines et al., *Stefan Zweig und sein Freundeskreis. Sein letztes Adressbuch 1940–1942* [Stefan Zweig and His Circle of Friends. Sein letztes Adressbuch 1940–1942] (Berlin: Hentrich & Hentrich, 2016).

32 See Dines, *Tod im Paradies* [Death in Paradise], 615.

33 AMIA/Comunidad judía de Buenos Aires (ed.), *Libro del Centenario 1894–1994* [Book on the Centenary 1894–1994] (Buenos Aires 1994).

34 The acquisition of the land, which was always the biggest hurdle due to the cost, was the responsibility of Mauricio Klabin, a native of Lithuania and one of the most important Jewish philanthropists in Brazil.

the question of secularism. In the Constitution of 1891, the Brazilian Republic distinguished itself from the Catholic Church, among other things with Article 72, which declared burial grounds to be secular and open to all denominations: "The cemeteries have to be secular and shall be run by the municipality. All religious communities may practice there the rites according to their faith, as long as they do not violate public morals and laws."[35]

The demand of the Jewish community as a religious minority for exclusivity in the cemetery question obviously collided with the secularization and equality aspirations of the Republic. The *halachah*, however, offers arguments to justify this difference. In a letter from the Jewish community to the responsible ministry, this desire is justified by Jewish law, according to which graves must exist for eternity and must never be levelled or reused. The latter was usually the case in Brazilian cemeteries once grave fees were no longer being paid. The Jewish community invoked the principle of equality of all citizens: it would be unjust to allow Jews to have graves in perpetuity, regardless of their economic situation, while the rest of Brazilians had ephemeral resting places that would be removed if payments ceased. The community (*kehillah*) offered a solution to this: the creation of its own cemetery, open to its members in perpetuity, and the maintenance of which it would pay for itself without government support. Later, the fact that the cemeteries – despite their secular and neutral character – were decorated with images of Christ and saints was also cited as reducing the acceptance of such a place by people of other faiths. The disputes dragged on until 1919. In 1923, there were renewed differences with the government over "Jewish affiliation" (*qualidade de israelita*),[36] i. e., the question of which persons were entitled under state law to be buried in the Jewish cemetery. The decision was particularly difficult in the case of interfaith marriages. Finally, a compromise solution was found enabling the burial in the Jewish cemetery of not only the non-Jewish intermarried spouse, but also other non-Jewish family members, neither of which the *halachah* traditionally allows.

After these differences were settled, an internal dispute arose. Beginning in the early twentieth century, a vast network known as *Sociedad Varsovia* (later *Zwi Migdal*) operated in Latin America for several decades, trafficking in women.[37] The

35 Cited in Monica Musatti Cytrynowicz and Roney Cytrynowicz, *Associação Cemitério Israelita de São Paulo, 85 anos. Patrimônio da história da comunidade judaica e da cidade de São Paulo* [85 years of Associação Cemitério Israelita de São Paulo. Historical Heritage of the Jewish Community and the City of São Paolo] (São Paulo: Narrativa-Um, 2008), 13.

36 Ibid., 27.

37 On the history of the *Zwi Migdal*, see Victor A. Mirelman, *En búsqueda de una identidad. Los inmigrantes judíos en Buenos Aires, 1890–1930* [In Search of an Identity. Jewish Immigrants in Bue-

Jewish community in both Brazil and Argentina began to crack down on this, expelling pimps as well as prostitutes from their institutions.[38] The harshest measure against these people was the denial of burial in a Jewish cemetery. For example, the statutes of the Association of Israelites of São Paulo explicitly stated that no certificate of Jewish affiliation would be issued to pimps or prostitutes (Art. 28).[39] As a result, participants in these networks formed associations – outside the official community – for mutual aid. Their main goal was to build their own cemeteries and synagogues so that they could live and die according to the Jewish rite, for example the *Associação Beneficente Funerária e Religiosa Israelita* in Rio de Janeiro in 1906, which consecrated the Cemitério de Inhaúma in 1916, and the *Sociedade Feminina Religiosa e Beneficente Israelita,* founded in São Paulo in 1924. The latter requested permission to open its own cemetery in 1925. The municipal authorities of São Paulo reacted with irritation, since an exception had already been granted, which was now apparently not enough for the entire community. The authorities argued that discrimination against individual members was an affront to the principles of the Republic and showed a lack of respect for its own dead.[40]

In Buenos Aires, the same internal conflict had arisen earlier. At the beginning of the 20th century, there were attempts to acquire land to be dedicated to a Jewish cemetery – a difficult undertaking due to the high purchase prices. The members of the *Zwi Migdal* offered to donate a large part of the sum, but after a lively discussion the offer was turned down because the money came from "unclean people." The *Sociedad Varsovia* then bought its own ground in the Avellaneda district, where pimps and prostitutes were buried. The official community did not manage such an acquisition until 1910 (Cementerio de Liniers).[41] In this context, the Chief

---

nos Aires, 1890–1930] (Buenos Aires 1988; Ricardo Feierstein, *Historia de los judíos argentinos* [History of Jewish Argentines] (Buenos Aires: Milá, 2006); Haim Avni, *Argentina y la historia de la inmigración judía, 1810–1950* [Argentina and the History of Jewish Immigration, 1810–1950] (Buenos Aires: AMIA, 1983); Haim Avni, *"Clientes," rufianes y prostitutas. Comunidades judías de Argentina e Israel frente a la trata de blancas* ["Clients," Pimps and Prostitutes. Jewish communities in Argentina and Israel against trafficking in women] (Buenos Aires: Leviatán, 2014).

38 This is a complex and interesting chapter of Jewish history, involving the liberation of hundreds of young Jewish women from the clutches of pimps, with the help of the London-based *Ezra Nashim Association,* among others.

39 Cytrynowicz and Cytrynowicz, *Associação Cemitério Israelita de São Paulo,* 36.

40 Ibid., 38–40.

41 See Mirelman, *En búsqueda de una identidad*; Ricardo Feierstein, *Historia de los judíos argentinos*; Slavsky, *La espada encendida.* I am grateful to Mirtha Shalom for information on the *Zwi Migdal* cemetery in Avellaneda.

Rabbi of Buenos Aires Reuven ha-Cohen Sinai is known to have said: "I would rather lie among honourable gentiles than among our unclean (*tmeym*).[42]

The 1970s

About thirty years after Zweig's suicide, another, even more dramatic political suicide occurred on September 11, 1973. After the military coup in Santiago de Chile, Salvador Allende (1908–1973) took his own life in the presidential palace, *La Moneda.* The situation on the subcontinent came to a head. In Brazil, a military dictatorship since 1964, journalists were forbidden to write about what was happening in Chile. Alberto Dines, then director of the most important daily newspaper *Jornal do Brasil,* solved the problem in a "Talmudic" way: the front page of the 12 September 1973 issue featured an article about the events in the neighboring country, but without a single headline or title. All copies of this extraordinary issue were sold – Dines lost his job some time later because of his critical political positions.[43]

Emigrants from Europe to Latin America experienced the nightmare of persecution, torture, and murder once again during this period. Even though the majority of members of the Jewish community in Brazil were not directly affected by the violence of the military dictatorship and suffered relatively few deaths and disappearances, they were not unaffected by these trials.[44] In 1975, Dines, who by then worked for another newspaper, tried to protect his "triple"-colleague, the Jewish

42 "Prefiero yacer entre gentiles honorables que entre nuestros tmeym" (cited in Ricardo Feierstein, *Historia de los judíos argentinos*, 297).

43 On Alberto Dines and his work against censorship, and for more detailed information on the newspaper issue without a headline, see the essay by Giuliano Galli, "O jornalismo brasileiro está em luto. Morreu Alberto Dines" (Brazilian Journalism Mourns. Alberto Dines Has Died). May 22, 2018, accessed June 7, 2021, <https://vladimirherzog.org/o-jornalismo-brasileiro-esta-em-luto-morreu-alberto-dines/>.

44 Here, reference is made only to the inconceivable experience of the Jewish community in Argentina, which, with a population share of only 0.8 percent, yet made up almost 15 percent of all *desaparecidos*, for whom it had to mourn. See, among others, DAIA (ed.), *Informe sobre la situación de los detenidos-desaparecidos judíos durante el genocidio perpetrado en Argentina, 1976–1983* [Report on the situation of Jewish prisoners and disappeared persons during the genocide perpetrated in Argentina, 1976–1983] (Buenos Aires 2007); COSOFAM (ed.), *La violación de los derechos humanos de argentinos judíos bajo el régimen militar (1976–1983)* [Human Rights Violations against Argentine Jews under Military Rule (1976–1983)], Buenos Aires 2006; Edy Kaufman, *Jewish Victims of Repression in Argentina under Military Rule (1976–1983),* in Holocaust and Genocide Studies 4 (1989), 479–499; Gabriela Lotersztein, *Los judíos bajo el terror. Argentina 1976–1983* [Jews under the Reign of Terror. Argentina 1976–1983], Buenos Aires, 2008.

communist journalist Vlado Herzog (1937–1975), who became the target of a military witch hunt.[45]

Vlado Herzog was born in Osijek (Kingdom of Yugoslavia) in 1937. His family escaped persecution during the war by fleeing to Italy and then making the crossing to Brazil in 1942, where Herzog later studied philosophy, becoming one of the country's best-known journalists and director of the famous TV station *TV Cultura*. On October 24, 1975, he turned himself in to the police in São Paulo, who had summoned him under the pretext of "clarifying" his relations with the banned Communist Party and summarily arrested him. Two comrades who were in jail at the same time heard his screams in the basement of the police building. The following day, the military claimed he had committed suicide on the basis of fake photos circulated to all the Brazilian newspapers, and handed the body over to his widow.[46]

The men of the *ḥevra kaddischa'* informed the community leadership that the body showed numerous traces of severe torture and that it could therefore be assumed that Herzog had not committed suicide. The family sounded the alarm: a murdered person should not be buried with the suicides in the back row. The contradiction between politics and *halachah* became public and attracted attention in Brazilian society. Rabbi Pinkuss came under increasing pressure. More than 600 people, including journalists, photographers, many of his non-Jewish comrades, and even Catholic priests from the resistance, attended Herzog's funeral. The Jewish cemetery was completely surrounded by police. *Halachah* (hesitantly) prevailed. Vlado Herzog was buried with a hurried ceremony in a "normal" row – though not quite in the center of the small cemetery.[47] This indirect, yet clear, indictment by the Jewish community exposed the military as liars and murderers, and resonated strongly in Brazilian society. A few days later, an ecumenical service was held in São Paulo Cathedral in memory of Vlado Herzog, attended by several thousand people, with the participation of Cardinal Paulo Evaristo Arns, Rabbi Henry Sobel, and Reverend James Wright. Both events heralded the beginning of a tenacious resistance movement.

45 On Jewish victims of the military dictatorship in Brazil, see Beatriz Kushnir, *Dez histórias mais uma para contar. Militantes (judeus) das esquerdas armadas mortos sob tortura no Brasil (1969–75)* [Ten stories and one more to tell. Activists of the Armed Left (Jews) Killed Under Torture in Brazil (1969–1975)] (paper presented at the 17th International Research Conference of the Latin American Jewish Studies Association, June 22, 2015).

46 On Herzog's death and the Jewish victims of the dictatorship in Brazil, see ibid.

47 Herzog is buried at the Cemitério Israelita do Butantã in São Paulo in Sector G, Row 28/64, see ibid.

Herzog, however, was not the first case to trigger such a conflict between *halachah* and dictatorship. Four years earlier, Chael Charles Schreier (1946–1969) had already been killed. The military had given the murdered man to the family in a sealed metal coffin. After washing the body according to the rules of the *tahara*, the men of the *ḥevra kaddisha* witnessed signs of brutal torture.[48]

The rabbis' actions and interpretations of the *halachah* varied greatly, especially in Latin America, where many victims of the dictatorship were considered to have disappeared. Some rabbis in Argentina tried to help families grieve by offering – based on the experience of *agunot*,[49] and also especially the Shoah – to say the Kaddish as soon as there was no longer any hope to find the family's loved one still alive.[50] Others refused precisely this possibility, for example in the impressive narrative *K: Relato de uma busca* by Bernardo Kucinski, who here literarily attempts to come to terms with the search for his missing sister Ana Rosa Kucinski Silva. The chapter *The Gravestone* recounts a conversation with the community Rabbi and his refusal to provide a gravestone (*mazeyve*) for Rosa: "No body no stone, so it is in Jewish law."[51]

The *halachah* was also sometimes not followed out of fear. When the 27-year-old psychologist Iara Iavelberg (1944–1971),[52] an icon of the Brazilian guerrillas, was murdered in 1971, the embalmed body was not handed over to the family until a month later. As with Herzog and many others, the cause of death was given as suicide, but this time the opening of the sealed coffin was explicitly forbidden by the regime. The family and community were shocked because Iavelberg was buried in the suicide section. In the 1990s, her siblings requested an autopsy from the Jewish community and, in the very likely event of a murder, demanded that the coffin be transferred to lie next to their parents' graves as a historical reparation. Although democracy had long prevailed in Brazil by this time, the *ḥevra kaddisha* refused the autopsy on halachic grounds.[53] Since the actual circumstances of her death suggested murder, it proposed a ceremony next to Iavelberg's

48 See Kushnir, *Dez histórias mais uma para contar*, 9, and "'Bendito seja o verdadeiro Juiz.' As narrativas dos fatos em momentos díspares, Chael, Iara e Vlado" ("'Blessed be the True Judge.' Narratives of facts at different times, Chael, Iara and Vlado") , in *Cadernos CONIB* 5 (2008), 53–61.

49 *agunot:* Wives unable to end marriage due to husband's lack of consent to divorce (either by his disappearance or refusal to consent to divorce).

50 See Liliana Ruth Feierstein, *Mourning and/or Melancholy.*

51 Bernardo Kucinski, *K. Relato de uma busca*[Narrative of a search], São Paulo 2014.

52 On Iara Iavelberg, see the biography by Judith Lieblich Patarra, *Iara. Reportagem biográfica* [Iara. Biographical Report], Rio de Janeiro, 1993 and Beatriz Kushnir, *A trajetória de Iara Iavelberg e o empenho familiar por seu sepultamento* [Iara Iavelberg's Career and the Family's Commitment to Her Funeral], in: Revista Estudos Judaicos [Journal of Jewish Studies] 8 (2005), 76–79.

53 In Judaism, disturbing the peace of the dead is strictly forbidden.

grave to give the site proper dignity. The family, however, disagreed, viewing the retention of the suicide grave as yet another victory of the murderers over truth and *halachah.* Iavelberg's family sued in civil court to challenge the decision and were eventually vindicated. In September 2003, after the court-ordered exhumation, Iara Iavelberg's remains were reinterred beside her parents'. In the same year, Vlado Herzog's family received a revised death certificate in which the cause of death was recorded as murder.

Conclusion

Heinrich Lemle – who, appropriately enough, had written his doctorate on the concept of tolerance in Moses Mendelssohn – had gone a step ahead as a liberal rabbi at the Zweigs' funeral in 1942 to respect demands of *halachah* and societal sensitivities in equal measure. Sixty years later, Brazilian justice dared to step into the Jewish cemetery to do historical justice to halachic interpretation. In the meantime, through CENTRA, the work of the German-speaking rabbis, cantors (*ḥasanjim*), and religious teachers, and all Central European immigrants, liberal Judaism has become the predominant trend on the South American continent.[54] *Di galochim senen schojn gekumn.*

Moses Mendelssohn concludes his work *Jerusalem or on Religious Power and Judaism* (1783) with the famous call: "Let no one in your states be a judge of hearts and minds; let no one arrogate to himself a right which the All-Knowing has reserved for himself alone! *If we give to Caesar what is Caesar's, you yourselves give to G-d what is G-d's! Love the truth! Love peace!*"[55] In history, the paths of God and the Emperor sometimes cross.

Two images, two laws: *halachah* and state power. In between, many rabbis, many rulers, and more than three hundred years. Different traditions of jurisprudence meet, different sources of authority, sometimes overlapping or mutually exclusive. Especially at funerals, these tensions reveal themselves. The dead inhabit a sacred place and the laws there count for something special. Death is a cosmic dis-

54 On the history of Central European rabbis and hasanim in Latin America, see Liliana Ruth Feierstein: *Das Erbe von Breslau: Zentraleuropäische Rabbiner in Lateinamerika* [The Inheritance from Breslau: Central European Rabbis in Latin America] In: Von Europa nach Südamerika – Deutsch-jüdische Kultur in der Emigration. LMU Munich, 2016/2, 77–81.

55 Moses Mendelssohn, *Jerusalem oder über religiöse Macht und Judentum* [Jerusalem or about religious Power and Judaism], Berlin 1783, 141 (author's emphasis).

ruption of the world: rabbis but also legal categories of the secular state try to restore worldly order through funerals.[56]

Dina de-malchuta dina is an ancient Talmudic principle that obliges Jews in the Diaspora to obey the laws of the land as much as necessary even where they do not conform to *halachah*. The conflicts which constantly arise as a result between legal categories of the secular state and Jewish Law are repeatedly being renegotiated – always politically and often productively. The sources of this essay offer some clues as to how Jews in the Diaspora were able to construct a relevant political praxis which did not have to choose uncompromisingly between both systems.

References

AMIA/Comunidad judía de Buenos Aires, ed. *Libro del Centenario 1894–1994* (Book on the Centenary 1894–1994). Buenos Aires, 1994.

Aries, Philippe. *Essais sur l'histoire de la mort en Occident du Moyen Age à nos jours* (Essays on the History of Death in the West from the Middle Ages to the Present). Paris: Seuil, 1975.

Avni, Haim. *Argentina y la historia de la inmigración judía, 1810–1950* (Argentina and the History of Jewish Immigration, 1810–1950). Buenos Aires: AMIA Comunidad de Buenos Aires, 1983.

Avni, Haim. *"Clientes," rufianes y prostitutas. Comunidades judías de Argentina e Israel frente a la trata de blancas* ("Clients," Pimps, and Prostitutes. Jewish communities in Argentina and Israel against trafficking in women). Buenos Aires: Leviatán, 2014.

Bar-Levav, Ariel. "We Are Where We Are Not: The Cemetery in Jewish Culture." *Jewish Studies* 41 (2002): 15–46.

Böckler, Annette. *The "Einheitsgebetbuch": History, Theology, and Post-War Reception of the Last Pre-War German Jewish Prayer Book* (unpublished manuscript).

Carassai, Sebastián. "Violencia política, dictadura militar y memoria. La Argentina de los años setenta y ochenta a partir del Archivo Marshall T. Meyer" (Political Violence, Military Dictatorship and Memory. Argentina in the 1970s and 1980s, starting from the Marshall T. Meyer Archive). *Estudios Ibero-Americanos* 43, no. 2 (2017): 380–396.

COSOFAM, ed. *La violación de los derechos humanos de argentinos judíos bajo el régimen militar (1976–1983)* (Human Rights Violations against Argentine Jews under Military Rule [1976–1983]). Buenos Aires 2006.

DAIA, ed. *Informe sobre la situación de los detenidos-desaparecidos judíos durante el genocidio perpetrado en Argentina, 1976–1983* (Report on the situation of Jewish prisoners and disappeared persons during the genocide perpetrated in Argentina, 1976–1983). Buenos Aires 2007.

Dines, Alberto. *Tod im Paradies: Die Tragödie des Stefan Zweig* (Death in Paradise: The Tragedy of Stefan Zweig). Frankfurt: Edition Büchergilde, 2006.

56 Here especially Laqueur, *The Work of the Dead*. Laqueur shows very convincingly that neither religious nor secular laws are indifferent to death.

Dines, Alberto, Israel Beloch, and Kristina Michahelles. *Stefan Zweig und sein Freundeskreis. Sein letztes Adressbuch 1940–1942* (Stefan Zweig and His Circle of Friends. Sein letztes Adressbuch 1940–1942). Berlin: Hentrich & Hentrich, 2016.

Durkheim, Émile. *Les formes élémentaires de la vie religieuse. Le système totémique en Australie* (Basic Forms of Religious Life. The Totem System in Australia). Paris 1912.

Feierstein, Liliana R. "'A Quilt of Memory': The Shoah as a Prism in the Testimonies of Survivors of the Dictatorship in Argentina." *European Review* 22, no. 4 (2014): 585–593.

Feierstein, Liliana R. "Trauer und/oder Melancholie. Religiös-kulturelle Spuren in der Trauerarbeit über politische Gewalt in Argentinien" (Grief and/or Melancholy. Religious-Cultural Traces in Mourning Political Violence in Argentina). *Jahrbuch Zentrum Jüdische Studien Berlin-Brandenburg* 2 (2015).

Feierstein, Liliana R. "Das Erbe von Breslau: Zentraleuropäische Rabbiner in Lateinamerika" (The Inheritance from Breslau: Central European Rabbis in Latin America). *Von Europa nach Südamerika – Deutsch-jüdische Kultur in der Emigration. Münchner Beiträge zur Jüdische Geschicte und Kultur, Ludwigs-Maximilians-Universität München* 10, no. 2, (2016): 77–81.

Feierstein, Ricardo. *Historia de los judíos argentinos* (History of Jewish Argentines). Buenos Aires: Galerna, 2006.

Galli, Giuliano. "O jornalismo brasileiro está em luto. Morreu Alberto Dines" (Brazilian Journalism Mourns. Alberto Dines Has Died). May 22, 2018, accessed June 7, 2021, <https://vladimirherzog.org/o-jornalismo-brasileiro-esta-em-luto-morreu-alberto-dines/>.

Gennep, Arnold van. *Les rites des passage* (Rites of Passage). Paris, 1909.

Graff, Gil. *Separation of Church and State. Dina de-Malkhuta Dina in Jewish Law, 1750–1848.* Tuscaloosa: University of Alabama Press, 2003.

Kaufman, Edy. "Jewish Victims of Repression in Argentina under Military Rule (1976–1983)." *Holocaust and Genocide Studies* 4 (1989): 479–499.

Klapheck, Elisa. "Das religiös-säkulare Spannungsfeld des Judentums" (The Religious-Secular Tension in Judaism). In vol. 1 of *Machloket*, edited by Elisa Klapheck. Berlin: Hentrich and Hentrich, 2015.

Elisa Klapheck. "Towards a Jewish Theology of Secular Law." In this volume.

Kononovich, Bernardo, dir. *Kadish.* 2009; Argentina.

Kucinski, Bernardo. *K. – Relato de uma busca* (K. – Narrative of a search). São Paulo: Cosac Naify, 2014.

Kushnir, Beatriz. "A trajetória de Iara Iavelberg e o empenho familiar por seu sepultamento" (Iara Iavelberg's Career and the Family's Commitment to Her Funeral). *Revista Estudos Judaicos* (Journal of Jewish Studies) 8 (2005): 76–79.

Kushnir, Beatriz. "Dez histórias mais uma para contar. Militantes (judeus) das esquerdas armadas mortos sob tortura no Brasil (1969–75)" (Ten stories and one more to tell. Activists of the Armed Left (Jews) Killed Under Torture in Brazil (1969–1975). Paper presented at the 17th International Research Conference of the Latin American Jewish Studies Association, June 22, 2015.

Kushnir, Beatriz. "'Bendito seja o verdadeiro Juiz.' As narrativas dos fatos em momentos díspares, Chael, Iara e Vlado" ("Blessed be the True Judge." Narratives of facts at different times, Chael, Iara, and Vlado.) *Cadernos CONIB* 5 (2008): 53–61.

Laqueur, Thomas W. *The Work of the Dead. A Cultural History of Mortal Remains.* Princeton: Princeton University Press, 2015.

Lemle, Heinrich. *O drama judaico* (The Jewish Drama). Rio de Janeiro: Edições Dois Mundos, 1944.

Associação Religiosa Israelita do Rio de Janeiro. "Em Memoria do grão-rabino Dr. Henrique Lemle z. l." (In Memory of Grand Rabbi Dr. Henrique Lemle of Blessed Memory). *Jornal do Brasil*. 1978.

Lotersztein, Gabriela. *Los judíos bajo el terror. Argentina 1976–1983* (Jews under the Reign of Terror. Argentina 1976–1983). Buenos Aires: Ejercitar La Memoria Editores, 2008.

Mendelssohn, Moses. *Briefwechsel (1761–1785)*. Edited by Reuven Michael et al. Vol. 20/2, *Gesammelte Schriften. Jubiläumsausgabe* (Collected Writings, Anniversary edition), edited by Alexander Altmann et al. Stuttgart: Frommann-Holzboog, 1994.

Mendelssohn, Moses. *Jerusalem oder über religiöse Macht und Judentum* (Jerusalem or about religious Power and Judaism). Berlin: Friedrich Maurer, 1783.

Mirelman, Victor A. *En búsqueda de una identidad. Los inmigrantes judíos en Buenos Aires, 1890–1930* (In Search of an Identity. Jewish Immigrants in Buenos Aires, 1890–1930). Buenos Aires: Milá, 1988.

Musatti Cytrynowicz, Monica and Roney Cytrynowicz. *Associação Cemitério Israelita de São Paulo, 85 anos. Patrimônio da história da comunidade judaica e da cidade de São Paulo* (85 years of Associação Cemitério Israelita de São Paulo: historical heritage of the Jewish community and the city of São Paolo). São Paulo: Narrativa-Um, 2008.

Patarra, Judith Lieblich. *Iara. Reportagem biográfica* (Iara: Biographical Report). Rio de Janeiro: Rosa dos Tempos, 1993.

Pinkuss, Fritz. *Lernen, Lehren, Helfen. Sechs Jahrzehnte als Rabbiner auf zwei Kontinenten* (Learning, Teaching, Helping. Six Decades as Rabbi on Two Continents). Heidelberg: Universitätsverlag Winter, 1990.

Rosenberg, Diego. *Marshall Meyer. El rabino que le vio la cara al diablo* (Marshall Meyer: The rabbi who looked the devil in the face). Buenos Aires: Capital Intelectual, 2010.

Slavsky, Leonor. *La espada encendida. un estudio sobre la muerte y la identidad étnica en el judaísmo*. Buenos Aires: Milá, 1993.

Umansky, Ellen M. *Lily Montagu and the Advancement of Liberal Judaism. From Vision to Vocation*. New York: Mellen, 1983.

Volcovich, Mariela. *Marshall T. Meyer. El hombre, un rabino* (Marshall T. Meyer: the man, a rabbi). Buenos Aires: Generico, 2009.

Washofsky, Mark. "Halakhah and Political Theory. A Study in Jewish Legal Response to Modernity." *Modern Judaism* 9, no. 3 (1989): 289–310.

Zweig, Stefan. *Der begrabene Leuchter: Eine Legende*. Frankfurt a. M.: Fischer, 1992.

V. Law and Literature in the Diaspora

Klaus Stierstorfer

Law and Literature in Diaspora: Gandhi's Autobiography

Mahatma Gandhi (1869–1948) has once again widely been celebrated, discussed, and studied on the occasion of his 150th anniversary in 2019. As a global icon of peaceful resistance and a politics without violence, he is also a major figure in the construction of Indian national identity today. If that is accepted, Indian identity has significantly been shaped by Gandhi's experiences with the law, much of it gained in a diasporic context, with those experiences always relating to a religious framework. Gandhi trained as a lawyer and subsequently discussed and struggled with the law, its practice, and its relation to sovereignty for the rest of his life. Much of his early legal experience was gained as a member of the Indian diaspora in South Africa and from this experience, he retained a strong interest in the fate of Indian diasporics and their connection to their homeland ever after. Literary studies can further illuminate these connections, as Gandhi, though never widely read, developed a strong position towards literature and literary education, not least as a most expansive writer himself: the official edition of his works is the outcome of "The Collected Works of Mahatma Gandhi" (CWMG) project of the Government of India, which began in September 1956, and was concluded on 2 October 1994 with the publication of the 100th volume.

It is unfortunate for anyone's ambition to construe a smooth and clear-cut analytical argument about the law, diaspora, and literature, just as it is unfortunate for any attempt at pigeonholing Gandhi's thought and work that, under further scrutiny, each of the key concepts mentioned for his characterization dissolve into fuzzy and multi-layered complexities. Although a lawyer, Gandhi appears highly suspicious of legal practice and is riven by doubts about the respectability of his chosen profession, while later he would both use and face up to the law in his protests. The question if his situation in South Africa is really diasporic also bears more than one answer. Although he joined his countrymen, who acted as a group away from home and showed clear hallmarks ascribed to diasporas, Gandhi, along with his fellow Indians in South Africa, was also one of his Majesty's subjects within the wider British Empire, and he repeatedly professed his faithfulness to this status. When it comes to literature, things get even more complicated. Al-

Note: I wish to thank Prof. Sridhar Rajeswaran, Mumbai, for all the inspiring conversations on Indian history and culture in general, and on Gandhi in particular. Without these, I would not have ventured on the present "experiments" with Gandhi.

https://doi.org/10.1515/9783111062631-011

though he had spells of intense reading on various subjects, Gandhi's concepts of "literature" and of "literary education" have little space for the modern concept of literature as a form of art, and his extensive writings hardly touch on the realm of *belles lettres*.

Thus, bringing together these central concerns and issues in Gandhi's life does not result in a smooth texture, but rather in a Gordian knot no sword will easily cut. The approach taken here, limited and modest as it is, reverts to Gandhi's own view on his lifelines drawn out by diaspora, law, and literature, as they can be found in his autobiography, *The Story of My Experiments with Truth*, which appeared in serial publication between November 1925 and February 1929. Gandhi's reflections on the impact of various diasporic experiences on his legal and writerly outlook will be outlined and analyzed, even if these endeavors again will be hampered by the fact that Gandhi, with some justification, keeps insisting that this is not a biography in the received generic mold.

The approach taken in the following is therefore based on a reading of Gandhi's autobiography, where his own view on the central concepts of this paper – law, diaspora, and literature – will be clarified in a serial analysis. They will then be brought together in their functions within his autobiography and the specific approach he took in its conception. Thus, we first turn to Gandhi's views on and practice of the law.

Born Mohandas Karamchand Gandhi on 2 October 1869 in Porbandar, Kathiawar (on the coast of today's Gujarat), which was, of course, part of the British Empire at the time, he had a religiously minded mother and a father who was, as his father before him, a chief minister of Porbandar, then Prime Minister in Rajkot and then in Vankaner, as Gandhi relates on the first page of his autobiography. His father was also, as Gandhi reports, "a member of the Rajasthanik Court," which, he continues, "is now extinct, but in those days it was a very influential body for settling disputes between the chiefs and their fellow clansmen" (3).[1] The law and political office clearly had been running in the Gandhi family for the last few generations. Gandhi writes about an indifferent schooling and an indifferent childhood, including his arranged child marriage at the age of 13, as well as his indifferent attempts to study at a college in Bhavnagar. After his father's death in 1884, a Brahmin friend of the family advised that he should go to England for his studies, as his father had intended him to follow in his political footsteps, which the Brahmin doubted could be achieved by local education. Gandhi's pref-

1 All quotations from the autobiography are given with page numbers in parentheses from Mohandas Karamchand Gandhi, *The Story of My Experiments with Truth. An Autobiography* (Nolida: Om Books International, 2010, repr. 2018).

erence for the medical profession was opposed, he relates, by both the Brahmin and his elder brother, because it was not seen as helpful on his way to high office, as the Brahmin averred, and because his father would not have liked someone from their caste, the Vaishnavas, to have anything "to do with dissection of dead bodies": "Father intended you for the bar" (40), was his brother's summary conclusion, which young Gandhi then followed.

From his family home, Gandhi set out to Porbandar to meet his uncle, who had followed his father as chief minister there, only to find him strictly opposed to his plans to become a lawyer. He quotes his uncle as remonstrating thus: "When I meet these big barristers, I see no difference between their life and that of Europeans. They know no scruples regarding food. Cigars are never out of their mouths. They dress as shamelessly as Englishmen. All that would not be in keeping with our family tradition" (41). In short, Gandhi's "going to England [...] was in his opinion an irreligious act" (42). This early doubt, first experienced from the side of his uncle, about the moral integrity of the legal profession and its potential incompatibility with Indian cultural and religious life would remain with Gandhi through much of his early career as a lawyer, and his troubled ruminations about the law form a main theme throughout his autobiography. This includes his (probably justified) lack of enthusiasm about his legal training in England, which can already be seen by its place in his autobiographical narrative: in part I, chapter 12, he describes his departure to England "for being called to the bar" (45). It is only in part I, chapter 24 ("Called – But Then?") that he finally begins addressing his legal studies. His report is worth quoting at some length:

> There were two conditions which had to be fulfilled before a student was formally called to the bar: 'keeping terms' equivalent to about three years; and passing examinations. 'Keeping terms' meant eating one's terms, i. e. attending at least six out of about twenty-four dinners in term. [...] The curriculum of study was easy, barristers being humorously known as 'dinner barristers'. Everyone knew that the examinations had practically no value. In my time there were two, one in Roman Law and the other in Common Laws. There were regular textbooks prescribed for these examinations which could be taken in compartments, but scarcely anyone read them. [...] Question papers were easy and examiners were generous. The percentage of passes in the Roman Law examination used to be 95 to 99 and those in the final examinations 75 or even more. (89)

These exams, Gandhi concludes, "could not be felt as a difficulty. But I succeeded in turning them into one" (89). Far from lowering his standards to the easy life of an English law student, he set out on a course of extensive readings, notably Roman law (in Latin, which he had started to study in earnest at the University of London). He read "Broom's *Common Law*," "Snell's *Equity*," "White and Tudor's *Leading Cases*," "Williams' and Edward's *Real Property*," and Goodeve's *Personal Prop-*

erty (90). Gandhi was called to the bar in June 1891, enrolled in the High Court, and immediately afterwards took the next ship home.

Back in India, he found that, despite all his very serious readings during his time in London, "it was easy to be called, but it was difficult to practice at the bar. I had read the laws, but not learnt how to practice law" (91). Trying to set up a legal practice in Bombay, he not only noted that he did not know anything about Indian law (which he began to study), either "Hindu or Mahomedan Law" (91), and so he summarizes: "This is how I began life. I found the barrister's profession a bad job – much show and little knowledge" (104). And in this endeavor he failed dramatically: when taking on a minor defense job in court, he could not find the heart to cross-examine the plaintiff's witnesses and had to leave the court in complete embarrassment and shame. He fled from Bombay back to Rajkot, where his brother would give him some legal office work, and he even considered abandoning the law completely and becoming a schoolteacher of English. It is quite possible that the trace of this failed barrister, who was too diffident for the clamorous life at the bar and too principled to get the elbowroom he would have needed in an increasingly competitive field, would have disappeared at this point; or rather, he would never have risen to the prominence attributed even to this failure by the wider public today. What jerked Gandhi out of the dismal situation encountered during the two years after his return to India in 1891 was a chance opportunity to go to South Africa in 1893 and help with a lawsuit of an Indian firm there. It is not too great a claim to say that his failing legal career as well as his trajectory towards a political leader and national icon was jumpstarted by joining the Indian diaspora abroad. He had, to take up his own words, "read the laws" in Britain and India, but he only "learnt how to practice the law" as a member of the Indian diaspora in South Africa (91). What was the reason for this climactic turnaround?

In his autobiography, this change is described in two connected areas: on the one hand, Gandhi's philosophical reconfiguration of the law in general and in legal practice in particular, and, on the other hand, the legal requirements posed by the diasporic situation in South Africa. In the first area, Gandhi was struggling for his own way of truth and honesty against his impression, instilled in him early on during his studies in England, that "the lawyer's profession was a liar's profession" (409). Gandhi's counterstrategy was to stick to truth and honesty no matter the requirements of a case, as he reports: "I warned every new client at the outset that he should not expect me to take up a false case or to coach the witnesses" (410). He goes on to relate his experience in a particularly complicated trial in South Africa, where his clients had made a mistake in the contentious accounting and Gandhi, as junior counsel, successfully persuaded the senior counsel and the clients to admit to that mistake in front of the court. Gandhi presented the case and they won to Gandhi's huge relief: "I was delighted. So were my client and senior counsel; and I was confirmed in my conviction that it was not impossible to practice law without compromising truth" (413). Gandhi's arrival at this arrangement of sorts happened in a law case in South Africa but was not specific to the diasporic situation. Nor would it completely put Gandhi at peace with legal practice in general, as he immediately continues his joyful remark with the following cautionary one: "Let the reader, however, remember that even truthfulness in the practice of the profession cannot cure it of the fundamental defect that vitiates it" (413).

That inbuilt defect of the law was, in Gandhi's view, systemic, as he writes earlier in the autobiography: "I became disgusted with the profession. As lawyers the counsel on both sides were bound to take up points of law in support of their own clients. I also saw for the first time that the winning party never recovers all the costs incurred" (149). And later he writes along similar lines: "I got disgusted with the legal profession. The very intellect became an abomination to me inasmuch as it could be prostituted for screening crime" (306). Gandhi's conclusion was that the current practice of the law as a confrontation of two factions, with him as lawyer serving one of the sides against exorbitant remuneration, could not satisfy him. In fact, he only discovers his true vocation as a lawyer in a case where, in a sense, he succeeds in bypassing legal procedure and bringing about an out-of-court settlement: "My joy was boundless. I had learnt the true practice of law. I had learnt to find out the better side of human nature and to enter men's hearts. I realized that the true function of a lawyer was to unite parties riven asunder" (150).

Although Gandhi was able to make peace with his legal occupation in this fundamental, philosophical way, a second element was missing to redeem the law as an important, albeit never undoubted, instrument; this element clearly stems from his diasporic experience in South Africa. When the shy and hapless barrister arrived in Durban, he encountered what he calls "the deep disease of colour prejudice" (127). On his way from the port of Durban to Pretoria he had first-hand experience of it. Although Indians formed various subgroups, such as indentured laborers, Arab merchants, or Parsi clerks, they were summarily and disparagingly called "coolies," and Gandhi became "known as the 'coolie barrister'" (122). During this first journey in South Africa, he immediately felt the full force of this racial prejudice: he was thrown out of a first-class train compartment, then denied a seat inside a coach and assaulted by a passenger for not getting down from the coach at his behest, before being refused a hotel room on arrival (129). Sheth Abdul Gani, his contact in Johannesburg, Gandhi reports, then "narrated to me the story of the hardships of Indians in South Africa" (130). Here, Gandhi found his true calling in taking up the cause of the Indian diaspora, both by helping his countrymen as a lawyer in court and by political activities that were to become famous precedents for the much bigger movements to come in India itself. Looking back in his autobiography, he emphasizes the importance of this time of germination:

> The year's stay in Pretoria was a most valuable experience in my life. Here it was that I had opportunities of learning public work and acquired some measure of my capacity for it. Here it was that the religious spirit within me became a living force, and here too I acquired a true knowledge of legal practice. Here I learnt the things that a junior barrister learns in a senior barrister's chamber, and here I also gained confidence that I should not after all fail as a lawyer. (147)

The three interconnected areas of religious identity, legal expertise, and political commitment were all decisively shaped through his diasporic experience. What he encountered in South Africa was a real need of the law to redress social injustice and discrimination. Whereas his experience of the law so far, both in Britain and India, was primarily that of often disingenuous haggling for financial advantage, he now came to see it as an important instrument in a wider, socio-political context. Gandhi's own self-awareness of the formative character of these years is clearly shown in his autobiography, and further elaborated in his earlier publication *Satyagraha in South Africa*,[2] to which he refers the reader of his autobiography at the beginning of part II, chapter 13 (144).

Both in his autobiography and, more extensively, in *Satyagraha*, Gandhi outlined the origins of the Indian diaspora in South Africa. The urgent need for a large labor force on the settlers' plantations had led to the idea to bring Indians from across the Indian Ocean from one part of the British Empire to the other. The first ship with indentured laborers arrived in Natal in 1860 and brought a workforce with a contract to work in the plantations for five years under the conditions stipulated in the indenture, and with the right to settle and own land after the expiry of the contract. This potentially beneficial arrangement for both sides – the supply of badly needed workers to the plantations, and the creation of job opportunities with land-ownership potential for Indians coming from usually dire economic prospects at home – did not work out as expected. In *Satyagraha*, Gandhi sums up the grievance of the indentured laborers, which he had elaborated in his *Green Pamphlet* of 1896 (187). He writes about the contracts of the Indian workers:

> Fairly good arrangements were made for their board. But adequate consideration was not given to the question as to how these illiterate labourers who had gone to a distant land were to seek redress if they had any grievances. No thought was given to their religious needs or to the preservation of their morality. The British officials in India did not consider

2 Mohandas Karamchand Gandhi, *Satyagraha in South Africa* (in Gujarati: 1924), transl. Valji Govindji Desai (Ahmedabad: Navajivan, 1928).

> that although slavery had been abolished by law, employers could not be free from a desire to make slaves of their employees. They did not realize, as they ought to have realized, that the labourers who had gone to Natal would in fact become temporary slaves.[3]

This was the situation where Gandhi found his lawyer's calling, as he shows in part II, chapter 20 with the example of Balasundaram, a Tamil indentured laborer. The man came to him for redress against his employer, who had severely beaten him. Gandhi took up his case and successfully sued the employer, with the result that his client's indenture was transferred to another employer. Gandhi's report of the outcome of the case shows the impact he made as well as the diaspora's connection to the homeland:

> Balasundaram's case reached to ears of every indentured labourer and I came to be regarded as their friend. I hailed this connection with delight. A regular stream of indentured labourers began to pour into my office, and I got the best opportunity of learning their joys and sorrows. The echoes of Balasundaram's case were heard in far off Madras. [...] There was nothing extraordinary in the case itself, but the fact that there was someone in Natal to espouse their cause and publicly work for them gave the indentured labourers a joyful surprise and inspired them with hope. (172)

While this legal work mainly concerned indentured employees' grievances, more wide-ranging issues developed with those who had finished their five-year stint and chose to settle in South Africa rather than return to India, an option clearly offered in the arrangement of the indentures. In his autobiography, Gandhi provides a sustained narrative of how the relations between the white settlers and the Indians recruited as farm labor turned sour, which is worth quoting at length here:

> These recruits were to sign an indenture to work in Natal for five years, and at the end of the term they were to be at liberty to settle there and to have full rights of ownership of land. Those were the inducements held out to them, for the whites then had looked forward to improving their agriculture by the industry of the Indian labourers after the term of their indentures had expired. / But the Indians gave more than had been expected of them. They grew large quantities of vegetables. They introduced a number of Indian varieties and made I possible to grow the local varieties cheaper. They entered trade. They purchased land for building, and many raised themselves from the status of labourers to that of owners of land and houses. [...] The white traders were alarmed. When they first welcomed the Indian labourers, they had not reckoned with their business skill. They might be tolerated as independent agriculturists, but their competition in trade could not be brooked. / This sowed the seed of antagonism to Indians. Many other factors contributed to its growth. Our different ways of living, our simplicity, our contentment with small gains, our indiffer-

---

3 Gandhi, *Satyagraha*, 20.

> ence to the laws of hygiene and sanitation, our slowness in keeping our surroundings clean and tidy, and our stinginess in keeping our houses in good repair – all these, combined with the difference in religion, continued to fan the flame of antagonism. (174)

The antagonism produced legislative consequences in the form of a bill to disenfranchise Indians and to impose a heavy annual tax on those Indians who did not either return home after the end of their contract or renew their indenture. A delegation was sent to Lord Elgin, then Viceroy of India, for approval of this tax. Massive agitation against the tax, in which Gandhi was a leading figure, eventually brought the tax down from the original proposal of twenty-five pounds to three pounds per annum. Generally, Gandhi felt called upon to fight for the rights of his countrymen in South Africa, as he saw that "the bulk of Indians who went to South Africa were ignorant, pauper agriculturalists, who needed all the care and protection that could be given them" (321). Throughout, Gandhi kept the wider, diasporic vision, linking up diasporic situations across the cultures from India to Europe to Africa. Taking up the concept of the ghetto as a particularly nefarious development for diasporas, he succinctly observes about the bad living conditions in the "coolie locations" (320) in Johannesburg and elsewhere:

> Some of the classes which render us the greatest social service, but which we Hindus have chosen to regard as 'untouchables', are relegated to remote quarters of a town or a village, called in Gujarati *dhedvado* […]. Even so in Christian Europe the Jews were once 'untouchables', and the quarters that were assigned to them had the offensive name of 'ghettoes'. In a similar way today we have become the untouchables of South Africa. (320)

It is therefore not too much to say that Gandhi's understanding of the law and of legal practice was deeply informed by his diasporic experience in South Africa. During this time, he had not only gained sorely needed motivation and experience as a barrister, but also his legal understanding had become integrated in a wider political and public agenda. This agenda had its focus in the Indian diaspora in South Africa, but quickly transcended this geopolitical context, as the quotation above has shown, to address all kinds of discrimination, including that of his home culture, where the "untouchables" acquired attributes of an internal diaspora for him.

While his individual course of action consisted in employing his legal training to support his countrymen in the Indian diaspora in the law courts, the public and political instrument which he developed was *satyagraha*. Gandhi developed the concept during his South African years, and the concept's central role in the ensuing independence movement in India is, of course, history, as they say. The report in his autobiography is brief, as he refers the reader to his book-length history of

Satyagraha in South Africa. The main point he makes in the autobiography is the reason for finding a special, Indian name for the concept:

> The principle called Satyagraha came into being before that name was invented. Indeed when it was born, I myself could not say what it was. In Gujarati also we used the English phrase 'passive resistance' to describe it. When in a meeting of Europeans I found that the term 'passive resistance' was too narrowly construed, that it was supposed to be a weapon of the weak, that it could be characterized by hatred, and that it could finally manifest itself as violence, I had to demur to all these statements and explain the real nature of the Indian movement. It was clear that a new word must be coined by the Indians to designate their struggle. (357)

What the Gujarati and Hindi word, meaning "holding on to truth," or "firmness in a good cause,"[4] powerfully expressed was not only the non-violent attitude, but also the readiness to suffer and a focus on essentials without any admixture of hatred or revenge.[5] Famously, it was the guiding principle of the resistance against racial discrimination against Indians in South Africa which Gandhi masterminded and which culminated in the famous march of over 2,000 Indians from Charlestown over the border into the Transvaal. The following wave of imprisonment of Satyagrahis swamped the prisons of South Africa and could not be upheld for long, facilitating Gandhi's ability to strike a deal with the Union Government represented by General Smuts, which has gone down in history as the Smuts-Gandhi compromise.[6] It brought significant relief to Indians in South Africa, after which Gandhi saw his mission accomplished and finally returned to India, taking with him the full complement of his social, legal, and political experience from the diaspora.

In sum, Gandhi's diasporic experience was crucial in the development of his understanding of the law from a theoretical field of study and area of highly ambiguous professional practice to an operationalization of both theory and practice within a wider social and political context. In this he was helped, as I will now show in my final point of argument, by the development of his literary understanding, which offers some surprising analogies.

Gandhi's attitude to literature and "literary education," as he frequently called it, appears as ambivalent as his views on the law. In his childhood, he remembers to have "had a distaste for any reading beyond my school books" (7), but immediately avers how deeply affected he was by two plays he encountered at the time,

---

4 *Oxford English Dictionary*, s.v. "satyagraha, *n.*," accessed December 30, 2021, https://www-oed.com.ezproxy.princeton.edu/view/Entry/171300?redirectedFrom=satyagraha&.

5 Gandhi, *Satyagraha*, 302.

6 See e.g., Denis Judd, *Empire. The British Imperial Experience, 1765 to the Present* (London: Harper Collins, 1996), 226–241.

one in his father's library, and one performed live. He struggled with readings in English, notably with Bentham's *Theory of Utility,* upon arrival in London, but took to reading the newspapers regularly (53). Further books he read at the beginning of his studies all served the practical purpose to help him survive as an Indian diasporic in Britain: they were books on vegetarianism to strengthen his conviction against eating meat, or on rhetoric, such as Bell's *Standard Elocutionist* (57). Another category of reading at the time served his religious search and included theosophy, Carlyle's chapter on Mohammed in *Heroes and Hero-Worship,* Bradlaugh on atheism and the *Bhagavadgita* (76–77), and, finally, the law books already mentioned above. When he confides in a mentor, Dadabhai Naoroji, in London about his failure as a lawyer, he gets the following advice from this seasoned practitioner: "I understand your trouble. Your general reading is meagre. You have no knowledge of the world, a sine qua non for a vakil. You have not even read the history of India. A vakil should know human nature. He should be able to read a man's character from his face" (92). This advice, far from suggesting extensive literary experience as educational, actually referred to the physiognomists. Although dutifully going off to read Johann Kasper Lavater, Gandhi found him "scarcely interesting": "I studied Shakespeare's physiognomy, but did not acquire the knack of finding out the Shakespeare's [*sic*] walking up and down the streets of London. Lavator's [*sic*] book did not add to my knowledge" (93).

Gandhi left England with his literary interests quite as undeveloped as his legal assurance and expertise. And much like his legal awakening, Gandhi's literary awakening had to wait until he joined the Indian diaspora in South Africa. It was only there that he started reading books on various religions (Edwin Arnold's *The Light of Asia* [1879] on Buddha, Washington Irving and Thomas Carlyle on Mohammed, Leo Tolstoy on Christianity, Max Müller's *India: What Can It Teach Us?* [1883] on Indian culture and religion, and a translation of the *Upanishads* published by the Theosophical Society). These few examples quickly show that Gandhi's readings were eclectic and his sources mostly Western. What is more, not only was his view of Indian culture and religion shaped by Western perceptions, but it took the diasporic distancing for him to develop a profound interest in Indian culture and religion in the first place. Especially the readings of Indian religious texts, notably the "Gita," helped him in his recalibrations of the law. Thus, he writes:

> I understood more clearly in the light of the Gita teaching the implications of the word 'trustee'. My regard for jurisprudence increased, I discovered in it religion. I understood the Gita teaching of non-possession to mean that those who desired salvation should act like the trustee who, though having control over great possessions, regards not an iota of them as his own. (295)

The book, however, that Gandhi casts as the greatest revelation in his reading life is John Ruskin's *Unto This Last* (1862). It is given a chapter of its own in part IV of his autobiography, entitled "18. The Magic Spell of a Book." Gandhi was given the book to read on a train journey by Henry Solomon Leon Polak, an English Jew whose acquaintance he had made in a vegetarian restaurant and who had become one of his closest advisors and friends. Gandhi wrote:

> This was the first book of Ruskin I had ever read. During the days of my education I had read practically nothing outside textbooks, and after I launched into active life I had very little time for reading. I cannot therefore claim much book knowledge. However, I believe I have not lost much because of this enforced restraint. On the contrary, the limited reading may be said to have enabled me thoroughly to digest what I did read. Of these books, the one that brought about an instantaneous and practical transformation of my life was *Unto This Last.* (333)

And he goes on to sum up, as he says, the "teachings of *Unto This Last* I understood to be":

> 1. That the good of the individual is contained in the good of all.
> 2. That a lawyer's work has the same value as the barber's, inasmuch as all have the same right of earning their livelihood from their work.
> 3. That a life of labour, i. e., the life of the tiller of the soil and the handicraftsman, is the life worth living.
> [...] I arose with the dawn, ready to reduce these principles to practice. (334)

Here, Gandhi clearly sets out his attitude to literature as such: although he values what he calls "literary education," and has qualms about not having provided enough of it for his own children (221), books are valuable when they have practical relevance in directly changing people's lives, and his own reading experience of Ruskin is emblematic thereof. Gandhi has no time for what might be called *belles lettres*; edification or entertainment are qualities he does not appreciate as literary qualities in their own right. Whenever he commends a book's style, as in his phrase "Williams' book read like a novel" (90), it is not to encourage novels as paradigmatic for good literature; it is a commendation of the law book's accessibility and efficacy in providing knowledge and information. In short, Gandhi displays no interest in aesthetic qualities of any kind in literature, unless they are conducive to producing the desired outcome. Hence, his approach to literature in general is rhetorical, rather than aesthetic. And here, law and literature come together in Gandhi's very specific, diasporic mode: he is neither looking for a poetics of literature nor, ultimately, for a philosophy of the law; rather, he is interested both in a rhetoric and pragmatics of law and literature. In the public sphere, law and literature are operationalized for and made instrumental to public service, which for Gandhi refers to the Indian diaspora in South Africa and, later, the wider Indian nation in its struggle for independence. In his private sphere, both law and literature become instruments in what Gandhi calls his search for truth, which has many facets for him, but ultimately becomes an emblem for God, as he writes:

> Truth is the sovereign principle, which includes numerous other principles. This truth is not only truthfulness in word, but truthfulness in thought also, and not only the relative truth of our conception, but the Absolute Truth, the Eternal Principle, that is God. There are innumerable definitions of God, because His manifestations are innumerable. [...] But I worship God as Truth only. I have not yet found Him, but I am seeking after Him. [...] But as long as I have not realized this Absolute Truth, so long must I hold by the relative truth as I have conceived it. (xiii)

This principle of Gandhi's is particularly manifest in his venture to write his autobiography. As with the law, which he came to know mainly in its English version, Gandhi perceived of the forms of literature available to him as ambivalent and part of civilization, which he does not cast as necessarily Western, but certainly as modern, and which he repeatedly criticized.[7] Gandhi quotes an unnamed friend in his introduction who articulated these doubts: "Writing an autobiography is a practice peculiar to the West. I know of nobody in the East having written one, except amongst those who have come under Western influence" (xii). Leaving aside a discussion about the arguable claim that autobiography is here cast as an essentially "Western" genre, it is clear that Gandhi had his problems with the form that went against the grain of the entire venture he wanted to express in it. In autobiography, author, narrator, and narrated content (the narrated "I") are one. What therefore typically emerges as the result of autobiographical narration, as commonly understood today in the tradition of Rousseau and others, is an identity, a persona which is formed in and through the self-reflexive story. This is not Gandhi's aim in his version of an autobiography whose "hero" was not the self, but rather truth, which, as the quotation above indicates, is ultimately a cipher for God in Gandhi's universe. Angelika Malinar observes:

> This spiritual quest [for truth; K.St.] is turned by Gandhi into an autobiography [...] by interpreting his life as a series of 'experiments' with the reality and realization of this truth. Since this calls for reducing rather than building up the 'individual', the ego-oriented self, it seems to contradict the purpose of a standard 'Western', ego-centred autobiography.[8]

---

7 See Angelika Malinar, "Mohandas Karamchand Gandhi," in *Handbook of Autobiography / Autofiction*, ed. Martina Wagner-Egelhaaf (Berlin and Boston: De Gruyter, 2019), 3:1703–1718, 1708.

8 Malinar, 1709. I thank Ari Kloke, LCSW, very much for her great support in translating this chapter into English.

In short, the form of an autobiography was a misfit for the content Gandhi wanted to convey, though it could, just like law and literature in general, be inflected to Gandhi's firm trajectory. He did so by signaling already in the subtitle that it was a "series of experiments with truth," and these various experiments are presented so that truth is clearly set as the vanishing point of the narrative. In fact, as Gandhi avers at one point, "writing it [the autobiography; K.St.] is itself one of the experiments with truth" (312). In that sense, Gandhi's autobiography is a text with the aim to abolish itself, or at least its subject which is intimately tied to its form: the self. However, in place of the vanishing self, Gandhi conjures up refractions of truth both in his private and public life and in an Indian nation; such refractions of truth emerge out of a constitutive diasporic experience in South Africa, and will later take root in the home country of an independent India. Neither Gandhi's understanding and practice of the law, nor his attitude to literature, nor his specific presentation of both in an innovative use of the genre of autobiography would have been possible without his diasporic experience. And if Gandhi is projected more than ever as an avatar of the identity of a modern India, that identity is a profoundly diasporic one.

References

Gandhi, Mohandas Karamchand. *Satyagraha in South Africa.* Translated by Valji Govindji Desai. Ahmedabad: Navajivan Publishing House, 1928.

Gandhi, Mohandas Karamchand. *The Story of My Experiments with Truth. An Autobiography.* Nolida: Om Books International, 2010, reprint 2018.

Judd, Denis. *Empire. The British Imperial Experience, 1765 to the Present.* London: Harper Collins, 1996.

Malinar, Angelika. "Mohandas Karamchand Gandhi." In *Exemplary Autobiographical/Autofictional Texts,* edited by Martina Wagner-Egelhaaf, 1703–1718. Vol. 3 of *Handbook of Autobiography / Autofiction.* Berlin and Boston: De Gruyter, 2019.

Caspar Battegay

Star Trek: Diaspora and Law in the German-Jewish Imagination

Universal Diaspora

Between August 1918 and March 1919, the former soldier Franz Rosenzweig lived temporarily in Freiburg im Breisgau. There he wrote his main philosophical work *Der Stern der Erlösung* (*The Star of Redemption*), which he had designed in the trenches of the Balkan front. Deeply connected linguistically with the German idealist tradition, while at the same time tied to biblical and rabbinical thinking, the book represents the systematic attempt at a Jewish existential philosophy. In the third and last part, the author outlines his political theology: an alternative to the liberal and bourgeois Jewishness of assimilation, but also to the Zionist understanding of the Jewish people as a modern nation – a Judaism as a community of timelessness. According to Rosenzweig, the Christian peoples are essentially organized as territorial states; they live in the medium of history and politics and move from revelation in the past to redemption in the future. For Judaism, however, the star of redemption always burns within, and redemption can take place at any moment. Rosenzweig does not use the term "diaspora," rather he speaks of exile and of a community that is constituted only by itself and not by a territory. He writes: "we have taken root in ourselves, without roots in the earth."[1]

In this context, the concept of law in the *Star of Redemption* is crucial. Rosenzweig states: "Therefore, the peoples are alive when they continuously change their today into new customs ... and at the same time set new law from their today for the tomorrow."[2] For Rosenzweig, the law, along with the soil and the language, is one of the three characteristics of a modern nation. To the Eternal People, on the other hand, these three categories are sacred. For Judaism, the Jewish Law is the "the only available path to redemption."[3] This sacred, even eschatological status of the law also means, however, that it is the subject of a traditional practice of interpretation; it can be interpreted, but not changed: "and whereas the peoples

---

1 Franz Rosenzweig, *The Star of Redemption*, trans. Barbara E. Galli (Madison WI: University of Wisconsin Press, 2005), 324.

2 Rosenzweig, *The Star*, 322.

3 Zohar Maor, "Redemption and Law: Rosenzweig's Critique on Max Brod" in *Faith, Truth, and Reason. New Perspectives on Franz Rosenzweig's "Star of Redemption,"* ed. Yehoyada Amir et. al. (Freiburg im Breisgau: Verlag Karl Alber 2012), 391–408, 406.

https://doi.org/10.1515/9783111062631-012

live in revolutions in which the law continuously sheds its skin, here [in Judaism] reigns the law that no revolution could repeal, and that can probably be evaded but not changed."[4]

In my contribution, I will not offer a new interpretation of Rosenzweig's complex philosophy of history. Rather, I would like to explore the connection between diaspora and law in the German-Jewish imagination in the decades after the First World War. In addition to a quasi-bourgeois literature of German Jews who understood themselves less as Jews than as Germans, and a Zionist literature aimed at building up a modern Jewish national culture, I will follow a narrow but clear line of Jewish writing that locates its creative element in the diaspora. In German-Jewish literature, we find a remarkable congruence with the use of the term "diaspora," which did not develop until the 1990s in postcolonial studies, and, in the course of what is known as globalization, has led to a successful new academic discipline called *diaspora studies.*[5] I want to show that "the powers of diaspora" are not only stated in retrospect, as Jonathan and Daniel Boyarin show in their admirable essay, in which they plead for understanding the diaspora as a cultural resource of Judaism and not only as a history of suffering and heteronomy, thus placing the emphasis more on the aspect of the diaspora community than on that of dispersion.

In general, it should be noted that the term diaspora is not used as frequently by modern Jewish authors as the three terms exile, *galut* (Hebrew), or *golus* (Yiddish). The negative connotation of the term diaspora is particularly widespread among authors with Zionist leanings. The young Martin Buber, for example, speaks of the "torments of the diaspora" ["die Qualen der Diaspora"] when he is concerned with developing a new Jewish autonomous self-image.[6] Under the impression of the devastating anti-Semitism of the German Nazi dictatorship, this assessment becomes even more radical.[7] In contrast, however, diaspora was already perceived as a cultural resource by a minority of German-speaking Jewish intellectuals of the early twentieth century. Interestingly, it is in a letter to Buber of all

4 Rosenzweig, *The Star*, 323.

5 Jonathan Boyarin and Daniel Boyarin, *Powers of Diaspora. Two Essays on the Relevance of Jewish Culture* (Minneapolis: Univerity of Minnessota Press 2002).

6 Martin Buber, "Jüdische Renaissance," in *Werkausgabe 3. Frühe Jüdische Schriften 1900–1922*, ed. Barbara Schäfer (Gütersloh: Gütersloher Verlagshaus, 2007), 146; Unless otherwise noted, all translations are my own.

7 One of the paradigmatic texts in this regard is an essay from 1936 by the historian Jizchak Fritz Baer, in which he denounces the exile ["galut"] as "political slavery, which has to be suspended" ["politische Knechtschaft, die restlos aufgehoben werden muß"]. Jizchak Fritz Baer, *Galut* (Berlin: Schocken, 1936), 101.

people that Stefan Zweig writes in the war-torn year of 1917: "The only thing that separates me from you and yours is that I never wanted Judaism to become a nation again .... That I love and affirm the Diaspora as the meaning of its [Judaism's] idealism, as its cosmopolitan, all-human vocation."[8] In what follows, I will trace the various formulations and conceptions of this "all-human vocation." One consequence of the German-Jewish existence and especially of its violent end is the differentiated (and certainly in many cases ambivalent) approach to the connection between legality, law, community and political existence, which was demonstrated, for example, by Hannah Arendt. Thus, for instance, she held that "the boundaries of positive law are for the political existence of man what memory is for his historical existence: they guarantee the pre-existence of a common world, the reality of some continuity which transcends the individual life span of each generation."[9] However, in my essay, I will not focus on the theoretical reflection of this "common world" but on non-systematic approaches by German-Jewish poets and writers.

To begin, I would like to look at a quote by the expressionist poet Alfred Wolfenstein (1883–1945), who was involved in the establishment of the Munich Soviet Republic together with Ernst Toller. In his essay *Jüdisches Wesen und neue Dichtung* (*Jewish Essence and New Poetry*) from 1922, he noted:

> In the present, no one bears the signs of transition as visibly as the Jew. War and revolution, the fraternal catastrophe, has stirred up all its problems. Perhaps the diaspora, as after the destruction of Jerusalem and the fall of the ghetto, began anew now. This time, however, it is a general human, a more connected dispersion. But I believe that the Jew is called to it forever (and this does not have to be better and not even more sorrowful than the rootedness).[10]

---

8 "Und von Ihnen und den Ihren trennt mich nur dies, dass ich nie wollte, dass das Judentum wieder Nation wird und damit sich in die Concurrenz der Realitäten erniedrigt. Dass ich die Diaspora liebe und bejahe als den Sinn seines Idealismus, als seine weltbürgerliche allmenschliche Berufung." Stefan Zweig, *Briefe zum Judentum*, ed. Stefan Litt (Berlin: Jüdischer Verlag im Suhrkamp Verlag, 2020), 49.

9 Hanna Arendt, *The Origins of Totalitarianism* (New York: Schocken Books, 2004), 599. See also *Hannah Arendt and the Law*, ed. Marco Goldoni and Christopher McCorkindale (Oxford: Hart Publishing, 2012).

10 "In der Gegenwart trägt keiner die Zeichen des Übergangs so sichtbar wie der Jude. Krieg und Revolution, die geschwisterliche Katastrophe, hat all seine Problematik aufgewühlt. Vielleicht begann die Diaspora, wie nach der Zerstörung Jerusalems und nach dem Fall des Ghettos, von neuem jetzt. Sie ist freilich diesmal eine allgemeiner menschliche, eine verbundenere Zerstreuung. Doch ich glaube, der Jude ist zu ihr (die nicht besser und nicht einmal leidvoller sein muss als die Verwurzelung) für immer berufen." Alfred Wolfenstein, *Jüdisches Wesen und neue Dichtung* (Berlin: Erich Reiss, 1922), 8.

In this quote, four remarkable aspects can be observed. Firstly, Wolfenstein suspects that the breakout of the First World War and the revolutions mark the beginning of a new diaspora. He parallels this beginning with the Roman conquest of Jerusalem in the year 70, and with Jewish emancipation in modern European societies ("fall of the ghetto"). Secondly, this new diaspora is in his words a "general human" diaspora. It is noteworthy, that Wolfenstein paradoxically describes his universal diaspora as "a more connected dispersal" in comparison with the two preceding historical stages of Jewish history (destruction of the temple, emancipation). Thirdly, "the Jew" nevertheless has a particular position, an ontologically prominent status in Wolfenstein's universalist diaspora model. For the "Jewish being" (which gives the essay its title *das jüdische Wesen*) is "forever called" into a diasporic condition. Fourthly, Wolfenstein's re-evaluation of the term diaspora is striking, for the term has still clearly a negative connotation at the beginning of the twentieth century; however, for Wolfenstein, the term seems to be rather neutral or even positive: "[The diaspora] does not have to be better and not even more painful than rooting."

The four aspects of this quote are thus meta-history, universalism, ontology and the re-evaluation of the concept of diaspora, the transition into a category which seems to tend to be positive.[11] We can observe these four aspects again and again in different texts that try to escape the hegemonic determinations of Jewish identity. Often these determinations are utopian or conceived according to the patterns of literary utopia, and thus focus on alternate realities. According to the German literary scholar Wilhelm Voßkamp, the genre of utopia, generally speaking, represents a response to history, insofar as it always depicts a state of community beyond historical confrontations.[12] Virtually, Utopia lies at the end of history, or more precisely, as Fredric Jameson proposes, it represents the invitation to imagine radical alternatives to possibility.[13] In this respect, Jameson considers the genre of utopia, as propagated by his theoretical inspirer Darko Suvin, to be a subgenre of science fiction. Thus, the title of my essay is not only a rhetorical suggestion, but also has implications for cultural theory.

It is quite obvious that Zionist *and* diasporic utopias gained urgency from 1933 onward in a moment of greatest existential uncertainty and under the conditions

11 For a general overview on the historical semantics of the term diaspora see: Stéphane Dufoix, *The dispersion: a history of the uses of diaspora* (Leiden: Brill, 2017).

12 Wilhelm Voßkamp, "Utopie als Antwort auf Geschichte. Zur Typologie literarischer Utopien in der Neuzeit," in *Geschichte als Literatur. Formen und Grenzen der Repräsentation von Vergangenheit*, ed. Hartmut Eggert et. al. (Stuttgart: Metzler, 1990), 273–283.

13 Fredric Jameson, *Archeologies of the Future. The Desire Called Utopia and Other Science Fiction* (London: Verso, 2005), 416.

of exile. In the next parts of this essay, I will concentrate on two examples: first, the political writings of Alfred Döblin, and second, Franz Werfel's utopian sci-fi novel *Star of the Unborn* (*Stern der Ungeborenen*). Both examples demonstrate the intertwining of a 'diasporic fantasy' with utopian imagination. Like the Zionist theory, this imagination is fed by a certain relationship, not always of the same kind, to religious patterns and to eschatological ideas in the Jewish tradition, as we can observe in the quotation above by Wolfenstein. However, the Jewish history of exile "remained a remarkably open-ended adventure,"[14] as Sidra DeKoven Ezrahi succinctly puts it. In contrast to Zionist ideology and the "Zionist pull of 'the *real*,'" the literary examples I examine in this essay are less concerned with political realities than with political alternatives and seemingly apolitical possibilities.[15]

Döblin's Diaspora

In 1938, the medical doctor and writer Alfred Döblin (1878–1957), who achieved fame with his modernist novel *Berlin, Alexanderplatz* (1929), wrote in an essay on the emigration of German writers after the takeover of the Nazis: "Emigration is not only a blow of fate, but also a trial by fire. The longer it lasts, the more it becomes a wandering in the desert."[16] Döblin's choice of words is remarkable. The biblical phrase "wandering in the desert" ("Wüstenwanderung") hints at the fact that Döblin combines his turbulent exile as a writer in Switzerland, France, and the United States with religious patterns of the Jewish tradition. Until his escape to America, Döblin had two strategies to deal with exile. At first, Döblin practically and politically committed himself to so-called 'neo-territorialism'. After disappointing experiences in exile politics, he turned completely to literary writing again starting in 1936. The focus was on a large-scale work about the colonization of South America, for which Döblin intended the title *Land Without Death*, but which is known and published today as the *Amazon* trilogy. This novel can also be read as a reflection and processing of his preceding political experiences. In

---

14 Sidra DeKoven Ezrahi, *Booking Passage. Exile and Homecoming in the Modern Jewish Imagination* (Berkeley: University of California Press, 2000), 10.

15 Ibid., 225.

16 "Die Emigration ist nicht nur ein Schicksalsschlag, sondern auch eine Feuerprobe. Je länger sie dauert, umso mehr wird sie eine Wüstenwanderung." Alfred Döblin, *Aufsätze zur Literatur* (Olten: Walter, 1963), 197.

this contribution, I deal exclusively with Döblin's political essays and their political contexts.[17]

Actually, "territorialism" was founded as a split from the Zionist movement in 1905 during the 7th Zionist Congress in Basel under the British writer Israel Zangwill (1864–1926). The organization consisted of delegates who refused to accept the so-called Uganda Plan, the British government's proposed Jewish settlement of East African territories, in favor of Palestine, but never had much impact and was disbanded after Zangwill's death. It was not until 1931 that there were renewed efforts in various places to activate the territorialist movement or the "Freeland Movement."[18] In July 1935, Döblin took part in a conference of leading territorialists in London, where the "International Freiland League" was founded and Döblin was elected to its central council. In parallel, Döblin described his concepts in his political-theological essays, which were collected and published as well in 1935 under the title *Escape and Community* [*Gathering*] *of the Jewish People* (*Flucht und Sammlung des Judenvolkes*).

In these texts, Döblin states "landlessness" [Landlosigkeit] as the crucial problem that prevents a *real* existence of the Jewish people. "In the Diaspora," he notes, strictly speaking, "there would be neither Jewish people nor Judaism, because neither is possible there, but only a succession that derives from the Jewish people and worships its kind."[19] However, in addition to the internal weakness, there is also an external pressure on Judaism. As Döblin puts it, "the Diaspora itself is under attack."[20] In this situation of internal and external threat, the multi-layered concept of diaspora in Döblin's work also has a certain relationship to the idea of law, understood as Jewish religious law. Here, Döblin represents a kind of anomic idea of Judaism; from his point of view, in order to vitalize in an existentialist way, Judaism must free itself from its orthodox works of law. Concerning these ideas, Döblin also carries on a correspondence with the Jewish publicist and ideologue Nathan Birnbaum, who at this time lives in exile in the Netherlands and, after his Zionist phase and his advocacy of Yiddish autonomy, is in the 1930s considered a *bal tshuva*, i.e., 'a convert,' and represents religious orthodoxy, although he also

---

17 See Battegay, "Jüdische und Postkoloniale Diaspora-Diskurse in Alfred Döblins *Amazonas*," *Internationales Alfred-Döblin-Kolloquium Zürich 2015. Exil als Schicksalsreise*, ed. Sabina Becker and Sabine Schneider (Bern: Peter Lang, 2017), 157–178.

18 See Adam Rovner, *In the Shadow of Zion. Promised Lands before Israel* (New York: New York University Press, 2014), 79–115.

19 Alfred Döblin, "Flucht und Sammlung des Judenvolkes. Aufsätze und Erzählungen", in *Schriften zur jüdischen Frage*, ed. Hans Otto Horch (Zürich: Walter 1995), 79–262, 110.

20 Ibid., 195.

takes certain dissenting positions within orthodoxy.[21] In a letter to Birnbaum from June 1934, Döblin attacks the validity of the Talmud and ritual regulations (to which he refers, using traditional vocabulary, as a "fence around the Torah"), which is rather rude to the religious Birnbaum on the one hand, but on the other hand also gives insight into Döblin's ideas of Jewish awakening.[22] Birnbaum, in turn, responds politely but tersely to Döblin's letter. He instructs the writer that, while he himself uses the term *Orthodoxy* "very unwillingly," he holds unreservedly to the metaphysical convictions and traditional status of the *halakha*, the Jewish law: "I prefer to say ancient Judaism, where ancient does not mean obsolete to me, but contains a reference to eternity."[23]

At this time, Birnbaum advocates a concept of a "ruralization" ("Verländlichung") of Judaism (which seems bizarre not only today but also according to the standards of the time), by which he meant religious Jewish colonies away from large urban centers, which should lead to a re-authentication of Judaism not as a nation, but as the people of God. Döblin follows up on this rejection of the territorial nation-state in Birnbaum and on the emphasis on the natural. But he rejects the turn to Jewish tradition, including messianism. In contrast to Birnbaum, who wants to religiously transform *golus* in a messianic perspective, Döblin explicitly uses the term diaspora, which is not understood as an eschatological concept but as a gathering space for a political Jewish renewal.[24] The "mobilization of the entire active diaspora" is based on the idea of a colonization of yet unexplored lands, although Döblin avoids any concrete geographical indication. Certainly, these ideas are under the desperate impression of the real search of European Jews for emigration possibilities. But the talk of free "colonization spaces" seems irritating against the backdrop of the radical critique of European colonialism in the first part of the *Amazon*-novel. For Döblin, diaspora in no way means peaceful multiculturalism. Rather, the idea of a society in ideological and physical turmoil emerges, preoccupied with conflicts and in constant (intentional and unintentional) dynamics. In contrast, his utopian idea of colonization or "world colonization" – this

---

21 See Jess Olson, *Nathan Birnbaum and Jewish Modernity. Architect of Zionism, Yiddishism, and Orthodoxy* (Stanford: Stanford University Press, 2013.)

22 Alfred Döblin, *Briefe II*, ed. Helmut F. Pfanner (Zürich: Walter, 2001), 89.

23 Birnbaum's letters are not published, I read and copied them in the *Nathan and Solomon Birnbaum Archives*, Toronto, ON, Canada.

24 Döblin even publishes three longer essays, which are then adopted in *Flucht und Sammlung des Judenvolkes*, in Birnbaum's journal *Der Ruf* [*The Calling*]. See Hans Otto Horch, "Nachwort des Herausgebers," in Alfred Döblin, *Schriften zur jüdischen Frage*, ed. Hans Otto Horch (Zürich: Walter, 1995), 525–580; Caspar Battegay, *Geschichte der Möglichkeit. Utopie, Diaspora und die jüdische Frage* (Göttingen: Wallstein Verlag, 2018), 243–249.

can only be hinted at here – tends to mean a transformation of capitalist society towards a collectivist-oriented community that sees itself as part of nature.[25] For Döblin, this movement always includes a liberation from the traditional legal thinking of Judaism.

Like Wolfenstein, Döblin sketches a three-part scheme of Jewish history. Up to the year 70, according to him there was "the people in Palestine", which is the first form of Judaism. The second form is diaspora, which lasted for almost two thousand years. Modernity now forms another turning point. He writes: "Now the diaspora itself is attacked and is to make itself the subject of its fate."[26] This modern autonomization is supposed to transfer Judaism into the third form, into the so-called "New Judah." The difference to political Zionism in this concept is that, despite all territorial rhetoric, a new Jewish state is not to be created immediately. Rather, Döblin conjures up a departure into an undefined area of dispersion and salvation – an area of transition. This area he calls the "desert". The departure into the "desert" explicitly does not only mean emigration, but the creation of a Jewish colony in an assumed "free country" – which also means a kind of a new, vanguard diaspora beyond the theology of exile and homecoming.

Of course, this could not be accomplished, for the diaspora had neither a "plan" nor a common organization, nor was there a "free country." What Döblin was striving for, then, was rather a new way of thinking about possibilities. The call for unity in dispersion is a call to become aware of the diaspora as a universal space of the possible. Döblin's rather obscure concept of the "New Judah" is not a political utopia in a traditional sense, but rather has a religious or spiritual agenda, which is another parallel to Wolfenstein's abstract utopian concept of a connected dispersion. The spirituality to be attained is supposed to reshape the Jewish people. Döblin dreams of a Judaism connected with nature, whereby "nature" is understood as Creation itself that can be reached through mystical experiences. For Döblin, diaspora is thus a kind of nowhere, where the particularized Jews of the modern age should gather and find their way back to the community (and thus to God), but also withdraw from their attachment to the law. However, the concept had a more private character and never became politically effective. Even before he emigrated to America, Döblin turned away from his territorialistic ideas and devoted himself entirely to literature, specifically to the genre of the historical novel, which, especially in German-language exile literature, generally serves as a space for reflection on contemporary discourses and problems.

25 Döblin, *Flucht und Sammlung*, 197–198.

26 Ibid., 195.

Astromental Diaspora

On August 26, 1945, the writer Franz Werfel died from a heart attack in Beverly Hills, California.[27] Only some days before, he finished the last chapter of his novel *Stern der Ungeborenen*, subtitled *Ein Reiseroman* [*Star of the Unborn. A travel fiction*] – a book that tells the story of a posthumous journey into the far future and back. The novel can be read as a giant allegory of an "absolute diaspora," that is, of an inherently irresolvable geographical and temporal dispersion.[28] Werfel, who was born a citizen of the Austrian-Hungarian monarchy and a member of the German-speaking Jewish minority of Prague in 1890, escaped the Nazis together with his famous wife Alma Mahler to the United States (like Döblin via France), where he was a part of the German exile community in California.[29] Werfel shared with Döblin not only the fate of emigrants, but also an interest in the Catholic faith.

Werfel's novel is typically structured with all the important plot elements of the modern utopian novel, and, in turn, its dystopian counterpart. It depicts a utopian science, which implies infinite progress but also the threatening aspects of advanced technology. The story opens with a spectral moment. The first-person narrator suddenly materializes himself more than hundred thousand years in the future after his virtual death. The narrator calls himself a "Forschungsreisender" – an explorer – who is sent away at nighttime against his own will. Until the end of the 600-page story it remains unclear if this expedition is the description of a dream, an eccentric fantasy of a near-death experience, or the account of a trip through a fantastic world that is real on the fictitious level. All in all, the narrator stays two and a half days and three nights in this so-called "astromental world." Back at home in Beverly Hills, he wakes up and decides to write down his account. This means that the action in the novel occurs either over a period of three days or one hundred thousand years; either the story happens in several moments or in "just as many eternities," for every time specification is – as the narrator explicitly states – only subjective.[30] This programmatic indeterminacy of time is embodied by the uncanny existence of the narrator who simultaneously lives in different times. With this construction, Werfel's novel deconstructs the notion of a rational or subjective time and subverts the causal and linear narration in favor of a meta-

27 See Caspar Battegay, *Geschichte der Möglichkeit*, 269–290.

28 See Paul North, "Absolute und Relative Diaspora: Borges und Ahad Ha'am," in *Exil – Literatur – Judentum*, ed. Doerte Bischoff (Munich: Edition text + kritik, 2014), 86–109.

29 See Erhard Bahr, *Weimar on the Pacific. German Exile Culture in Los Angeles and the Crisis of Modernism* (Berkeley: University of California Press, 2007).

30 Franz Werfel, *Star of the Unborn*, trans. Gustave O. Arlt (New York: Viking Press, 1946), 528.

temporal thinking. Thus, the genre of utopia is used to construct a literary space of infinite possibilities in contrast to the real historical situation of political powerlessness and exile. This is a movement that parallels Döblin's retreat from politics and his turn to the historical novel, though Werfel projects this textualization of the world not onto history but onto the future, or more precisely, onto a supra-temporal space of possibility. In this regard, the title *Star of the Unborn* refers to the possible and to the potentiality of literature. The novel transforms the individual exile towards an alternative notion of space and time. This alternative model correlates with the traditional perception of time in the Jewish diaspora as a collective experience, an exile which implies a potential redemption as a homecoming.

In Werfel's fictitious future, the "astromental" technology is advanced in such a way that the visitor from the twentieth century has the impression of an immaterialized or "mental" technology. For example, the so-called "Mentelebol" allows people to stop traveling through space, simply moving the destination towards them – something that of course sounds quite familiar in our digital age. But also the political structure of this mental age is utopian. Thus, the head of the "panopolis," the president of the world state, is elected only if the person absolutely does not want to take office. However, despite the utopian laws, there are serious political tensions, and during the narrator's presence a violent conflict breaks out, which leads to a global war. It is impossible to sum up the extensive story. I can only state that the "astromental" culture seeks to control life and death absolutely, but there are also zones where this control fails, and people can mutate into horrible monsters and become a kind of human waste. The book contains some allusions to the terror of the National Socialist dictatorship and the Holocaust, to the extent that Werfel was already aware of them. Of particular value is probably his critique of biopolitically motivated extermination and the intersection of racism and medical discourse, a critique of the control over who is allowed to live and who must die. This critique stands out in what is otherwise often quite a stereotypical novel. At the end, the critique of absolute ideologies becomes universal. The christological motif of a boy who sacrifices himself reveals that, for Werfel, religion is the opposite of the techno-biological utopia/dystopia. The indefinable time frame of religious expectations stands against the technological and political control of human lifetime.

The basic motif of *Star of the Unborn* is the issue of time, or rather the issue of timelessness. In this respect, it is also significant that the narrator meets the so-called "Jude des Zeitalters" (a representative of all Jews of the utopian time). This Jewish character seems to be a traveler as well because he is the symbolic outsider of the "astromental" society, and the representative of an alternate sense of time. Remarkably thus, in this novel, we find a thought similar to that of Rosenzweig. In a circularly structured time travel narrative, the protagonist encounters

Jewish figures, who, in a kind of eternal or absolute diaspora, measure time and space and are only conditionally subject to the laws of society.

The experience of synchronicity – a kind of mystical unity of all things in the universe – is a central issue of the novel. The so-called "spiritual time" is described as the most important goal of the "astromental" science. A look at Werfel's exile library shows that he concerned himself with modern physics and books by Einstein and other physicists and scientists (for example, he read about solar astronomy).[31] Yet Werfel used these readings for satirical fictionalization: *science* turns into *fiction*. His references do not aim at a narrative exploitation, a paraphrase, or an illustration of the relativity of space and time in modern physics. This includes a conscious ignorance of the mathematic and scientific facts, but also a transformation of the physical universe into a literary universe of an absolute presence, a time without past or future. In the narrative, this is shown by the time traveler, who paradoxically remembers the future, a future which is his past, but also the present of his narration.

The paradoxical entanglements of different time levels are of course formative for every time travel narrative, but in Werfel's novel they become highly self-referential. This is evident in the motif of the so-called "Isochronion" – the most important tool of the utopian world, which is also described as an unknown substance or a drug of the "astromental" science. The "Isochronion" is the counterpart of the "Mentelebol," in that it does not suspend space but rather opens a metatemporal dimension; it de-temporalizes the human perception and allows an experience of synchronicity for its user. Werfel's depiction of the "Isochronion" goes beyond scientific comparisons; it instead refers to Jewish tradition, specifically the *tfillin*, the phylacteries worn by Jewish men in morning prayer.

> Externally, the Isochronion was a small hexagonal metal box with a belt on each side. It was reminiscent of the phylacteries, the Jewish prayer straps, where a capsule is also fixed in the middle of the forehead of the prayer. The Isochronion seemed to be an unknown tool to switch the atomic consciousness of the terrestrial man into the omniscient consciousness of the heavenly man, to let the earthly diversity of time [die irdisch-winzige Verschiedenzeitigkeit] flow into the simultaneity of the whole [Gleichzeitigkeit des Ganzen]. For those who knew how to use the Isochronion, there was therefore no successive, but only an infinite togetherness, a simultaneity beyond all boundaries. At every moment his soul contained all as-

31 Christian Zemsauer, "Regierung der Nichtgeeigneten. Zur gesellschaftspolitischen Ordnung in Franz Werfels Stern der Ungeborenen," in *Das Mögliche regieren. Gouvernementalität in der Literatur- und Kulturanalyse*, ed. Roland Innerhofer et al. (Bielefeld: transcript Verlag, 201), 231–248.

> sociations and all connections in nature, the falling of a lime leaf thousands of years ago, the explosions of a star of light millions of years ago.[32]

The transformation from "Verschiedenzeitigkeit" ('diversity of time' or 'multichronicity') to synchronicity, from a historical and chronological perception towards an experience of the whole universe is compared with the time of praying in traditional Judaism. This eschatological order of time is the time of the diaspora, the time of waiting for a messianic event, where history would come to a standstill. And so it is that, in the course of these events, the narrator learns there cannot be any linear progress. Since the fall of man, mankind is moving away from God – yet it also circularly moves towards God. Werfel describes this theological paradox as follows: "The straight line of time bends in each of its seconds before the Creator in adoring curvature. And so we are safe, because distance is nothing but a form of approach."[33]

The Star of the Unborn relies on prophecy and eschatology. The history of the world and the story of the narrator's journey are both circular; the end of the narration leads back to its beginning. This narrative entanglement of time correlates with the time model of the diasporic narrative, in which the collective displacement leads to a return, and the exile to a homecoming. Werfel leaves no doubt that in this narrative his Jewish characters are situated in an eternal or an absolute diaspora, even if Werfel does not use this term. It is their role to perform the possibility of staying outside of history; they are the true utopian inhabitants of the star of the unborn, because they are outside the law, or better still, because they follow a law that cannot be changed, even under the conditions of an "astromental" revolution.

---

32 "Äußerlich war das Isochronion eine kleine, sechseckige Metallkapsel mit je einem Riemen an jeder Seite. Sie erinnerte an die Phylakterien, an die Gebetsriemen der Juden, wo ebenfalls eine Kapsel inmitten der Stirne des Beters befestigt wird. ... Das Isochronion schien ein unbekanntes Hilfsmittel zu sein, um das atomare Bewusstsein des Erdenmenschen in das Allbewusstsein des Himmelsmenschen einzuschalten, die irdisch-winzige Verschiedenzeitigkeit in die Gleichzeitigkeit des Ganzen verströmen zu lassen. Für den Eingeweihten, der das Isochronion anzuwenden verstand, gab es daher kein Nacheinander mehr, sondern nur ein unendliches Miteinander, eine Simultanität über alle Fassungsgrenzen. Seine Seele enthielt in jedem Augenblick alle Assoziationen und alle Zusammenhänge in der Natur, das Fallen eines Lindenblattes vor Jahrtausenden, die Explosionen eines Lichtgestirns vor Jahrmillionen." Franz Werfel, *Stern der Ungeborenen. Ein Reiseroman* (Stockholm: Bermann Fischer, 1946), 633–634.

33 "Die Gerade der Zeit beugt sich in jeder ihrer Sekunden vor dem Schöpfer in anbetender Krümmung. Und so sind wir geborgen, weil die Entfernung nichts anderes ist als eine Form der Annäherung." Ibid., 657.

As refugees, Werfel, Döblin and Wolfenstein suffered tremendously from their faith. They experienced that – in Hannah Arendt's words from 1943 – "being a Jew does not give any legal status in this world."[34] Unlike Arendt, however, they did not only reflect on *this* world, and hardly reflected on the connection of laws and politics, but as poets and writers chose to imagine a *possible* world where the laws of their time were suspended. As German Jews, they chose literature and imagination, which are the universal conditions and expressions of diaspora. The last sentences of Wolfenstein's short book on the connection between poetry and Jewish fate read: "The ground can be lost, the fate can repeat itself furiously always, ... eternal dispersion – Jerusalem can be destroyed again: the [our] floating [rootless] mission can never be destroyed.[35]

References

Arendt, Hannah. "We Refugees." In *The Jewish Writings*, edited by Jerome Kohn and Ron H. Feldman, 264–274. New York: Schocken Books, 2007.

Arendt, Hannah. *The Origins of Totalitarianism.* New York: Schocken Books, 2004.

Baer, Jizchak Fritz. *Galut.* Berlin: Schocken Books, 1936.

Bahr, Erhard. *Weimar on the Pacific. German Exile Culture in Los Angeles and the Crisis of Modernism.* Berkeley: University of California Press, 2007.

Battegay, Caspar. *Geschichte der Möglichkeit. Utopie, Diaspora und die 'jüdische Frage'.* Göttingen: Wallstein Verlag, 2018.

Battegay, Caspar. "Jüdische und Postkoloniale Diaspora-Diskurse in Alfred Döblins *Amazonas.*" In *Internationales Alfred-Döblin-Kolloquium Zürich 2015. Exil als Schicksalsreise*, edited by Sabina Becker and Sabine Schneider, 157–178. Bern: Peter Lang 2017.

Boyarin, Jonathan and Daniel Boyarin. *Powers of Diaspora. Two Essays on the Relevance of Jewish Culture.* Minneapolis: University of Minnesota Press, 2002.

Buber, Martin. "Jüdische Renaissance." In *Werkausgabe 3. Frühe Jüdische Schriften 1900–1922*, edited by Barbara Schäfer, 143–147. Gütersloh: Gütersloher Verlagshaus, 2007.

Döblin, Alfred. *Briefe II.* Edited by Helmut F. Pfanner. Walter: Zürich, 2001.

Döblin, Alfred. "Flucht und Sammlung des Judenvolkes. Aufsätze und Erzählungen." In *Schriften zur jüdischen Frage*, edited by Hans Otto Horch, 79–262. Zürich et. al.: Walter 1995.

DeKoven Ezrahi, Sidra. *Booking Passage. Exile and Homecoming in the Modern Jewish Imagination.* Berkeley: University of California Press, 2000.

Dufoix, Stéphane. *The dispersion: a history of the uses of diaspora.* Leiden: Brill, 2017.

34 Hannah Arendt, "We Refugees," in *The Jewish Writings*, ed. Jerome Kohn and Ron H. Feldman (New York: Schocken Books, 2007), 264–274, 274.

35 "Der Boden kann verloren gehen, das Geschick kann sich wütend immer wiederholen, ... ewige Zerstreuung – Jerusalem kann wieder zerstört werden: die schwebende Sendung nicht." Wolfenstein, *Jüdisches Wesen und neue Dichtung*, 54.

Goldoni, Marco, and Christopher McCorkindale, eds. *Hannah Arendt and the Law.* Oxford: Hart Publishing, 2012.

Horch, Hans Otto. "Nachwort des Herausgebers." In Alfred Döblin. *Schriften zur jüdischen Frage*, edited by Hans Otto Horch, 525–580. Zürich: Walter 1995.

Jameson, Fredric. *Archaeologies of the Future. The Desire Called Utopia and Other Science Fiction.* London: Verso, 2005.

Maor, Zohar. "Redemption and Law: Rosenzweig's Critique on Max Brod." In *Faith, Truth, and Reason. New Perspectives on Franz Rosenzweig's "Star of Redemption."* Edited by Yehoyada Amir et. al., 391–408. Freiburg im Breisgau: Verlag Karl Alber, 2012.

North, Paul. "Absolute und Relative Diaspora: Borges und Ahad Ha'am." In *Exil – Literatur – Judentum*, edited by Doerte Bischoff, 86–109. München: Edition text + kritik, 2014.

Olson, Jess. *Nathan Birnbaum and Jewish Modernity. Architect of Zionism, Yiddishism, and Orthodoxy.* Stanford: Standford University Press, 2013.

Rosenzweig, Franz. *The Star of Redemption.* Translated by Barbara E. Galli. Madison WI: University of Wisconsin Press, 2005.

Rovner, Adam. *In the Shadow of Zion. Promised Lands before Israel.* New York, London: New York University Press, 2014.

Voßkamp, Wilhelm. "Utopie als Antwort auf Geschichte. Zur Typologie literarischer Utopien in der Neuzeit." In *Geschichte als Literatur. Formen und Grenzen der Repräsentation von Vergangenheit*, edited by Hartmut Eggert et. al., 273–283. Stuttgart: Metzler, 1990.

Werfel, Franz. *Star of the Unborn.* Translated by Gustave O. Arlt. New York: Viking Press, 1946.

Werfel, Franz. *Stern der Ungeborenen. Ein Reiseroman.* Stockholm: Bermann Fischer, 1946.

Wolfenstein, Alfred. *Jüdisches Wesen und neue Dichtung.* Berlin: Erich Reiss, 1922.

Zemsauer, Christian. "Regierung der Nichtgeeigneten. Zur gesellschaftspolitischen Ordnung in Franz Werfels *Stern der Ungeborenen.*" In *Das Mögliche regieren. Gouvernementalität in der Literatur- und Kulturanalyse*, edited by Roland Innerhofer et al., 231–248. Bielefeld: transcript Verlag, 2011.

Zweig, Stefan. *Briefe zum Judentum*, edited by Stefan Litt. Berlin: Jüdischer Verlag im Suhrkamp Verlag, 2020.

About the Authors

Ino Augsberg, Professor of Philosophy of Law and Public Law at Kiel University. His research focuses on the margins of law, namely the intertwinements between law, religion and literature. Recent publications include Elemente einer Theorie des expositiven Rechts (2021); Theorien der Grund- und Menschenrechte (2021), and Schmitt-Lektüren (2020).

Caspar Battegay, Lecturer (Privatdozent) in Modern German and Comparative Literature at the University of Basel. Head the section for Culture & Communication at the School of Engineering of the University of Applied Sciences Northwestern Switzerland. Recent publications include Geschichte der Möglichkeit. Utopie, Diaspora und die 'jüdische Frage' (2018), Judentum und Popkultur. Ein Essay (2012) and German Psycho. The Language of Depression in Oliver Polak's Der jüdische Patient, in: Garloff / Mueller (Ed.), Germn Jewish Literature after 1990 (2018).

Liliana Ruth Feierstein, Professor for Transcultural Jewish History at the Humboldt University Berlin and the Selma Stern Zentrum für Jüdische Studien. Fellow at the Seminario Rabínico Latinoamericano. Recent publications include Diaspora* (Lo Sguardo N. 29, 2019), "A Quilt of Memory": The Shoah as a Prism in the Testimonies of Survivors of the Dictatorship in Argentina (European Review, Cambridge, Vol. 22) and Habitar la Letra. Judaísmo, escritura y transmision (2011)

Charlotte Elisheva Fonrobert, Professor in the Department of Religious Studies at Stanford University and Director both of the Taube Center for Jewish Studies and the Program in Feminist, Gender and Sexuality Studies. Her publications include the award-winning Menstrual Purity: Reconstructions of Biblical Gender in Rabbinic Judaism and Christianity (2000), and The Cambridge Companion to the Talmud and Rabbinic Judaism (edited with Martin Jaffee, 2007). She edited, together with Amir Engel, the English translation of Jacob Taubes' From Cult to Culture: Fragments toward a Critique of Historical Reasoning (2009). Her recent essays on rituals of Jewish diaspora are being worked into a book on Re-Placing the Nation: Judaism, Diaspora, and Neighborhood.

Martin Heger, Professor at the Faculty of Law of Humboldt University of Berlin, Chair of Criminal Law, Criminal Procedure, European Criminal Law and Legal History. Guest professor at UWC, Capetown, University of Athens and University of Regensburg. President of the Berlin Scientific Society (BWG), Speaker of the Berlin Studies of Jewish Law and the Network of student's exchange East-West, Member of the Academic Senat and Council of Humboldt University and the Faculty Board, Member of the Berlin Institut of Islamic Theology. Among his publications: „Der Nießbrauch in usus modernus und Naturrecht" (2004); „Die Europäisierung des deutschen Umweltstrafrechts. (2009); „Der strafrechtliche Schutz der Religion in Deutschland – Geschichte, aktuelle Herausforderungen und kriminalpolitische Überlegungen" (Zeitschrift für evangelisches Kirchenrecht, 2016).

Susannah Heschel, Eli M. Black Distinguished Professor and Chair of the Jewish Studies Program at Dartmouth College. She is a Guggenheim Fellow and has also held research grants from the Carnegie Foundation and the Ford Foundation. She has been awarded five honorary doctorates and held year-long fellowships at the National Humanities Center and the Wissenschaftskolleg zu Berlin. She is the author of Abraham Geiger and the Jewish Jesus (1998), The Aryan Jesus: Christian Theologians and the Bible in Nazi Germany (2008), and Jüdischer Islam: Islam und jüdisch-deutsche Selbst-

https://doi.org/10.1515/9783111062631-013

bestimmung (2018). She has also published several co-edited volumes, including The Muslim Reception of European Orientalism (with Umar Ryad 2018).

Elisa Klapheck, liberal rabbi in the Jewish Community of Frankfurt am Main and Professor of Jewish Studies at the university of Paderborn. Before her ordination in 2004, she obtained a degree in Political Science and worked for many years as a political journalist. Particularly important to her is the discourse on rabbinic-Talmudic texts in the light of current sociopolitical issues and questions. Among her publications are the books Fräulein Rabbiner Jonas – The Story of the First Woman Rabbi (1999, English translation 2004), Margarete Susman – Religious-Political Essays on Judaism (2022) and Zur politischen Theologie des Judentums (2022).

Serdar Kurnaz, Professor for Islamic Law at the Berlin Institute for Islamic Theology at the Humboldt-Universität zu Berlin. He was director of the Swiss Centre for Islam and Society at the University of Fribourg in Switzerland and Associated Professor at the Hamburg University at the Academy of World Religions. His main research areas are Islamic Theology, Islamic Law and Legal Theory, Islamic Ethics, Philosophy of Law, Epistemology and Hadith and Qur'anic Studies. He is the author of „The maqāṣid-cum-maṣlaḥa Approach as a Theological Basis for Islamic Social Work: A Critical Analysis and an Alternative Proposal" in H. Schmid/A. Sheikhzadegan (eds), Exploring Islamic Social Work. Between Community and the Common Good. (2022); "Ibn Rushd's legal hermeneutics and moral theory for a "living Sharīʿa" – an alternative approach to Islamic Law in Ibn Rushd's Bidāyat al-mujtahid" (Oxford Journal of Law and Religion, 8/1, 2019) and "Who is the law giver? – The Hermeneutical Grounds of the Methods of Interpreting Qur'an and Sunna (istinbāṭ al-aḥkām)" (Oxford Journal of Law and Religion, 6/2, 2017).

Stephan M. Probst, medical doctor and senior physician in charge in the Department of Hematology, Oncology and Palliative Medicine of the Klinikum Bielefeld, Universitätsklinikum OWL der Universität Bielefeld, Campus Klinikum Bielefeld, Germany. There he is head of the Palliative Care Unit and chairman of the clinical ethics committee. Dr. Probst is also member of the ethics committee of the German Medical Association (Zentrale Ethikkommission bei der Bundesärztekammer). He is a specialist in internal medicine, hematology, oncology and palliative care, and an expert in Jewish medical ethics. Publications include „Die palliativmedizinische Begleitung jüdischer Patienten und Palliative Care aus jüdische Sicht", (Zeitschrift für Palliativmedizin 2019); Vom Umgang mit Verlust und Trauer im Judentum (ed. 2018). Hirntod und Organspende aus interkultureller Sicht (2019).

Klaus Stierstorfer, Chair of British Studies at the University of Muenster, Germany. He has published widely on literary history, British drama and aspects of literary theory. He is series editor of the current 13-volume series Grundthemen der Literaturwissenschaft with De Gruyter. His ongoing research interest are in diaspora studies, law and literature. Spokesperson of the Collaborative Research Centre 1385 "Law and Literature" funded by the Germany Research council, and the project "Literary Modelling and Energy Transition", funded by the Volkswagen Foundation. Recent Publications include Enzyklopädie Recht und Literatur (edited with Thomas Gutmann and Eberhard Ortland, 2022), Citizenship, Law and Literature (edited with Caroline Koegler and Jesper Redding, 2018), Diaspora, Law and Literatur (edited with Daniela Carpi, 2016).

Daniel Weidner, Professor for Comparative Literature at the Martin-Luther-University Halle-Wittenberg. His research focuses on the relation between literature and religion, on the history and theory of literary studies and cultural theory, and on German-Jewish Literature. Recent Publications include:

The Father of German Mysticism. The Writing of Gershom Scholem, (2022); Prophetic Politics (Special Issue of Political Theology, ed. with Nitzan Lebovic, 2020); Handbuch Literatur und Religion (ed., 2016).

Index

Abduh, Muḥammad 111
Aboab da Fonseca, Isaac 171 f.
Adler, Samuel 28
Adorno, Theodor 45
Adret 68, 71
Agamben, Giorgio 46
al-ʿAlwānī, Ṭāhā Jābir 100, 106, 110–113
al-Būṭī, Muḥammad Saʿīd Ramaḍān 112
al-Fārābī, Abū Naṣr 101, 103 f.
al-Ghazālī, Abū Ḥāmid 101–103, 107
al-Qaraḍāwī, Yūsuf 100, 106, 110–113
Alarich II. 123
Allende, Salvador 182
Altmann, Alexander 45
Altmann, Lotte 172
ar-Raysūnī, Aḥmad 109
Arendt, Hannah 207, 217
Aristotle 38, 103
Arnold, Edwin 200
Arns, Paulo Evaristo 183
Asad, Talal 87
Āshūr, aṭ-Ṭāhir ibn 108 f.
Auda, Jasser 109

Bachmann, Ingeborg 46
Baeck, Leo 152
Baer, Jizchak Fritz 206
Baron, Salo 58, 88
Bedir, Murteza 105
ben Chalafta, Yose 163, 166
ben Gurion, David 27 f.
ben Teradyon, Chanina 156, 158 f.
Bentham, Jeremy 200
Berdichevsky, Micah Joseph 26
Berkowitz, Beth 85
Berman, Harold 51–54
Biale, David 46, 139
Birnbaum, Nathan 210 f.
Blaustein, Jacob 27
Blidstein, Gerald 68, 73
Bodin, Jean 126
Bouhafa, Feriel 103 f.
Boyarin, Daniel 31 f., 206

Brodsky, David 94
Buber, Martin 142–144, 206
Burg, Avrum 25
Butler, Judith 33

Carlyle, Thomas 200
Celan, Paul 46
Cover, Robert 43
Crow, Jim 29

d'Argentré, Bertrand 128
Darwish, Mahmoud 32
Derrida, Jacques 42
Dines, Alberto 171, 174 f., 182
Döblin, Alfred 209–214, 217
Dorff, Elliot N. 161
Douglass, Fredrick 29
Durkheim, Émile 165

Edrei, Arye 62–64, 79
Eger, Salomon 157
El Fadl, Abou 105 f.
Emden, Jacob 173
Eshed, Avital 25
Ezrahi, Sidra DeKoven 209

Feinstein, Moses 77, 160
Fischer, Shlomo 57, 61, 63
Fleischmann, Israel 172, 175
Fowler, Francis George 38
Fowler, Henry Watson 38
Franke, Patrick 110
Freud, Sigmund 37, 179
Frisch, Max 46
Furstenberg, Yair 90 f.

Gandhi, Mahatma 191–203
Gani, Sheth Abdul 195
Geiger, Abraham 23
Gerondi, Nissim 70
Glenn, Patrick 54
Goethe, Johann Wolfgang 43
Goldschmidt, Georges-Arthur 37

https://doi.org/10.1515/9783111062631-014

Graetz, Heinrich 83, 97
Graff, Gil 85, 87f., 173

Ha-Levi, Yehuda 73
Ha-Meiri, Menahem 81
Ha-Nasi, Yehuda 157
Harding, Vincent 30, 33
Hegel, Georg Wilhelm Friedrich 146
Herman, Geoffrey 88
Herzl, Theodor 24
Herzog, Vlado 183–185
Heschel, Abraham Joshua 178
Hirsch, Samson Raphael 139
Horowitz, Isaiah 28

Iavelberg, Iara 184f.
Ibn Adret 68
Ibn Rushd 101–104

Jackson, Vicki 80
Jaffee, Martin 83
Jameson, Frederic 208
Josephus 17
Justinian 123

Kahane, Meir 22
Kaplan, Mordechai 60
Karaman, Hayreddin 101, 105
Karl der Große 123, 126
Karl V. 129
Klabin, Mauricio 179
Kloke, Ari 202
Koogan, Abraham 175, 179
Kucinski, Bernado 184

Laqueur, Thomas W. 176, 186
Lavater, Johann Kasper 200
Leibowitz, Yeshayahu 65, 73, 75, 168
Lemle, Heinrich 171f., 175–177, 185
Lieberich, Heinz 124, 127
Linder, Amnon 83f.
Lorberbaum, Menachem 72, 84, 86f., 89
Luzzatto, Simone 21, 30, 33

Mahler, Alma 213
Maimonides 63, 68–72, 95, 141, 160
Malinar, Angelika 202
March, Andrew 99, 113
Mendelssohn, Moses 45, 59f., 85, 173, 176, 185
Mestiri, Mohamed 112
Meyer, Marshall 178
Mitteis, Ludwig 124, 127
Moltmann, Jürgen 20
Montagu, Lily 176
Montefiore, Claude 176
Müller, Max 200

Nachmanides 71
Neumann, Aron 173
Nussenbaum, Henrique 175

of Berdichev, Levi Yitzchak 22
of Kotzk, Menachem Mendel 23
of Samosata, Lucian 38
Opwis, Felicitas 100, 108f.

Philo 17, 74
Pinkuss, Fritz 177, 183
Polak, Henry Solomon Leon 201
Poznanski, Gustav 28

Rabbi Akiva 92–94, 167
Rabbi Eliezer 19, 139
Rabbi Goren 63f.
Rabbi Ishmael 19, 137
Rabbi Judah 19, 155, 158f.
Rabbi Shimon 92–96
Rabbi Yochanan 18, 161
Rahman, Fazlur 106
Rajeswaran, Sridhar 191
Rakover, Nahum 141
Ramadan, Tariq 108f., 111f.
Rashi 77f., 91f., 95
Raz-Krakotzkin, Amnon 32f.
Reinhart, Kevin 104f.
Riḍā, Rashīd 109f.
Rosenzweig, Franz 142–147, 205f., 214
Rousseau, Henri 202
Ruskin, John 201

Said, Edward 24, 167
Sandford, John F.A. 130
Santos, Boaventura de Sousa 54, 82

Saunders, Cicely 164
Schleiermacher, Friedrich 39, 41
Scholem, Gershom 20
Schreier, Chael Charles 184
Scott, Dred 130
Seligmann, Caesar 177
Shalom, Mirta 181
Shapiro, Haim 70
Sherwin, Byron L. 160
Shilo, Shmuel 84, 88
Shiloh, Shmuel 76 f., 81
Slabodsky, Santiago 32 f.
Sobel, Henry 183
Spinoza, Baruch 57, 59, 172
Suvin, Darko 208

Tchernichovsky, Saul 26
Titus 17 f.
Toller, Ernst 207
Tolstoy, Leo 200
Tzekinovsky, Mordechai 174 f., 179

Urbach, Ephraim 85

Vargas, Getúlio 173, 175
Vespasian 18
von Bismarck, Otto 121
von Jhering, Rudolf 43 f.
von Savigny, Friedrich Carl 123
Voßkamp, Wilhelm 208

Werfel, Franz 209, 213–217
Wessely, Herz 23
Wolfenstein, Alfred 207–209, 212, 217
Wright, James 183

Yisraeli, Shaul 65, 79–81
Yuval, Israel 14, 16–18, 23, 32

Zangwill, Israel 210
Zweig, Stefan 171–177, 179, 182, 207

Printed and bound by CPI Group (UK) Ltd, Croydon, CR0 4YY

13/09/2026

14961091-0002